STO

The

Maryknoll

Fathers

BY THE SAME AUTHOR

The White Fathers

The Woman God Loved

Equatorial Africa: New World of Tomorrow

The Papal Princes:
*A History of the Sacred
College of Cardinals*

GLENN D. KITTLER

The
Maryknoll
Fathers

THE WORLD PUBLISHING COMPANY • CLEVELAND AND NEW YORK

Published by The World Publishing Company
2231 West 110th Street, Cleveland 2, Ohio

Published simultaneously in Canada by
Nelson, Foster & Scott Ltd.

Library of Congress Catalog Card Number: 61-6648

First Edition

WP361

For Leslie, Florence, and Shirley

—my brother and sisters

Contents

The
Maryknoll
Fathers

I

For over a year there had been no news of him. No one could be sure that he was even alive. From time to time rumors about him seeped through the Bamboo Curtain. According to some, he was very ill and in a prison hospital; others claimed that he had been brainwashed and would soon be put on public trial, now that the Communists were confident of him; yet others had him still stern and immobile, still strong and arrogant against the Communists, an unconquerable man. But no one was sure.

Then on March 17, 1960, came the official announcement from Shanghai. Bishop James Edward Walsh, aged sixty-nine, the last American Catholic bishop on the China mainland, had been tried by a People's Court and found guilty of spying for a foreign power, of plotting to overthrow the Chinese government, and of corrupting youth. He was sentenced to twenty years in prison. At his age there was little chance that he would live long enough to serve his term.

The Chinese announcement gave no report of what Bishop Walsh might have said in his own defense or whether he said anything at all.

That same day, at a press conference in Washington, D. C., Secretary of State Christian A. Herter declared:

I find it difficult to emphasize sufficiently the revulsion that I, personally, and the United States government feel today. I am instructing our ambassador at Warsaw to lodge the strongest possible protest with the representative of the Chinese Communist regime at their next meeting Tuesday, March 22. I am certain that the rest of the world will join me in condemning this action taken against an innocent citizen of the United States and distinguished member of the Catholic clergy.

But the Bishop was not entirely innocent. There were grounds to the charges against him: the Communists were clever enough to see to that. In Communist terms, he was indeed a foreign agent. If he did not actually work to overthrow the government there was, nevertheless, no question that he was belligerently opposed to it and by his presence in the country urged others to oppose it. As for the youth of the country, at least the Communist evaluation of youth, he had most certainly attempted to corrupt as many as he could.

In a unique sense, Bishop James Edward Walsh was without doubt a very guilty man. His greatest crime was that he loved the Chinese.

In 1956, he wrote an American friend: I have always liked China, but it's just Grand Opera to me now. I wouldn't trade it in for a farm. Nobody knows the human race in all its glory until he has lived in China. At least that's the way it seems to me."

For harboring this sentiment, he was an enemy of the country to which he had devoted his life.

He always gave the impression of being a small man. He stood five feet nine inches, but he was thin. He never weighed more than one hundred forty pounds in his life. The long robes he wore, first as a seminarian, then as a priest, then as a bishop, gave him a boyish grace he never outgrew. Even after his black hair had turned white and his blue eyes had been dimmed by too much reading over mission oil lamps and the years had furrowed his face and bent his shoulders, there was still much of the boy in his walk and in his attitudes. He moved quickly, he possessed a restless curiosity, there was a crisp directness to his speech that dismayed less acute men who felt he was always trying to cut them off. At twenty-one, some people thought he was too old to begin the long years of study for the priesthood, and with typical firmness he told them, "I believe I have a vocation for the missions and I intend to see it through."

Years later the Chinese Communists were not prepared for this kind of stubbornness. They wanted to get rid of him, they wanted to get rid of all missionaries, they wanted to get rid of Christianity itself because as long as it existed in the country they could not wholly impose their own moral standards upon the people. By pressure, threat, and murder they had terrorized most missionaries out of China. Others stayed until they were evicted or called back by their superiors. But Bishop Walsh refused to budge. He wrote home:

I am a little tired of being pushed around because of my religion. My religion is all right; I don't see anything wrong with it. And that, come to think of it, is probably the world's prize understatement. Well, anyhow, I don't feel inclined to get off the earth just because some people dislike my religion—or me because of it. I don't hold it against them, good souls; that's another matter. But what I say is let them come and put me off. Is there anything wrong in that? I hope not. It seems merely normal and natural to me.

So they tried to put him off the earth. They might have executed him had they not feared the repercussions within China itself. So they distorted his very reasons for being in China into crimes against the government, they tried him, and they sentenced him to prison for twenty years.

When the news about him broke in America, two hundred young men went into a church overlooking the Hudson River some forty miles north of New York City and prayed for him. At the same time, scores of other young men, dedicated to the same purpose as these, entered a dozen chapels across the country and said their own prayers. And in Korea, Japan, the Philippines, Formosa, in Central and South America, and across the Atlantic in the heart of Africa hundreds of other young men knelt in prayers for Bishop Walsh. They were all his spiritual brothers, and they were where they were because one day, long before most of them were born, two priests had sat together in the lobby of a Montreal hotel and discussed a dream.

They were both looking for jobs.

The
First
Decade

I I

In SEPTEMBER, 1910, an International Eucharistic Congress was held in Montreal, the twenty-first such gathering in the history of the Catholic Church. The purpose of the Congress was to provide the Catholic clergy and laity the dramatic occasion to convene in large numbers to affirm their faith publicly in the true presence of Jesus Christ in the Blessed Sacrament and to stimulate devotion to this vital Catholic precept. The first such assembly had been held in Lille, France, in 1881, at the suggestion of Pope Leo XIII, who saw in it an effective gesture to revitalize French Catholics who, influenced by Freemasonry, Protestantism, materialism, and embryonic Communism, were drifting away from the Church. So successful was the first Congress that subsequently the meetings were held almost annually, mostly in France.

The Montreal Congress was the first conducted in the Western Hemisphere. By now, the Congresses had taken on the nature of religious pilgrimages, attended by leading members of the world hierarchy and all priests, nuns, and laymen who could afford the trip. Holding the 1910 Congress in Montreal was a welcomed convenience for men and women whose duties or limited finances had prevented them from attending the Congresses in Europe.

One such man was Father James Anthony Walsh, a priest of the Boston diocese; another was Father Thomas Frederick Price, who belonged to the North Carolina vicariate.

Actually, neither man should have been in Montreal. Price couldn't afford the trip, and in addition he was having difficulties with his bishop. His presence in Montreal was somewhat like the last meal granted a condemned man: he knew that when he returned to North Carolina he would probably be assigned a remote parish and never be heard from again. Walsh was in a similar situation. He was in Montreal as, if anything, a hastily chosen substitute. The priest he replaced had remembered at the last minute that he was scheduled to preach a retreat at a Boston convent: Walsh was allowed to go because there was no time to choose anyone else. Walsh, too, was at odds with his superior—an archbishop. In Montreal he tried to put out of his mind the dread thought that when he returned to Boston he would be appointed to a suburban parish where he could be easily forgotten.

And yet these two men, each in his own way, were soon to take part in the American development of their Church to such an extent that their names would forever outshine those of their two superiors who were trying to get rid of them.

Price's parents were converts. His mother became a Catholic at eighteen, an act for which her family disowned her. Homeless, she moved in with the family of Dr. Frederick Gallagher while she finished her education. Through the Gallaghers she met Alfred Lanier Price, and they were eventually married. Alfred subsequently became the editor of the *Wilmington Daily Journal,* North Carolina's first daily newspaper, and it was in Wilmington that the ten Price children, five boys and five girls, were born.

Thomas Frederick Price, the sixth child and the third son, was born on August 19, 1860, and he was six years old the Christmas his father became a Catholic. The boy made the unusual remark, "This is the best Christmas present I could ever have." He was, obviously, deeply religious, a trait he acquired from his pious mother. The Prices lived next door to St. Thomas's Catholic Church; Clarissa Bond Price was at Mass every morning, accompanied by as many of the children as were old enough, and the parish priests were frequent guests in the Price home. At eight, young Fred Price was serving the daily Masses of Father James Gibbons, who had been appointed from Baltimore to be the vicar apostolic of North Carolina. Gibbons later became the cardinal-archbishop of Baltimore and remained Price's lifelong friend.

Wilmington had no Catholic school taught by Sisters, but in the basement of St. Thomas's two of the Price daughters, Mary and Agnes, conducted classes for Catholic children. Fred Price was, of course, one of their pupils; later in life he often joked that he couldn't escape being a good student because of the pressure of having to live with his teachers. Both girls eventually joined the Sisters of Mercy and they worked with Price after he became a priest. Mary Price particularly had a strong influence on her brother, a situation that was to stir severe criticism.

Clarissa Price wanted one of her sons to be a priest. Willie, the second son, actually studied three years for the priesthood at St. Charles College in Maryland, but then he changed his mind, went home to Wilmington, got a job in a bank, married, and raised a family. When, therefore, Fred announced at sixteen that he wanted to enter a seminary, Mrs. Price was both happy and eager to pave the way. The education his sisters had given him qualified Price for the second-year high school level, which was remarkably good under the circumstances. The college readily accepted him.

The best way to travel from Wilmington to Baltimore in 1876 was by sea. A few years earlier, the youngest Price boy had drowned in the Cape Fear River; the necessity of the voyage, then, was the only aspect of Fred's vocation that Mrs. Price disliked. On the morning of Friday, September 15, she accompanied him to the pier, four miles downstream from Wilmington, and helped him settle in his cabin aboard the steam packet *Rebecca Clyde.*

"Now, be careful," she told him repeatedly.

"Of course I'll be careful," he assured.

"I mean, don't go near the railing or anything," she said. "You know you can't swim."

He laughed. "Don't worry. I'll be all right. I'll write you as soon as I get to Baltimore."

"Yes, do that," she said. She glanced at the cabin walls, appraising their sturdiness. "I wish you were there already."

"So do I," said Fred. "I wish I were ordained and back here."

He was uneasy about leaving her. His father had died when he was twelve; his two older brothers were married and his two older sisters were away in a convent; he was practically the man of the family. Knowing he would be away from his mother for most of the next nine years discomforted him.

"Be careful," she said again. Then she kissed him and went ashore.

The *Rebecca Clyde* reached the open sea at noon on Friday and turned north. Within an hour, storm clouds caught up with her from the south. The barometer dropped quickly to a dangerous low, a wind struck, and the sea burst into savage whitecaps. Some of the passengers tried to calm themselves with coffee in the ship's lounge, but Price was too sick for coffee or company. He lay on his bunk, stiff and frightened, his rosary clutched in his hands. When he heard the dinner call, a stab of nausea made him grimace. He rolled over and buried his face in his pillow.

Saturday the storm was worse. The vicious wind sent giant waves crashing against the ship, knocking her off course and rolling her precariously to port. When Price failed to appear for breakfast or lunch, a steward came to check on him.

"You ought to eat something," the man suggested.

"I can't," Price said.

"I'll bring you some coffee and a sandwich," the steward offered. "You can have it when you want."

"No," said Price. "Thanks. I'll be all right. Just leave me alone."

He tried to sleep. At one point the wind shook the *Rebecca Clyde* so fiercely that Price was tossed to the floor. He heard a crash at his side: while he had slept the steward had brought a tray of food and now it was on the floor beside him. He salvaged what he could and put the tray on a chair. Sitting on the edge of his bed, he stared at the tray realizing how hungry he was. Several minutes passed before he got the courage to reach for the sandwich and try it. Two bites were enough. He stretched out again and put an arm over his face to hide the sight of his clothes, swinging wildly on hooks.

That night the heart of the storm hit the ship like a lightning bolt. The sea grabbed at the ship, pulling her deep into the violent waves, then throwing her brutally back at the black sky. All night Price heard the crew scurrying across the wind-beaten decks, futilely struggling with the cargo. Near morning, a steward banged on the door. "Go to the lounge," he cried. "The captain wants all passengers in the lounge."

It was hopeless. Price tried to stand, but his legs were too weak to hold him. Just then a mountain of water crashed down on the ship's bow and held it under. Cargo broke from ropes and smashed the steering gear. Price lost his balance and careened across his cabin hitting the opposite wall hard. Dazed and hurt, he slid to the floor, watching helplessly as furniture piled on top of him. Suddenly there was silence, and for a moment Price wondered if he had lost consciousness. He looked at the door and saw water seeping into the room.

From above came a man's shout: "We've hit the shoals! Abandon ship! Abandon ship!"

It was impossible for Price to move. He remained there, pinned down by the heavy furniture, watching the water flow into his room. Then the ship seemed to settle, and the weight upon him lessened. He could move his arms; he pushed some of the furniture aside and struggled to his feet.

The water in the corridor was up to his ankles. He stumbled his way up the stairs and outside to the deck. The noise, the wind and rain and the cold stormed at him. Most of the passengers and crew had already donned life jackets and were jumping over the side. Price went to the big box where the preservers were kept, but they were all gone. Frantic, he looked around for somebody to help him. He gripped the rail and inched his way forward, and before he had gone half the length of the ship he realized that he was the last person aboard.

He did not know what to do. Too terrified to move, he tightened his grasp on the railing and stared out at the sea. Then he saw it: the gigantic wave, rising a hundred feet from him, growing in height and power and roaring down at him.

The defeated ship shivered and began to break up. The great wave slammed against the ship with such force that Price felt the railing disintegrate in his hands. He skidded along the deck for several feet, then fell down. He was aware of being scooped up and flung over the side.

He cried, "Christ Jesus, save me or I perish!" And then the sea closed over him.

When he bobbed to the surface a moment later he saw something he was too startled to question. Years passed before he spoke to anyone about it.

He saw, poised in the air above him, a woman he immediately recognized as the Blessed Virgin. She seemed untouched by the storm; she was calm and peaceful and she was smiling at him. Then she pointed. Price looked to his right and saw a big plank that had been ripped from the ship's deck. By flailing his arms and legs he was able to reach it and he threw his arms around it.

In an instant he lost all concern for himself. He could think only of the apparition he had just experienced. He looked all around him, hoping the Virgin would still be there but she was gone. He felt warm and safe and very happy. The cold wind still ripped at him, the water was like ice, and the rain pounded his head, but he did not care. He began to recite the Litany of the Blessed Virgin, and there was so much joy in him that he almost sang it.

He was in the water over six hours before the storm pushed him close enough to shore for his feet to touch bottom. When he dragged himself onto the beach he was still holding on to the plank. He heard voices and he was aware of people. He let himself drop to the sand.

Someone cried, "Here's another one over here. It's a man—no, a boy." Then closer, "Are you all right?"

Price could not bring himself to answer.

"Where's the doctor? Doc, there's another one over here."

Then, "Here, drink this."

A bottle was put to Price's lips and a bit of bitter, burning liquid filled his mouth. He spat it out. It was the first time he had tasted whiskey, and he did not taste it again until an equally strange night forty years later.

The *Rebecca Clyde* had hit the Hatteras shoals at Pamlico

Sound, and the storm had carried Price almost twenty miles to shore near the village of Portsmouth. It had been the worst storm in the history of the area. The villagers, knowing that other storms had forced ships onto the shoals, had set up a watch in case any accidents happened this night. When they were sure there would be no more survivors, they took Price and the others to their homes for rest and food and medical attention. One passenger had drowned, so had the captain and ten members of the crew. When Price told them later that he did not know how to swim they said that surely his survival was miraculous. He agreed with them.

Five days after leaving Wilmington, Price was back home. He remained until the following February when, this time by land, he made the journey to Baltimore and entered the spring term of St. Charles College for his preseminary training. Upon his graduation in 1881, he entered St. Mary's Seminary close by for five more years of intensive study. He worked hard and held his own, but there was no subject in which he was particularly outstanding. When his classmates talked about him years later they spoke mostly of his fervent devotion to the Blessed Virgin; they admired him for it, but only one of them ever discovered the dramatic background of it when Price told him long afterward.

On June 20, 1886, he was ordained in his home parish in Wilmington, the first native North Carolinian to become a secular priest. His only sadness was that his mother was not present: she had died six months before.

His ambition was to convert everybody in North Carolina. This would have been an impossible task even if all the priests in the state had dedicated all their efforts to it exclusively. There were, actually, few priests in the state at the time—about eight secular priests scattered in remote areas and a dozen Benedictines at an abbey near Belmont, west of Charlotte. The bishop of North Carolina was a Benedictine—Bishop Leo Haid, who was also the abbot of the monastery. The Benedictines had moved to North Carolina from their parent house at Latrobe, Pennsylvania. The men were either Germans or had been strongly influenced by Germans. In a highly rural state that still lived in an atmosphere of Elizabethan Protestantism, the monks were considered, even by many of the Catholics, to be foreigners, therefore suspect and un-approachable.

In deciding to convert all of North Carolina, then, the young Father Fred Price had picked himself a tough job. His first assignment was his home parish in Wilmington, where he filled in for several months for his pastor who went back to Ireland on vacation. Price was next assigned to Asheville, again as a substitute. In 1887, he was appointed to New Bern, on the coast, where he was made pastor of St. Paul's Church and seventeen mission chapels scattered over an area of three hundred square miles.

His particular advantage was that he was a native Tarheel. If at first his Roman collar scared off North Carolinians, his speech, his mannerisms, and his attitude showed him to be one of them and they gradually warmed to him. He encountered the usual obstacles of a Catholic priest in the South at that time. Once while riding a stagecoach a woman asked him, "Are you one of them papist priests?"

"I am a priest of the Roman Catholic Church," he clarified.

"Is it true," she asked, "that popish priests have horns?"

"I am only a young priest," Price said. He took off his hat and pointed to a pimple on his forehead. "Mine are just beginning to come out."

He traveled almost constantly, preferring to walk as often as he could because this gave him the opportunity to chat with farmers along the way and to visit towns off the normal transportation routes. He had the typical North Carolinian's concern for everything that happened in the state, and so he was able to talk to farmers about crops, to merchants about business, and to innkeepers about the woes of the world. And yet, conversation with strangers was often difficult for him. He was inclined toward shyness and solitude, and because he could not easily be casual he was more apt to be silent. Because of this he was usually considered to be a gentle person, but on the other hand he had no talent for diplomacy and in matters that were important to him he expressed himself directly, almost to the point of being sharp. At other times, when events around him did not hold his interest, he retreated suddenly into his own thoughts so deeply that he might just as well have left the room.

By early manhood he had lost most of his brown hair. He developed a short, square body that gave the impression he was heavier than he actually was. His steel-rimmed glasses fitted tightly against his face and he always seemed to be squinting. He walked with a heavy, tense step, his head thrust forward expectantly. His dislike for inactivity showed in his awkwardness with his hands: he never knew what to do with them, and they usually ended clasped firmly in front of him or pressed flat against his chest. He loathed having his picture taken, and when he couldn't get out of it he either hid himself in the back row of a group of people or turned away from the camera or frowned fiercely.

Putting himself forward in the course of his ministry must have been an ordeal for him, and yet he was successful at it. Several men who worked with him in later years admitted he was unusual but they were openly devoted to him. Despite the anti-Catholic sentiments during his early days in North Carolina, he won many friends and was welcomed as a man in homes where he was at the same time resented as a priest. He delighted in telling of how, one morning, after spending the night at a farmhouse, he had set up his portable Mass kit and was in the middle of the ceremony when the tiny daughter of the family came in, tugged at his vestments, and said, "Mamma says come eat your breakfast now, mister. You can finish that later."

He earned a reputation for excellent sermons. During his New Bern assignment, the Raleigh newspaper carried an article about him, mentioning the towns he visited regularly and urging people to go to hear him speak. The remarkable feature about the article was that it appeared at all and it showed clearly how Price was able to get along with people despite their attitude toward his religion.

Throughout his nine years at New Bern he retained his desire for broad-scale evangelization of the state. He left no record of how many he might have converted at New Bern, but he still wanted a try at the whole of North Carolina. In October, 1896, he went to Belmont to see Bishop Haid and he said, "I want permission to start a Catholic magazine for North Carolina."

"A magazine?" the Bishop said. "Who will buy it? There are only eight hundred Catholics in the whole state."

"It will be a Catholic magazine for Protestants," Price explained. "I want to call it *Truth*, and it will contain articles explaining the Catholic faith."

"But what experience do you have in running a magazine?"

"My father was a newspaper editor," said Price. "I learned a lot from him."

The Bishop was not impressed. "How do you expect to pay for this?"

"I have thirty-five dollars," Price said. "I've already talked to a printer in Raleigh and he said that's enough to bring out a first issue of five hundred copies."

"What about the second issue?"

Price shrugged. "I will have to trust to God and Mary to provide."

The Bishop nodded knowingly. "Well, if you want to throw away your money, go ahead," he said. "Just remember that I have none to give you."

Money did not prove to be a problem. In ten years, *Truth* acquired a circulation of twelve thousand throughout the South and West. Most of the copies were given away free to Protestants of every social and professional level, with support coming from Northern Catholics who were anxious to give an explanation of themselves to Protestants. At the outset, Price wrote that the magazine would not deal with controversial subjects but was dedicated purely to the definition of Catholic ideas. But controversy was inescapable. Protestant ministers denounced the magazine from their pulpits, suggesting that its name be changed to *Lies,* and many recipients sent it back untouched. Some wrote letters heavy with familiar accusations of popism, foreignism, Mary-worship, scandalous priests and nuns, and a secret plot to take over the world by force. Soon Price was busy turning out defensive articles that returned the attacks with fresh attacks and the magazine eventually became a battleground.

When Bishop Haid permitted Price to start *Truth* he also released him from parish work. Now Price was free to travel the entire state. One of his aims was to confront his accusers, in private discussion or public debate, whichever they preferred, but his most vitriolic opponents refused to have anything to do with him. Price therefore spent the time with Catholic groups or with individual Protestants he knew to be possible converts. He often said that the best argument for the Catholic Church would be one good Catholic family in each town, but again his success at this work was not recorded.

As he traveled around he became increasingly aware of the number of orphans in the state, especially in the cities, and he was haunted by the desire to do something for them. One day he encountered one of his New Bern parishioners on the streets of Raleigh and after a brief conversation he announced, "I am going to start an orphanage."

"That's a fine idea," the man said. "Where?"

"I've seen some property about three miles west of town," Price said. "Six hundred acres."

"Will the Bishop be in on it with you?"

"I haven't discussed it with him yet," Price said.

"What if he says no?"

Price said, "I don't think he will. It's not going to cost him anything."

"Where are you going to get the money?"

"That I don't know," said Price. "I just know that I'm going to start an orphanage."

He did. Where he got the money nobody ever discovered. But he bought the land, changed over the house into dormitories, and convinced the Sisters of Mercy to send him some nuns to take care of the children. A group of five Sisters arrived, headed by his own sister Mary. He called the orphanage Nazareth. At first he had only a few boys, but by the end of a year their number was up to forty. To support them, he started another magazine, called *The Orphan Boy,* and, although it did not reach a circulation that could possibly pay all the bills, Price somehow found the money to add an industrial school to the orphanage where the boys could learn trades.

So he had two magazines, an orphanage, and a school to occupy him, plus his continued travels throughout the state in search of converts. He could never put the converts out of his mind. When paper work kept him at Nazareth too long, he would become restless and testy, eager to get back on the road. More and more, he turned Nazareth affairs over to his sister, until the day came when she was practically in charge. He realized that if he was to fulfill any part of all his plans he would need an assistant; in June, 1900, Father Michael Irwin was assigned to work with him. Like others who were to follow him, Irwin discovered that he had to take orders as much from Mary Price as from Fred Price, a situation that eventually proved unpleasant; but unlike most of the others, Irwin did not let this discolor his admiration for Price himself.

The plain truth was that Price was an exceedingly disorganized administrator. He had no conception of money; his books were a mess; he never had the slightest idea of how much he had in the bank. Business forms, whether those of the Bishop or the state, bewildered him, when he gave them any attention at all. His office and his room at Nazareth always looked as if they had just been ransacked. Whenever his sister or Father Irwin pleaded with him to find a missing document he would brush them off with "Well, it wasn't important anyway. And if it was, then they'll send us another copy." This unconcern for business affairs was the cause of his frequent hasty recalls to Nazareth to raise money to buy food for the orphans, to pay the printer, to meet a bank note, or soothe some impatient creditor, but the emergencies never disturbed him enough for him to take any preventive steps about them.

He was the same way with himself. He never cared what he ate or what he wore or how he looked. At meals, if there was no special topic to keep him talking excitedly, he quietly put away his food, his mind miles away. He was indifferent to the variety of spots on his suit and cassock and he paid so little attention to clothes that he would go on trips dressed in anything handy, regardless of its color or cut. He simply had no concern for the outer man and could not understand anybody who did.

These shortcomings were to have their cost. In his anxiety for converts, Price decided that a good step would be to have North Carolinians get used to seeing working priests with some regularity. With this in mind, he wrote Northern seminaries and invited students to spend their summer with him on missionary treks into rural areas. Because of *Truth,* the students knew about him, they admired him and what he was trying to do, and in their youthful zeal they were impatient to get into the fray. Thus, for the next three or four summers, there were always a dozen of them eager to volunteer to work in the backwoods of North Carolina. They were, however, both young enough and practical enough to want a decent meal once in a while, to have their clothes washed occasionally, and to have a place where they could get in out of the rain without having to rely on the uncertain hospitality of an isolated farmer startled by the sudden appearance at his door of a cluster of black-robed young men. Therefore, although there were always students ready to go to North Carolina for the summer, there were none who were ready to go back.

Nevertheless, they did good work. If the people still did not tip their hats to Price when they saw him in the winter, at least they no longer threw things at him. One day, while Price was giving a street-corner sermon in a farm town, he was pelted with a particularly heavy barrage of cabbages, potatoes, tomatoes, and onions. He announced, "Now, if somebody will kindly throw a piece of meat up here, I should be able to make a good stew out of all this." They laughed, and then they listened to him.

Price felt he was now ready for his next step. He wanted to organize a new society of priests to work among the Southern Protestants—North Carolina first, then the rest of the South. But North Carolina first.

Bishop Haid was against it. In the first place, he was wary of what he was convinced would be serious repercussions when North Carolinians found out that a band of priests was being organized to convert them; the time was not ripe for that sort of thing. In the second place, even had he been for the idea, experience had forced him to suspect that Price was not the man to do the organizing. There would be so much red tape involved, all the way to Rome. Also, there were the additional problems of money, housing, training facilities—no, it was too much.

But Price had a way of getting what he wanted from the Bishop. This was not based on any great affection between the two men because, actually, they were always quite reserved with each other. Nobody was ever able to explain why. If they had argued or if there had been a breach between them there would have been evidence of it in their diaries or personal files, or their separate friends would have heard of it. But there was nothing like that. Most likely the problem was simply one of personalities, or perhaps it was one of a bishop who thought a priest was reaching beyond his grasp and a priest who thought a bishop would not reach at all. In any event, the two men were stuck with each other. Their relationship in public was restrained; others observed it and remembered it. If in their private discussions Price always seemed to come out winner, it might well have been that Bishop Haid lacked the stamina to resist Price's unemotional stubbornness once he made up his mind. In the end, the Bishop gave his consent.

Price built a new house at Nazareth for what he hopefully expected would be a deluge of volunteers. He wrote to seminaries in the North, explaining his plan. Students would undergo a year of spiritual formation at Nazareth, then enter the Benedictine monastery at Belmont to finish their studies. He also sent news of his plan to Northern bishops, asking them to pass it on to any priests who might be interested. Price called both the new Nazareth house and the new program Queen of Apostles—Regina Apostolorum.

It was doomed from the start. The first serious problem was the national shortage of priests. No bishop was about to release one of his seminarians or one of his priests to go to work in North Carolina unless he suspected there was something wrong with the man. Price failed to take this into consideration. Thus the men he got were not exactly prize catches. They were seminarians who, for any number of reasons, were not making the grade where they were and, had they not joined Price, might have given up their studies altogether. And they were priests who had proved to be such malcontents that, despite the shortage, their bishops were relieved to get them out of the diocese. The second serious problem was Price himself.

Between 1902 and 1907, the Regina Apostolorum population, at Nazareth and Belmont, averaged about twenty a year. The turnover was heavy; most of the students did not return after their vacations. Of all the students, there was only one who completed the entire course of studies, was ordained, then joined Price's work. A few of the others did become priests, but they either joined the Benedictines or went out to some other diocese. The priests who entered the movement made a similar showing. Most of them left after a few months, many of them bitterly. They

complained about Price's bad management, his indifference toward their material welfare, the unnecessarily Spartan routine he
imposed, and they resented the broad authority that Mary Price
wielded. In 1905, the building burned down, but the undiscouraged
Price rebuilt it. Bishop Haid was very discouraged, distressed to
see so much money, time, and effort achieve so little, but he felt
there was nothing he could do but sit back and watch the movement die of its own dead weight.

One good thing that came out of it was the wide attention it
earned for Price. Church experts in mission work thought he had
a good idea, and undoubtedly he did; they sought him out. During Easter Week, 1904, Price was invited to Washington, D. C., to
address a mission conference. He spoke on "The Progress of Localized Missions." On the same program was Father James Anthony
Walsh, director of the Boston office of the Society for the Propagation of the Faith. In his paper on the foreign missions, Walsh
said, "While conscious of the need of priests in many parts of our
country, I believe that to send some of our young men and women
to more remote districts would stimulate vocations for home needs,
and especially for the more remote missions of the United States."

Price liked that. It made sense. He realized that one of the problems with his own project was that North Carolina offered none
of the drama that might attract a young man or woman who
sought the exciting life of missionary work in distant lands. But
it seemed reasonable to him that if the Church in America took
aggressive action in the foreign missions, which it could not possibly have done to date, inevitably some of the vocations among
youngsters not eager to go too far from home would fall to North
Carolina.

After the conference, Price told Walsh how much he had enjoyed the talk and he promised to help the foreign missions any
way he could. An early issue of *Truth* contained an article about
the Propagation of the Faith Society, urging support of it. Walsh
saw the article and sent Price a note of gratitude. Price was not
the type to stop there. He had an idea; he was determined to give
it life. In a subsequent issue of the magazine he published an
article on how the Church in America could start in the foreign
mission field. He suggested that a major seminary be established
in affiliation with the Catholic University, which the American

hierarchy had founded in 1887 at Washington, D. C. The future missionaries could live in their own house, undergoing their spiritual formation and special training there while taking their regular classes at the university. Meanwhile, preparatory seminaries could be built in the major cities—high schools where aspirants for the priesthood could study closer to their own homes. Those who successfully completed the preliminary courses and were found worthy could then go on to Washington. Price offered to donate his services to what would amount to America's own missionary society, and he asked his readers for reactions. From Boston, Walsh wrote enthusiastically, urging Price to go ahead, promising that his office would provide all the help it could. But the idea seemed to die with that; years passed and nothing happened.

Nothing was happening with the Regina Apostolorum, either. Bishop Haid reached the point where he felt that the effort, no matter how noble, was never going to get off the ground and he let it be known that he was considering its dissolution. In August, 1908, the handful of secular priests in North Carolina met at Belmont for a retreat, during which the Bishop indicated to Price that his days were numbered.

The Belmont retreat brought another change, a quite different one, into Price's life. He made a resolution to "Write a letter every day to my own dear Mother Mary—even if one line only." It was an unusual resolution, and it showed his deep love for the Virgin Mary. He kept his resolution to the day of his death, writing daily almost without exception. The letters amounted to a diary, a most intimate one, revealing his intense piety and his consuming preoccupation with spiritual affairs. When the diaries were transcribed after his death, they totaled fifteen hundred typewritten pages. They revealed, too, his devotion to Bernadette Soubirous, the French girl who, in 1858, experienced apparitions of the Blessed Virgin at Lourdes. Price's friends knew of his attachment for Bernadette: he spoke about her often, in the years to come he visited her home and shrine at Lourdes, and he edited a translated French book about her, but no one could have imagined until the contents of his letters became known the extraordinary extent of his feelings.

After the retreat, Price plunged back into work. He tried several times to attract more men to Regina Apostolorum, hoping that by stirring new life into it he could protect it from Bishop Haid's growing impatience, but he had thin luck. He continued to travel a great deal, giving speeches, building chapels, urging North Carolina Catholics to be more overt in the practice of their religion so that the Protestants might outgrow their apprehensions. He avoided Haid as much as he could in order to postpone as long as possible what he realized would be the discussion that would close the doors on his pet project. The two men went weeks, even months, without seeing each other, which was unusual in so small a vicariate. Then Price heard that the Bishop was also thinking of absorbing the orphanage as a vicariate program, thereby taking its administration out of Price's hands. He was very unhappy. A life as a parish priest loomed ahead of him and he knew his heart would be chained by the restrictions.

He wanted to get away and think. The International Eucharistic Congress was soon to take place in Montreal. Without the slightest notion of how little money he had in the bank, he wrote a check to pay for his transportation and took off.

III

JAMES ANTHONY WALSH was the son of Irish immigrants who both arrived in America in their childhood and settled in Boston. When Walsh was born, on February 24, 1867, his father was the owner of a liquor store which, located as it was in the heart of the Irish colony, proved to be a gold mine. With his profits, Walsh senior bought real estate and invested in stocks, thereby acquiring a social stature that the liquor store alone could not provide. The family lived in a large house at 14 Greenwich Park and had a summer cottage at Ocean Spray, Winthrop; they also owned a horse and two carriages. They were considered well off.

Despite the steadily growing Irish population, Boston remained predominantly Protestant, particularly in the zones of social influence. There was only one Sister-taught Catholic school, and it was overcrowded. At the age of six, therefore, young James Walsh entered the Dwight Public Grammar School on West Springfield Street. However, Walsh's mother saw to it that her six children, four boys and two girls, received a proper Catholic training. They were baptized, received their First Communion, and were confirmed as soon as she felt they were ready; they all attended Sunday School regularly at Immaculate Conception Church, and the boys learned to serve Mass. From their mother, the children learned music, French, and a taste for the arts. The family kept a good-sized library in the house and the children grew up with a fondness for books. While they were still very young, Mrs. Walsh felt she detected definite proclivities in two of her sons: Timothy, the second boy, would be an architect, she was sure, and James would be a priest. She died when both boys were in their early teens, but they never forgot what she expected of them.

James had been his mother's pet. From their close association he had assimilated a great deal about housekeeping matters and after her death he took her place in the family with effective ease. He saw to it that the servants did their work, that the household needs were met, and that life went on as normally as possible; all this was to serve him well in the years ahead.

He was a bright boy, charming, well mannered, mature, and he had the Irish gift for a phrase. At nine he had won an elocution contest in the Boston public school system, the prize for which was the privilege of reciting a poem at a dinner for the Emperor of Brazil, Pedro II, who was visiting the city. In high school, he won a twenty-five-dollar prize in a debate on the subject of woman suffrage. He was against it.

Despite his mother's ambitions, there was little evidence during his teens that young James would become a priest. He remembered later that his only interest in the missions occurred when he was ten, when a Jesuit missionary told his Sunday School class about the plight of Chinese children who were abandoned by their parents. Cards were passed out to be filled with twelve pennies to help such children. James could easily have got the money from his father, but he preferred to collect the twelve cents by begging door to door in his neighborhood. This, too, served him well in later years. But outside of that, there was no clue of a vocation.

At seventeen, James was graduated from Boston College High School, a Catholic school. Connected with the school was Boston College, but since the college did not award the usual degrees it was presumed that any young man who entered it intended to go on to the priesthood. James entered, but still he said nothing about his plans. At the end of the year, his father's real estate and stock investments took a bad turn. Timothy Walsh was then an apprentice with a firm of architects and was earning practically nothing. In order that Timothy could continue with his

studies, James gave up his. The liquor store, which had wisely
been retained, provided a family income until the financial
crisis passed. A year later, James's father said the boy could go
back to college if he wished. Instead of returning to Boston
College, however, James entered Harvard, and that, everybody
thought, would be the end of the priesthood for him.

Harvard was then on the threshold of a new religion: the worship of brotherhood on the altars of social services. It acknowledged God, but merely as everybody's big brother; it denied the
supernatural, redemption, and sin; it made each man a priest,
whose theology was the Golden Rule, whose ritual was good
manners, and whose sacraments were municipal charity. But it
was a comfortable religion because it provided a sense of belong-
ing to a high-minded organization that had no commandments
except fellowship.

James Walsh lived at home, which protected him from becoming involved in either the plans or the parties of his classmates. He could not have been too interested in them or in the
school because, oddly enough for a young man who had already
proved himself to be a brilliant student, of the six courses he
carried at Harvard he managed with Latin and Greek, he scarcely
passed German and English, and he completely ignored mathe-
matics and chemistry. He spent just a year there. Later he said,
"The most important thing I learned at Harvard was that I
didn't belong there." In September of 1886 he boarded a horse-
car near his house, rode out to the Brighton hills, and entered
St. John's Seminary, the training center for the Boston diocese.

He was nineteen, a little shy, a little displaced by this, his
first time away from his family. He was dressed too well, which
his classmates attributed to his Harvard adventure. His thick,
arched eyebrows and his aquiline nose gave the impression that
he was always looking down at people, which the students took
to be another Harvard trait. He had arrived prepared for a
somber atmosphere: the boisterous bursts of the seminarians so
surprised him that he had difficulty unwinding with them. It
was the custom for the students to take a long walk every Thursday, paired off in a line behind one of the faculty priests. Walsh
disliked the military spectacle the line made; the regimentation
took all the pleasure out of the walk for him, and he suspected

it did for the others. On the third walk, the students encountered a similar line of orphans, hurrying along in the same puffing double row, behind a quick-stepping nun. The priest leading the seminarians saw the orphans and smiled at the amusing sight of them, wholly unaware that the students behind him looked equally amusing. Walsh spoke up, "Well, for a moment there I didn't know if we were coming or going." The seminarians laughed.

The priest glanced over his shoulder and quickly recognized the ludicrous similarity between the two groups. He stopped. "You can walk slower," he said, "and you need not stay in pairs."

After that the walks were less like calisthenics, more enjoyable, and the students knew they had Walsh to thank for it. And with that he became one of them.

The seminary faculty, comprised entirely of Sulpicians, were pioneers in preparing a curriculum for the secular priesthood and they remained leaders in the field for centuries. Until the early nineteenth century, Americans who wanted to be secular priests usually went to France to study under the Sulpicians. But the anticlericism that was part of the French Revolution had lingered long after it and forced the Sulpicians to close some of their schools and move out of the country. Bishop John Carroll of Baltimore, the first American to become a bishop, invited the society to come to the United States and start a seminary in his diocese. As new dioceses opened, the Sulpicians were asked to establish seminaries in Boston and New York. There was only one thing wrong with this—or at least some people thought so. It was customary, when a new bishop was to be appointed, for the Vatican to consult with neighboring bishops for suggestions. In the early years of the nineteenth century—for a good part of it, actually—there were few American bishops to consult. Thus the Vatican did the next best thing: the Sulpicians, who had trained all the secular priests in the country, were asked to suggest a man. As a result, the Church in America was in Sulpician hands for a long while. Unquestionably, they did a good job, but nevertheless the time came when there were enough American bishops for consultation, who soon discovered that the Sulpicians were still making the choices, and a bit too often the

choices were French priests who had come over during the
sporadic outbursts of French persecutions and gone into mission
work in the fast-developing West. Some American bishops, although Sulpician trained, resented what appeared to be a permanent Sulpician prerogative, and in future years Walsh became
involved in it.

Walsh loved the Sulpicians he met at the Boston seminary.
Two of them—Abbé Hogan and Father Gabriel André—remained
his friends for life. Their intense interest in the foreign missions
sparked Walsh and he was soon corresponding with several
members of the Paris Foreign Mission Society, then the largest
society of its kind. From his Sulpician friends, Walsh learned of
Théophane Vénard, a young Frenchman who, in 1852, worked
in the Paris society's missions in Tonkin. Vénard was a holy man,
an inspiration to all who knew him. He often said his ambition
was to become a martyr, an ambition that was shortly fulfilled
when anti-Christian Tonkinese savagely beheaded him. He had
left behind a voluminous collection of letters. Walsh read them
and developed a deep attachment for the man. Later Walsh
wrote a book and magazine articles about Vénard and spoke
about him as often as Fred Price spoke about Saint Bernadette.

It was surprising that after six years of such influence Walsh's
concrete interest in the missions should seem to wilt the day he
was ordained. This was on May 20, 1892. He was assigned to St.
Patrick's parish, Roxbury, and was quickly absorbed in the duties
of a young curate. He was busy enough. In addition to his
sacerdotal duties, he was put in charge of the Holy Name Society, the Young Ladies Sodality, and the altar boys, and he was
responsible for the decoration of the sanctuary. To keep former
altar boys active in the church he organized the Sanctuary Boys
Alumni, and from this group a dozen young men went on to the
priesthood. He also organized the Catholic Young Men's Association and the Catholic Young Women's Association to check-
mate the Protestant influence of similar organizations. His neighborhood had no public library; he convinced the City of Boston
to open a branch in one of the parish halls. His interest in his
people was more overt than that of the patient curate who waited
for parishioners to drop by the rectory. He was out every day

into the homes of parish families, particularly those who did not make much of a habit of visiting the church.

He liked to spend his vacation in the woods, most often with Father James F. Stanton, a classmate who had become a devoted friend. Their favorite haunt was at Long Lake, in the Adirondacks. There they met Harry Harper, of the publishing family, who gave them an acre of his own shore property for a camp. For the next few years, the two priests were there, frequently with other Boston priests, for two weeks of a routine so different from their daily lives in the city that they could not help but return refreshed. In 1902, Walsh and Stanton obtained permission for a two-month vacation in Europe. It was on this trip, most likely, that Walsh's interest in the missions was revived. In England, he visited the Mill Hill Fathers, the British missionary society; in Italy, he visited the Milan Foreign Mission Society; in France, of course, he called on the Paris Foreign Mission Society. He was allowed to examine the room of Théophane Vénard and read letters in the Frenchman's own handwriting: this part of the visit was something of a pilgrimage for him. Abbé Hogan was dead; Walsh visited his grave. Father André, then assigned to Avignon, came up to Paris to spend a few days with Walsh. Walsh returned home stirred up again about the missions, and soon he was to do something about it.

There existed an organization called the Society for the Propagation of the Faith. It had been started in Lyon, France, in 1819 by Mademoiselle Pauline Jaricot for the purpose of supporting foreign missions. In earlier days, the Church had received funds for its mission work from the crowned heads of Europe, but some of the crowns had turned out to be a little crooked, others had slipped considerably, and others had fallen on Protestant heads. To support the missions, the Vatican consigned as a means of support certain properties held in Europe to the Sacred College of Propaganda Fide, a Vatican administration department which supervised mission efforts. Church property was confiscated during the French Revolution and the income from France was thus cut off. Pauline Jaricot's plan was to have French children donate a penny a year to help the missionaries. The program was so successful that it spread to other countries and Mademoiselle Jaricot soon found herself with a great deal of money to disburse every year. The mission world was so wide that she could not possibly know how to allocate the funds to the best advantage, but she realized that of course the Vatican knew. The program was then made part of the Sacred College of Propaganda Fide.

In 1822, American Catholics sent their first contribution to the Society—six dollars. They were obviously ready to do more, but they needed to be organized. The program was then carried on at the parish level, but the United States was itself a mission territory and it was natural that many pastors were reluctant to send elsewhere money which they themselves needed. Nevertheless, the program held a certain attraction and Americans wanted a bigger part in it. Gradually it moved up to the diocesan level, but it still needed organization. On a trip to France, Cardinal Gibbons discussed the Society with Father André, whose interest in the missions he knew. André was invited to return to America to give the movement some direction, which he did with considerable success. It was then suggested that more could be achieved if the independent diocesan branches of the Society were linked in a national organization. This was done; the first national offices were in Baltimore, and later they were moved to New York.

In 1903, the national director was Father Joseph Freri. His assistant was a convert layman named Moses Hale Douglas, whose cousin, a Boston Episcopal minister, had also become a Catholic and taken a job in the Boston Public Library. On a visit to Boston, Douglas had met Walsh during his efforts to get a library branch for his neighborhood. The Boston director of the Society was Father Joseph Tracy. One day Walsh read in the *Pilot,* the Boston diocesan paper, that Tracy was ill and would resign his position.

Walsh looked up from the paper and said out loud, "I am going to be the next diocesan director of the Society. I know it as well as I know I'm sitting here."

When Tracy went to Baltimore to submit his resignation, Freri asked, "Do you know anybody else in Boston who might replace you?"

Tracy said, "I can't say. I haven't given the matter any thought."

Douglas remembered the only priest he had met in Boston. "What about Father Walsh?" he suggested.

"James Walsh?" Tracy asked. Tracy knew Walsh slightly.

"Yes," said Douglas.

"Maybe he'd take it."

A week later, Walsh was strolling in the rectory garden, reading his breviary, when he saw a bearded priest approach the rectory door. "That," he said, "is Father Freri, and he has come to offer me the job."

He was right. The housekeeper led Father Freri into the garden, and he said, "I am Father Freri, of Propagation."

"Yes, I know," said Walsh.

"Father Tracy is resigning because of ill health," said Freri. "Your name has been suggested as his successor."

"Yes, I know," said Walsh. Freri looked at Walsh quickly, then decided he had heard of the suggestion through rumors. But he had not; he had not discussed it with anyone. Walsh said, "I am indeed very interested in the work, Father, and I appreciate the offer."

"I have talked to Archbishop Williams about it," Freri said. "It is all right with him."

"That's good," said Walsh. "May I think about if for twenty-four hours, Father, and give you my answer tomorrow?"

"Of course," Freri said. "I am staying at the cathedral. You can reach me there."

"I will," said Walsh, "the first thing in the morning."

Walsh used the time to discuss the offer with Stanton and with Father John I. Lane, another seminary friend and summer-camp companion. They all agreed it was an excellent opportunity. Then Walsh checked the Archbishop's office to be sure the transfer would be approved. In the morning he telephoned Father Freri and said that he would take the job. He reported for work the following Monday morning.

As he sat at his desk for the first time, he looked around at the roomful of books, maps, files, and mission paraphernalia, and he said, "I am going to stay at this work in some form or other for the rest of my life."

He spent his first weeks putting his office in order. He was by nature a meticulous man, neat to the point of fetish. A misplaced document completely unnerved him; unfinished business

haunted his dreams. The office was on the second floor of an old
building at 62 Union Park Street, opposite the cathedral. It was
a large room, shared with a secretary, and it was jammed with
the accumulations of the six years Tracy had spent there. But
in two weeks everything had its place, and Walsh knew where
it was. He then made his quick trip to Europe, returning with
a suitcase bulging with notes and photographs. He dived immediately into a full schedule of writing, lecturing, preaching,
organizing and canvassing. At the end of a year he had raised
over thirty-four thousand dollars in cash, plus forty-five thousand in bequests—three times more than Boston had donated
the previous year and one third of the total raised in the entire
country. Walsh quickly became known as a leader in missionary
work. He was invited to Philadelphia to reorganize its branch of
the society, and did so. Distressed because New York was not
more active, he approached Archbishop John Farley with the
idea of organizing the city at the diocesan level.

"Yes," said the Archbishop, "but who will do the work after
you go back to Boston?"

In New York Walsh was staying at the Church of St. John
the Evangelist, where he had met a young curate he liked. He
said, "Father John Dunn, over at St. John's."

The name meant little to the Archbishop, but he presumed the
two men had already talked about it. "Go ahead," he said.

Walsh hurried back to the church and found Dunn teaching
a catechism class. He announced, "You've just been made director of the S.P.F."

"The S.P.F.?" Dunn asked. "Is that the animal outfit?"

"You've got a lot to learn," said Walsh. Dunn learned, and in
doing so his life was changed.

At Eastertime, 1904, Walsh attended the mission conference in
Washington, where he met Fred Price. In a year, Walsh had become a celebrity in mission circles; his fame, his achievements,
his charm, and his openness made him the star of the conference. He met many men in Washington, but it was Price who
followed up the encounter with letters. Price's article in *Truth*
on the kind of American mission society he would like to see
made a deep impression on Walsh and he wrote articles on the
subject himself. He further showed his interest in Price when

Nazareth burned down; he wrote about it in a Boston magazine and urged contributions. He sent a contribution of his own.

In 1906, Walsh made another tour of the European mission societies, and when he returned he asked Stanton, Lane, and Father Joseph Bruneau, a Sulpician, to meet with him.

"I think," he told them, "it's about time we do something about starting an American foreign mission society."

"We?" Lane asked.

"Yes. You might as well all face it: you're in on it with me."

Stanton grinned, pleased. "What's your idea?"

"Right now I haven't the vaguest idea," Walsh admitted. "But I don't think that should prevent us from starting something, somehow."

Bruneau said, "It will be very difficult. America itself is still a mission country."

"We won't always be," Stanton put in.

"And we ought to prepare for that," said Walsh.

"All right," said Lane. "How?"

"Well, we could start by getting people used to the idea," Walsh said. "I brought back some wonderful stories from Europe that could be used especially for this project, but I don't want them to get lost in general magazines. They ought to have a place of their own."

"You want to start your own magazine?" Lane asked.

"Yes. I've already got a name for it—*The Field Afar*."

"Very romantic," Stanton said.

"I mean it to be. It'll catch people's interest."

"And the magazine," asked Bruneau, "the Archbishop will permit it?"

"I think he will," said Walsh. "But here's the point. I don't want the magazine to belong to the archdiocese; I want it to belong to us—or to the American foreign mission society, if you prefer. Now, the three of us, Father," he said to Bruneau, "belong to the archdiocese and we'll be doing this work on archdiocese time, and I suspect the Archbishop will expect any money we raise to go into the archdiocese office of the Propagation Society. That's all right with me."

"What else can we do?" Lane offered, in agreement.

"For the time being, anyhow," said Walsh, "all I want is an

outlet to start the country thinking about an American mission society and I think a special magazine is the best way. Do you agree?"

They all agreed.

"Good," said Walsh, "because if the Archbishop approves only on the condition we pay for the magazine ourselves I'll be expecting all of you to kick in."

In their poverty they groaned.

The Archbishop approved. He accepted Walsh's plan completely; the magazine could be started on Propagation funds, with the understanding that the income would go to the Boston office until the mission society was founded. Furthermore, the prelate said, the archdiocese had a little property outside of town; if, when the society was ready to begin, a place was needed to build a seminary he felt arrangements could be made. He would, in fact, be happy to have the seminary in his archdiocese.

"You are thinking much farther ahead than we are, Your Grace," Walsh said, "but it is wonderful to know that we'll have a home when we need one."

The first issue of *The Field Afar* appeared in January, 1907. In the masthead it was identified as a publication of the Catholic Foreign Mission Bureau. "Bureau" was considered a safer word at this point than "society": it precluded too many questions and any premature action. Walsh was listed as editor. It was to be issued bimonthly for fifty cents a year.

In the first issue, Walsh stated the magazine's aim: to stimulate active interest in the foreign missions by alms, prayers, and personal participation. He wrote:

The worthy young man who, out of love for his country, goes into voluntary exile and runs the danger of losing his life stimulates and strengthens the patriotism of his fellowmen. The soldier of Christ who, for the love of souls, leaves all—home, friends, and country forever—to bare his neck, if need be, to the sabre cut of one whom he could save or to pass his days in the awful weariness of exile must certainly appeal to the heart of the American Catholic and make him love more dearly the faith which can prompt such sacrifice as this.

He also observed, "We see by the local papers that seven Boston Protestant laymen have left for the mission fields. This is very worthy and noble of them. But where are the Catholics?"

There were, in 1907, just fourteen American Catholics in the missions. Two were New Englanders who had joined the White Fathers, the French mission order devoted to Africa; eight were Marist teaching brothers, stationed in Japan; three were members of the Society of the Divine Word, a German order that had settled at Techny, Illinois; one was a nun, Mother Paul, of New York, who was in Uganda with the British Franciscan Medical Missionaries. The difficulty, as Walsh saw it, was that, with one or two exceptions, the mission society training centers were all abroad and any American who wanted to join any of them was faced with the expense of traveling to the center and most likely had to learn a foreign language before the training could begin. As things stood, France was supplying two-thirds of the Church's missionaries and providing half of the mission funds. This predicament gave native populations everywhere the idea that the Catholic Church was a French church, which was not only wrong but unwise. Also, they were getting the impression that America was a Protestant country. American Protestant missionaries were very busy in the Orient and in Africa. American Catholic businessmen returning from those areas told Walsh that the people could not believe they were Catholics: the Protestant missionaries had said there were no Catholic Americans.

There were, in fact, well over ten million of them, but they were not making their presence felt for several reasons. First, a great number of them were immigrants or the children of immigrants, and they were so relieved to be away from the hardships that had sent them to America that they did not want to think about any other place, almost to the point of isolationism. Secondly, the Church in America was suffering the expenses of growing pains: there was so much to be built here—churches, missions, schools, hospitals, orphanages—that the Catholic purse was already flat in many areas. The local needs for priests, brothers, and nuns was the third reason why so few were going to the missions. Fourth—and extremely important—parents who knew that many missionaries were being killed either refused to let their children go into the missions or did all they could to discourage them.

Walsh hoped that through the pages of *The Field Afar* he could overcome these obstacles one by one. To be Catholic, he

felt, meant to be missionary, and he was convinced that once
the American interest in the missions was stirred the people
would rush to the challenge. At this point, the challenge could
best come from the pages of the magazine. Walsh wrote most of
the copy himself, using the first pages for editorials on the state
of mission affairs and filling the rest with adventurous excerpts
from letters missionaries wrote him. For several issues he ran a
digest of his book on Vénard; frequently he used pious quota-
tions from Vénard's writings as fillers. Walsh had a light, breezy,
conversational style of writing that was easy and pleasant to read
and created the impression that everybody was as interested in
the missions as he was. In a short time many people were. In
two years, the magazine had a circulation of five thousand.

Archbishop Williams died in the summer of 1907; Archbishop
William O'Connell, who succeeded him, said of *The Field Afar*,
"It is certainly gratifying to testify to its great improvement upon
the sort of missionary literature we were accustomed to not so
very long ago." But there was not much more about *The Field
Afar* project that the Archbishop did like.

Archbishop O'Connell was one of the prelates who had grown
to dislike the extensive Sulpician influence in the American
Church and it was his opinion that the magazine, and Walsh
himself for that matter, was too French-influenced. He said little
about this at first, but his attitude gradually became quite clear.
Walsh was responsible directly to him; as the months passed, their
relationship grew increasingly strained. Walsh sensed it, but he
felt there was not much he could do about it. After all, the French
dominated the mission field; it was impossible to put out the
magazine without a few stories about them. Walsh's missionary
hero, Vénard, was a Frenchman, and Walsh could never publish
too much about him. And Walsh hoped that the mission society
he would one day establish would be modeled on the Paris Foreign
Mission Society, with which he maintained close ties. To top
things off, Father Bruneau, a Frenchman and a Sulpician to boot,
was a dear friend and a staff member and Walsh had no intention
of asking him to withdraw from either capacity merely for the
sake of peace with the Archbishop.

The rift between the two men broadened and deepened and

reached a state beyond repair. Openly they gave no hint of it. Walsh often wrote about the Archbishop in the magazine, praising him for his interest in the missions. O'Connell readily admitted that Walsh was doing a good job: each year more money came in for the missions, each year the magazine circulation expanded. Boston was becoming known as the mission center of the country, which pleased both men. But more and more O'Connell let it be known that he felt the magazine was getting repetitious and he thought it needed new blood. To Walsh, that indicated one thing: a transfer.

In the summer of 1910, Walsh went abroad again and when he returned the talk of Boston was the International Eucharistic Congress to be held at Montreal. Walsh felt he would like to go, but he had a great deal of work and occupied himself with it. He also knew that the head of the Boston entourage would be the Archbishop; he did not expect to be included, and he wasn't.

A few days before the Congress began, Walsh received a telephone call from Mother Michaud, a Canadian who was superior of the Boston convent of the Grey Nuns, a Canadian congregation. "Are you going to the Congress, Father?" she said.

"I'm not sure, Mother," said Walsh.

"I'll tell you why I ask," she said. "My nephew is the mayor of Maisonneuve, just outside Montreal. I had made arrangements for the rector of your cathedral to stay with him during the Congress, but now Father tells me that he must preach a retreat and cannot go. I thought if you were going and you needed a place. . . ."

"That's very kind of you, Mother," Walsh said. "I had not definitely made up my mind—" He glanced at his desk— "I have already been out of my office so much this year—" He gave a thought to the Archbishop—"but I suppose a few more days won't hurt. You are very kind, Mother."

That night he boarded the train to Montreal, determined to enjoy himself, aware that making the trip without permission might be construed by the Archbishop as disobedience, but sadly resigned to the fact that at this late stage nothing he did could make much difference anyway.

IV

At montreal, Fred Price was staying at the Hochelaga Convent and James Walsh was staying with the Michauds. In a week crowded with meetings, conferences, seminars, and religious ceremonies there was every likelihood that the two men should run into each other, but because of the thousands of people in the city there was actually little chance that they would. The night before the principal event, the field Mass, the Maisonneuve band gave a concert on the Michaud lawn. Walsh was there. So was a priest friend of his from Pittsfield, Massachusetts. They chatted briefly during the intermission. After the concert the Pittsfield priest returned to his room at the Hochelaga Convent. The convent was busy the next morning, what with a succession of Masses by the visiting priests and a succession of their breakfasts. It so happened that when the Pittsfield priest went into the refectory for his breakfast Fred Price was among the half-dozen priests already there.

Someone greeted the Pittsfield priest with "Where were you last night? I couldn't find you."

"I went to a band concert out at Maisonneuve," he said. "By the way, I saw Father Walsh there."

Price looked up from his eggs. "Father Walsh of *The Field Afar?*"

48

"Yes. He's staying there at Mayor Michaud's house."

"Just the man I want to see," Price said. He hurried to a telephone.

At Maisonneuve the telephone was answered by Madame Michaud, who did not speak English well. "Who?" she asked. "Preece? Father Preece? He is not here. Prize?"

Walsh was standing nearby. "Let me help you," he said. He took the phone. "This is Father Walsh."

"This is Father Price of Nazareth."

"Oh, hello!"

"Father, I must see you right away," Price said.

Walsh glanced at the hall clock. "But, Father, we're just leaving for Fletcher Field."

"I can be there in a few moments. It's very important."

The Michauds were putting on their coats. "Very well," Walsh said. "But please hurry. I can't hold up the others."

With his conflicting values of time and money, Price came by slow tram. Walsh and the Michauds were standing outside at a carriage, their gaze impatiently in Price's direction.

Price hurried up and took Walsh's hand. "I want to know what is in your mind about foreign missions."

"Plenty," said Walsh.

"Are you serious about—"

Walsh took Price's elbow. "We must be on our way."

The Michauds entered the carriage, then Price, then Walsh. Price turned to Walsh. "Father, this mission society you've been writing about—"

Walsh held up his hand to halt Price. He indicated the Michauds. *"Madame, je vous presen—"*

Price touched his broad-rimmed hat. "How do you do." He took the Mayor's offered hand. "Enchantay." He was back at Walsh. "How far have you carried this idea of yours about an American society?"

"Just what you've read in the magazine."

"Have you decided when you might start it?"

"No. You see—"

"What do you think of my idea of tying in with Catholic U?"

"It has definite advantages, but—"

"And the minor seminaries scattered all over the country?"

"That's good too, and—"

"Do you run the show alone up in Boston?"

"No, there are three others with me, but we haven't dared think—"

"We've got to get this thing started right away, Father."

"We?"

"Of course."

Walsh sat back, stunned. He tried to remember what Price had been like in Washington: he had seemed much less aggressive. He remembered the letters Price had written him, addressed *carissime,* most endeared, which was about as extravagant a display of affection between two men that Latin allowed, but now he was ready to hear Price call him son.

Price talked all the way out to Fletcher Field. Friends of the Michauds had a house at the edge of the field and the party assisted at Mass from there. Price talked on. To silence him at one point, Walsh said, "Father, please, the Consecration."

When the Mass was over, Price said, "Can we go some place and talk?"

Walsh regarded the Michauds. "I don't know. I am their guest, and maybe I ought not—"

"When are you going back to Boston?"

"Tomorrow morning."

Price pursed his lips. "There isn't much time, then, is there? Well, we've got a few hours." He gripped Walsh's arm and led him to a line of taxis.

They settled in the lobby of the Windsor Hotel in leather chairs placed close together. At first Walsh only listened, evaluating Price, his ideas, his enthusiasm. Over the past two or three years various priests had approached Walsh about his foreign mission society idea and they had urged him to begin. He was reluctant; he was unsure of himself. It would be such an enormous task, and he was not convinced he was the man for it. Yes, he wanted the society, wanted it badly, but all along he had half expected that someone else would be its instigator. If by showing the need and the possibility he could be accredited with bringing the society into being, Walsh would be content. But now here was a man who had dumped the whole thing into his lap and climbed in with it.

"The trouble is," Price was saying, "I'm sure there are all kinds of headaches."

"There are," Walsh said. "I remember once talking about just this idea with the Mill Hill Fathers in England and—" And now he was off. An hour passed, two, three.

Walsh said, "There's one other thing we ought to settle now. You're in the North Carolina diocese and I'm in the Boston diocese. Just how are we supposed to get together?"

"We'll get our bishops to release us," Price said. "Mine will be glad to."

"I'm not so sure about mine," Walsh said.

Price reflected. "The magazine is too important, I suppose."

"It's more than that," Walsh said evasively. "It's all kinds of things."

"Oh?" Price said with recognition. "You too?"

Walsh rolled his eyes.

"Well, never mind," said Price. "Bill O'Connell was a classmate of mine. I'll talk to him about you."

"You know the Archbishop?"

"I haven't seen him for years, but I knew him at school. I'll come up to Boston and talk to him."

A voice interrupted. "Father Price."

Price looked up and saw Bishop Donahue of Wheeling, another classmate. He stood and introduced Walsh. Walsh took the Bishop's hand, bowed, and kissed his ring. Donahue said, "Did you forget you're supposed to have dinner with me?"

"I did," Price said. "We got talking."

"I know," said Donahue. "I've been standing here for ten minutes trying to get a word in."

They all laughed. Walsh said, "You have your dinner. I'm late now where I'm supposed to be."

"All right," said Price. They shook hands firmly. "I'll see you in Boston."

They both had a lot to think about. The step they were about to take was immense, the complications grave, the responsibilities severe. Walsh felt almost trapped. He was in the uncomfortable position of being about to have a dream come true and he was not sure he could cope with it. The event was too sudden for him.

He was both happy and apprehensive, like an infant soon to be born but uncertain that it was really a good idea. He had his doubts about Price. How overwhelming the man was! Even so, enthusiasm was not enough. If indeed they embarked on their plan they would be treading a path where only saints could survive. Walsh did not consider himself a saint and he felt he did not know Price well enough to make any decision about him. Evidently Price was confident; he was certainly aggressive, almost arrogant. Walsh wondered if Price were the kind of man he would work with—or work for. Having achieved his own position in the mission field, this was a factor with Walsh. He would have preferred a man he knew better, a man like Stanton, perhaps, who openly admired him, respected him—followed him. He had met Price only twice, the first time being so brief that it could scarcely count. And they had exchanged a few letters. Admittedly, Price had been unusually overt in his letters, as if they were old and dear friends, and yet in both Washington and Montreal he had been almost indifferent to other people, withdrawn, cool, disinterested. He had, true, hinted at friendships with classmates and yet he obviously had had no contact with them for great lengths of time: the friendships could not be very close. Friends would be important to anybody starting so bold an adventure. But then there had been Bishop Donahue: maybe Price was the sort who could renew friendships abruptly, regardless of the changes of time or place. That was the word for him—abrupt.

Price had a word for Walsh—blessing. On the train going back to North Carolina Price was quietly jubilant. He kept thinking of questions he wished he had asked Walsh and he made mental notes to remember the questions the next time they were together. That must be soon. Now that they had agreed to start, they must start at once. Price considered himself extremely fortunate to have paired off with Walsh. What man in the country knew more about foreign missions? Who had better connections in mission work, either in this country or abroad? Who more impatiently shared his eagerness to make America active in the missions? Who had more clearly shown himself capable of maneuvering through all the complications ahead? Yes, they would make a good team. If it seemed that Walsh had been a bit cautious, that, Price felt, was all to the good. The project would need a cautious man, a perceptive man, a man of details. Price knew these things were beyond him. Walsh's difficulty with his boss was no serious problem; lived there a priest who, at one time or another, had not been called on the carpet by his bishop? Price had Bishop Haid to consider; he hoped that the Bishop had not made plans for him already. Yet, even this possibility did not dim his high spirits. He was convinced that what he wanted to do was God's design for him, he would trust to Mary and to Bernadette to see him through. They had before. All that mattered was the work ahead.

Neither man realized that already there was a difference of opinion between them. For Walsh, the missions meant the Orient —millions of pagans to be brought into the Church. For Price, the missions meant an area where there was already a Catholic atmosphere—South America, perhaps, where because of poverty, government opposition, and shattering ignorance the Church had been unable to make her presence adequately effective.

One day this difference of opinion would make both men wonder how in the world they had managed to get so involved with each other.

At Belmont, Bishop Haid wondered if he had heard correctly. "You want what?"

Price said, "I want to be released."

"From what?"

"From the diocese. At least from any assignments in it."

The Bishop sank back in his chair. "Now what are you up to?"

"When I was in Montreal I had a long talk with Father Walsh of *The Field Afar,*" Price said, and he told Haid what they had discussed. In his uncomplicated confidence he gave the impression that the plans were definite, that all initial problems had been solved, and that the only remaining obstacle was the permission of Haid and O'Connell to free him and Walsh from their present duties.

"Have you any idea," Haid asked, "of the enormity of such a project? Where are you going to get the money? and the men? Where do you propose to settle down? What makes you think any bishop will turn you two loose in his diocese? You'll need approval from Rome; America has just been removed from the mission category itself: do you think Rome considers this country

ready to enter the mission field at the level you plan? Father, I'm
afraid that once again you're rushing into something without
sufficient reflection."

"Oh, no," said Price. "Father Walsh and I have been working
on this through letters for years. At Montreal we went over the
whole thing again, and we're convinced now is the time to start."

"You're both going in over your heads," Haid said.

"Maybe we are, but we won't know until we try. I'm asking you
for permission to try."

"What about Nazareth?"

"I had the impression," Price said, "that you were beginning
to feel Nazareth had developed enough to be able to get along
without me."

The Bishop raised a piqued brow. "Perhaps," he said. "Nevertheless, you know how short of priests we are here. If you were
not at Nazareth you could be somewhere else in North Carolina."

That was precisely what Price dreaded. "I suppose I could," he
said, "and maybe some day I will be. But I think it's important
to give the mission society a try: we should know in a year whether
or not we can do it."

"I give you three months," Haid said flatly.

Price grabbed at the challenge. "Thank you, Excellency. I'll
keep in touch with you." He was out of the room before Haid
realized that what he had meant to be discouragement had been
taken as approval.

Price went back to Boston. Walsh had now had time to think
and he was ready. He was still unsure of himself but he was sure
of something else: he would not let Price's enthusiasm sweep him
away again.

Price said, "You know I have this property in North Carolina.
On my way up here, it occurred to me that we can use Nazareth
as our seminary site."

"But I thought you were giving up Nazareth?" Walsh offered.

"Yes, but I'm sure we can fix things to get one of the buildings
for our own use."

Walsh considered it. "Don't you think it would be better if
the seminary were nearer a large Catholic population? It would
simplify matters like getting vocations and raising funds."

"It would be more expensive."

"But it would be more advantageous in the long run."

Price shrugged. "Yes, you're right. What about Washington, then? Remember, I wrote you that we could use the Catholic University for the students. And Washington would give the society a national scope; I think that's important."

"It is," Walsh said. "But Washington isn't Catholic enough either, I would say. I was thinking more in terms of New York, perhaps, or Philadelphia."

Price raised his hands. "Well, then, what is more Catholic than Boston?"

Walsh shook his head.

Price understood. "I'm seeing the Archbishop this afternoon."

"You are? That should decide several matters. Tell me, Father, if I find I can't join with you now, will you go ahead on your own?"

"I suppose I'll have to," Price said. "But I hope you will join me."

"I hope so, too," Walsh said. "And if I do, am I to look upon you as organizer and founder and superior of the society?"

"Oh, no," Price said quickly. He was a little hurt. "We would be partners, equal partners, all the way. Sooner or later, I guess, we would have to write out a rule for the society; Rome would want that. We can decide then which of us will be the superior. But I tell you now, Father, it makes no difference to me who runs the society. I just want to get it started."

Walsh nodded. "I mention it," he explained, "simply because there are some men here who for several years have been planning to join *me* in forming a mission society and—"

Price cut in. "Father, I would never step in the way of you or anyone else undertaking such a work. I am quite sure I would rather die any death than interfere with or prevent any work for God, especially so great a work as one of this kind. If your people are ready to go, then I would happily give up my own plans. And if I could help you in any way I would be more than willing."

"Well, actually we're far from ready," Walsh admitted. "It's just that we have been thinking about it. The purpose of *The Field Afar* has been to prepare the way. I merely wanted you to know."

"Thank you," said Price. "But now what about us?"

Walsh thought about it for a moment, then, "Father, do you think it's possible that God has brought us together just for this reason?"

"I believe it with my whole soul," Price said.

"I am beginning to think I do, too."

They regarded each other for a brief silence, very seriously, and as the idea seeped into them a certain contentment suffused them. Then Walsh returned to realities. "How much money do you have?"

"*Truth* makes a profit of about two thousand a year," Price said. "I've been putting all of it into the Nazareth project, but now it can be ours."

"That would come in handy," Walsh said. "But I wonder if there might be some conflict between the intentions of *Truth* and the society?"

"How? I've written editorials in *Truth* about the missions."

"I know, and they've been good. But *Truth* is aimed at Protestants, and the mission editorials have been almost parenthetical. Don't you think it would be better to have just one magazine, a magazine that would be specifically missionary, something the public would identify directly with the society?"

"*The Field Afar?*"

Walsh nodded. "In the arrangement I had with Archbishop Williams, *The Field Afar* belonged to me, and when and if I ever became involved in establishing a mission society I was to take the magazine with me. I don't expect Archbishop O'Connell will insist on any change in that. Now, people already associate *The Field Afar* with a mission society; we've talked about it since our first issue. It seems to me, Father, that there would be less confusion in the public mind and at the same time it would be more profitable for the work if we put our energies exclusively into one publication."

It sounded reasonable. "All right," said Price.

"Good," said Walsh. "Now what in the world do we do next?"

"I suppose the next thing is for me to make a free man out of you," Price said. "I'd better get over to the cathedral and talk to your boss."

Walsh had forgotten about that. "Oh, dear, yes. I hope we haven't been too fast off the mark."

They did not see each other again for almost a month, during which Walsh had his first experience with Price's annoying habit of disappearing into a vacuum of silence. With the exception of a single telephone call, Walsh had no idea where Price had gone to or what he was doing. He worried, about both the man and the project. Now that he had made up his mind to go ahead with it he was uneasy when he was not fully aware of everything that might be going on. He had talked to Stanton and Lane about the proposed society. They were both enthusiastic and said they wished they could have met Price. Walsh was somewhat disappointed when Stanton did not immediately volunteer to join the project. But Lane did. "I am almost crippled with arthritis," he said, "and there's not much I can do. But I want to fit into the picture somewhere. Let me know when you're ready."

"I wish I knew myself," said Walsh, "but right now I don't even know where my partner is."

Price was busy.

After leaving Walsh's office he had gone across the street to the cathedral where he was heartily received by Archbishop O'Connell. "What are you doing up here in Yankee country?" O'Connell asked.

"I'm about to organize an American foreign mission society," Price said.

"Really? Splendid. Here in Boston?"

"I don't know about that," Price said, "but I expect to be working with a Boston man."

"You do? Who?"

"Father Walsh."

O'Connell was surprised. He pointed out the window to Walsh's office. "That Father Walsh?"

"Yes."

"Why him?"

"Because he's the best man in the country."

The Archbishop grunted. "I'd be less surprised to hear he wanted to start a *French* society."

Price's expression asked the question.

O'Connell said, "An Irishman who goes French is almost as bad as an Irishman who goes English. Your friend's magazine is full of Frenchmen, he talks about them all the time, and he's forever running out to the Frenchmen at the seminary. I've had enough of it."

"Well," said Price, "it is a fact that the French are doing most of the missionary work in the Church."

O'Connell shrugged. "I sometimes get the impression they think they're running the whole show."

"Then it's time we get into the act as Americans."

"What are your plans?"

For the next hour Price outlined all he and Walsh had discussed. "And what do you want from me?" the Archbishop asked. "And don't ask for money."

"I want Father Walsh," Price said. "I want you to release him to work on this with me."

"Why hasn't he asked me himself?"

"He will," said Price, adding with a rare flash of diplomacy, "but since I'm here I thought I might as well put in a plea of my own."

The Archbishop frowned and looked away. "Well," he said, "I have been thinking it's about time we get a new director for our Propagation Society office." He looked back at Price. "Walsh is a capable man; I grant him that. But a fund-raising program like Propagation needs fresh ideas." He looked away again. "We haven't been very close." He turned again to Price. "All right, you can have him. But you'd better brush up on your French."

Price wanted to rush across to Walsh with the news, but O'Connell held him.

"You say you haven't decided where to set up your headquarters," he said. "I think I can make room for you at the House of Philosophy at the seminary. Then if you need any special help in Rome I'll be in a position to arrange it for you."

Price recognized the hint of outside control. "Thank you," he said. "That's very encouraging."

"You will have to keep me well informed of your progress."

"Oh, by all means." Price made a move to leave.

"Have you seen any of the fellows from school lately?" O'Connell asked. And for the rest of the afternoon Price was chained to his chair by reminiscences.

When he finally escaped, Price saw that he had twenty minutes to catch a train South. Instead of going across to Walsh, he telephoned him from O'Connell's reception room.

"Everything is all right," he said. "He said yes."

"I'm to be released?"

"Yes."

"Glory be to God!"

That struck Price as a sufficiently Irish ejaculation. "There's a train in twenty minutes," he said. "I'd better get back to Nazareth and clean up my affairs there."

"We should have dinner tonight and celebrate," Walsh suggested.

"I'll feel more like celebrating when we actually get started."

"When will I see you?"

"In a few days. A week, I guess. It shouldn't take longer than that at Nazareth. But I'll write you."

"Fine." Then, "Fred, I'm very happy about all this."

"So am I. I'll write you. Now I must hurry for the train."

Walsh in his office and Price rushing across the city shared a thought. A few weeks ago they had both been suffering the discomfort of knowing that their bishops were dissatisfied with them. In such circumstances—and in whatever other circumstances there might be—the bishops, by the mere possession of their crosiers, were ineluctably in the right. For the priests there could only be submission to a transfer, a short period of disappointment and sadness, then an effort to forget what had happened and apply themselves to their new chores, all the while guarding against any recurrence of similar reprimands by regarding suspiciously any subsequent adventurous ideas beyond prescribed duties. But a chance meeting in Montreal and a scramble for survival had put flesh on the skeleton of a dream and saved Walsh and Price from obscurity. Perhaps, indeed, their separate misfortunes had been God's way of uniting them for the titanic purpose to which they were now dedicated. In any event, Walsh in his office and Price rushing across the city were both full of great hopes and great relief. They had jobs.

V

Price arrived in New York at midnight. On the train it occurred to him that the best way to prevent any bishop's interest in the new society from becoming too possessive was to spread the idea around. He decided, therefore, to make a New York stopover on his journey to Nazareth and pay a call to Archbishop Farley. He was at Farley's Madison Avenue residence early the next morning and gave a report on the new mission society with effective enthusiasm.

"I felt you would want to know about it as soon as possible," he said.

"By all means," said Farley. "This is very exciting, Father."

Price said, "It's good to hear the hierarchy say things like that. Archbishop O'Connell was very encouraging."

"Will you be working out of Boston?"

"We haven't decided yet."

"Let me assure you," said Farley, "that you'll be most welcome here in New York. Naturally, I would want to do all I could to help."

Price squirmed a little. "That's very kind of you."

Too much help could be as dangerous as no help at all. And the particular danger might well be with an overly generous prelate who, responsible for Church affairs in his diocese, might put strings on his generosity, first in the form of specific advice and

60

then in the form of orders. It was not unthinkable that an exceptionally interested prelate might also expect to be the superior
of the new society, and if that happened the risk arose that neither
Walsh nor Price would have much to say. Wary, Price left
New York the next day and went on to Baltimore to see the
prince of the Church he had known since boyhood: Cardinal
Gibbons. With Gibbons, Price could be more outspoken.

"We're going to have to settle in some diocese," Price said,
"and when we do we'll need the bishop's permission. But we
don't want permission to be turned into submission."

Gibbons asked, "How do you expect to get around that?"

"I'm not sure," said Price, "but it's occurred to me that maybe
you, holding the American primate, could announce that the
society is to be a national organization, not subject to any diocesan
rules."

The Cardinal chuckled knowingly. "You don't really expect
me to get tangled up in any diocesan wrangles, do you? Fred, I
can't tell any bishop or archbishop what to do."

"It was just an idea," Price offered.

"Here's another idea, then. Why don't you go over to Washington and talk to the Delegate about it? If he's in favor of it, he
can speak for Rome. That will put you on a national basis right
off."

Price went to Washington. The Apostolic Delegate to the
United States was Archbishop Diomede Falconio, a Franciscan
who had been in Washington eight years. He knew of Price's work
and therefore received him promptly when he arrived without an
appointment. Once again, Price gave the details of his plan
with Walsh.

"Very good," said Falconio. "I will write the Holy Father about
it immediately. He will be pleased."

"You see," Price pressed his point, "we don't intend to be a
religious society like the Redemptorists or the Holy Cross Fathers
or anything like that. We will be secular priests living in a community with our own rule."

"Yes, of course, I understand," the Delegate said.

"We are to be a national organization, subject to all bishops
but not to any one of them in particular."

"Yes, yes, I know."

"We want our superiors to be members of the society."

"Naturally."

"We want that clear from the start."

"Obviously."

Price dropped his guard. "But we don't know how to declare that without offending anyone."

"Ah." The Delegate understood. "Well, now. The American archbishops will be holding a conference soon. Do you know that?"

"No."

"They will. It is a periodic thing and a good idea. Do you have any special friends among them?"

"More than we can handle."

"Ah. So. But is there one with whom you can discuss your position frankly?"

"I've known Cardinal Gibbons all my life."

"Good. Then why don't you ask His Eminence to submit a proposal to the conference, suggesting approval by the archbishops of your society in the precise terms that you now plan it?"

"Do you think that will work?"

"I don't see why not. When it is placed before them in so neat a package, they must all either approve or disapprove as a group. Is there any reason they might disapprove?"

"I can't think of one."

"So. Why don't you do that? If they approve—and I believe they will—you will need the approval of Rome because of your circumstances. I shall be more than happy to write to the Holy Father about you."

"Thank you very much, Your Grace."

"Just one thing more. Will you be able to support yourselves?"

"I think so. We have a successful magazine going."

"Good. You will have difficulties enough: you will not want to worry about money as well." As he took Price to the door, the Delegate said, "I will pray for you, Father. You will have many problems, but you must not despair. Do you remember an experience Saint Teresa had? She started many convents in Spain, as you know, and always with great obstacles. But there was an exception with one. She was able to obtain the money with no trouble, the building went up so quickly it seemed to be constructed by Saint Joseph with his own hands, and soon the convent was full of postulants. Most people would have been relieved, but Saint Teresa knew that those who desire only to serve God must expect many difficulties, and she said, 'There is something wrong going on here that I cannot see as yet.' Keep that in mind, Father. God demands sacrifices and suffering from those who would serve Him. In the years ahead, when you are surrounded by troubles, do not think God has abandoned you: He will be very close."

Price went back to Baltimore and told Cardinal Gibbons what the Delegate had suggested.

"I'll do it," said Gibbons, "but you'd better write the statement yourself so that you get in all you want."

"Maybe Father Walsh ought to write it," Price said. "I'll go to Boston."

Instead, he went to Nazareth. Work had piled up during his absence and he was busy with it for several days. Then he went to Belmont to see Bishop Haid to initiate the legal process necessary to transfer the authority of Nazareth to him. Also, he arranged to sell *Truth* to the Catholic Truth Society for one dollar. A month after leaving Boston, Price walked into Walsh's office.

"Where have you been?" Walsh demanded, with a mixture of annoyance and relief.

"Everywhere."

"What have you been doing?"

"Everything."

"Didn't you get my letters and telegrams?"

"Yes, but there was no time to answer them."

"In a month?"

"So much has been happening."

"Good or bad?"

When Price finished his report, the two men agreed that everything seemed to be for the good. Most important was the statement for Cardinal Gibbons. Having talked and planned themselves to exhaustion, Price and Walsh decided to write the statement the next day.

"It might save time if we each wrote a separate statement and then combined the best of both," Walsh suggested. Price agreed. Next morning, they sat in Walsh's office and read what the other had written.

Walsh said, "You say too much."

Price regarded Walsh's effort. "You don't say enough."

"Look at it this way," said Walsh. "All we want at this point is the approval of the archbishops. We ought not give them too much to consider—just in case of any of them have any reservations."

"If I had to make the decision, I'd want to know more," Price said defensively.

It was Walsh who won out in the end. The statement they wrote declared only that America should take its place in the mission world, that the opportunity now existed to establish a national society, that it should be grasped, and that two experienced men were available to do the work, both of whom had received the release and the blessings of their bishops to do so. One safeguard was taken against the only objection that might be voiced at this stage by any archbishop, particularly from the Midwest, who was suffering a priest shortage. Into the statement went a remark by Cardinal Manning, made when the British hierarchy had similar reservations about the organization of the Mill Hill Fathers. Manning had said:

It is quite true that we have need of men and means at home, and it is because we have need of men, of more men and more means by a great deal than we as yet possess, that I am convinced we ought to send both men and means abroad. If we desire to find the surest way to multiply immensely our own material means for works at home, it is by not limiting the expansion of charity and by not paralyzing the zeal of self-denial.

When they had finished with the statement, Walsh said, "If you still think I'm being too vague, let's let Cardinal Gibbons decide. If he wants more detail, you are free to insert anything you like."

The Cardinal had one observation. "You don't mention where you might locate."

"Do you think we should?" Price asked.

The Cardinal thought about it. "Maybe not. This way they'll all think they're going to get it." He smiled at the idea, then teased, "But you're coming to Baltimore, aren't you?"

The statement was issued to the American archbishops in the form of a letter on March 25, 1911. The subject was then listed on the agenda for the archbishops' conference, to be held at the

Catholic University on April 27. A week before the session, Price wired Walsh: "CARISSIME: I AM BACK IN BALTIMORE WITH MY SLEEVES ROLLED UP FOR BUSINESS." On April 25, Price moved over to Washington to mingle with the archbishops as they arrived. He decided it would be unwise to be too aggressive; he merely paid his respects to the prelates and made himself available to them. None of them sent for him. The morning of the conference he was in the corridor outside the meeting room, as amiable as his natural reserve allowed. He was not permitted to attend the conference, but he waited outside all day in case he was summoned for explanations. The doors were opened only for lunch to be taken in. Price remained in the hall, his fingers restless upon his rosary. It was after six when the archbishops, flush with achievement, came noisily from their room.

Price caught Gibbons' eye and raised his brows hopefully. The Cardinal nodded vigorously and smiled. Price sank back against the wall. Still smiling, Gibbons waited for Price to recover and make his way to him.

"You did say yes?" Price tested.

"Yes, I said yes. They approved it."

"I was so worried," said Price. "You were in there so long."

"Well," Gibbons said archly, "there were other things to discuss besides you." Then he mellowed. "Actually the whole thing was simple. There was little discussion. I expected there would be some question about location, but when I suggested that the decision be left to you, everybody immediately agreed. The conference secretary will issue a statement this afternoon approving the society and you and Walsh will be instructed to go to Rome to clear things with Propaganda."

Price telegraphed Walsh: "CARISSIME: THIS IS THE DAY WHICH THE LORD HAS MADE."

Price went to Nazareth to finish his business there. On May 21 a farewell ceremony was held, and after it Price left for Boston to meet Walsh. In Boston, Walsh moved his personal papers out of the Propagation Society office and turned the work over to Father Joseph F. McGlinchey, appointed his successor by Archbishop O'Connell. About three blocks away Walsh found a small shop which he made the temporary headquarters of the newly born but still-to-be-baptized Catholic Foreign Mission Society of

America and the editorial offices of *The Field Afar*. The June–July issue of the magazine carried the news of the archbishops' approval and instructions that Walsh and Price should go to Rome. Walsh arranged with Father Lane to run the new office during his absence.

They were to sail on the *Franconia* from East Boston on May 30. On the morning of the departure, Walsh paced his office impatiently, wondering where on earth Price had vanished this time. "I'm afraid," he said to Lane, "that I'm going to have a problem with Fred Price."

"He knows today's the day, doesn't he?" Lane asked.

"Certainly. He wrote me three weeks ago that he had bought his ticket from a Raleigh travel agency."

"Is it possible he thinks the ship is sailing from New York?"

"I hope not." Walsh shuddered at the thought, then shook it off. "Of course he knows it's Boston."

"Maybe he went directly to the dock."

"He might have," Walsh conceded, "but I was sure we were to meet here. I expected him long before today."

Lane glanced at the wall clock and warned, "You haven't got much time."

"Yes. I'd better start. You're coming with me?"

"Of course. I'll leave word with the secretary that Father Price should go to the ship in case he shows up here."

They went to the waterfront for the ferry that would take them across the bay to East Boston. Walsh grew increasingly annoyed as each man who came aboard proved to be a stranger. When the ferry pulled out, he muttered to Lane, "This is so frustrating." The frustration mounted after they boarded the *Franconia*, checked in with the purser, and went to Walsh's second-class stateroom to deposit his brief case; he saw that the rest of his luggage was already there. They went out on deck to the gangplank to watch for Price. In the midst of the merry travelers, Walsh alone was silent and frowning.

"If by chance," he said wearily, "he misses the boat have him take the next one and look for me at the Mill Hill Fathers in London."

"He'll show up," Lane said with faint optimism. Walsh grunted his doubt.

The last warning to visitors was called. Lane tried to change the atmosphere. "Well, have a good time," he said. "Send me some post cards. And good luck in Rome."

"Yes, thank you."

"And don't worry about anything here."

"No, I won't."

"It's a fine ship."

"Yes, it's very nice."

"Have a good time."

"Yes."

The effort failed. They shook hands and Lane went to the gangplank. He waved and began to descend with the crowd. He was almost at the bottom when he was crushed to one side by a priest who was slowly making his way up. Lane heard Walsh call, "Father Price!"

Lane thought: Thank God he made it. He reached the dock and turned around to wave good-by again but Walsh was not looking at him. Instead, he was glaring at Price, now free of the crowd of visitors but still slowly making his way up the gangplank as if he had all the time in the world. Price no sooner set foot on the deck than the gangplank was swung away.

"Really, Father," Walsh said.

Price asked, "Is anything wrong?"

"Why, you almost missed the ship."

Price glanced around. He was aboard. They were still at the dock. He could not see any crisis. But he said, "I'm sorry."

The ship's horns snorted, then screamed. Visitors on the dock pushed forward and shouted and threw streamers; travelers aboard the ship pushed forward and shouted and threw streamers. Walsh looked for Lane, found him, and waved, his anger now mellowed to a pout. Price stepped back and watched all the others with unconcern. Ropes fell away, tugs nosed in, and the *Franconia* slid quickly and gently into the stream.

"Where's your stateroom?" Walsh asked.

"I don't know," said Price. He fished in a pocket for his ticket and handed it over.

Walsh said, "Good heavens, Fred, you're practically traveling steerage. Why didn't you get yourself a room?"

"I didn't want to spend the money."

"We'll see the purser and fix you a better place."

"No, that won't be necessary. I'll be all right. Besides, I have a lot of work to do." He held up a small suitcase. "I won't even notice."

"Where's the rest of your luggage?"

"This is it." He hoisted the suitcase again. "I don't need much."

"But we'll be traveling for weeks," Walsh pointed out.

"I know. I have enough." A thought came to him. He dug into his pocket again and drew out two checks and a wad of crumpled bills and he handed everything to Walsh. "You'd better be the treasurer." It was all he possessed in the world: one hundred and twenty-five dollars.

Walsh studied Price and slowly shook his head. It was impossible to remain angry with the man.

They did not see much of each other on the eight-day trip to Liverpool. Price had found a table in his quarters far below deck and occupied himself with articles he wanted to do for *Truth* and a book he planned to edit about Bernadette Soubirous. One afternoon Walsh came looking for him and suggested, "Why don't you get some fresh air?"

"All right," Price said with a resignation that was almost obedience. They went topside and made several rounds of the deck. They did not speak. From the movement of Price's hand in his jacket pocket Walsh deduced he was saying the rosary. At last Price said, "That was enjoyable. But now I must read some breviary." And he left. Watching him go, Walsh considered what an unusual man he had for a partner. Unquestionably an affection existed between them, but there was also a canyon, a canyon which Walsh knew would never be entirely bridged. It was strange indeed to realize that his life was now linked with a man he had seen only half a dozen times and who still could not bring himself to address him by his first name. Price could not be casual; Walsh knew that. He also knew that most likely all their conversations, no matter how long they worked together, would be about the work and little else. Perhaps this was best. It was for the work, after all, that they had united; otherwise there was little chance that the two men would ever be attracted to each other—they were so different in their backgrounds, their attitudes, their tastes, their whims. Nevertheless, Walsh admitted, there was much in Price to admire. He was dedicated, he was a hard worker, he was pious. Thinking of these things, Walsh went to his room and to his own breviary.

They spent four days with the Mill Hill Fathers, during which time Walsh took copious notes on their observations. Their main interest was in learning how to run a seminary. Although they had not decided which of them would be in charge of their seminary when it was built, Walsh seemed to assume the position naturally and it was he who did most of the talking during their interviews. He noted, for example, that the sons of average middle-class families showed more stability in the religious life. The rich or the poor had difficulty adjusting to the rigid discipline. It was also evident that an exceptionally brilliant student or an extravagantly pious one was a bad risk: both were too preoccupied with being individuals to conform to the character formation that was the mark of a priest. Walsh listed the Mill Hill daily schedule: the boys were busy from five in the morning to nine at night with prayers, studies, and chores. A boy with the wind run out of him was less apt to get into trouble. No boy was shown any favoritism, and the boys were not permitted any favoritisms among themselves: personal friendships were prohibited. At regular intervals the faculty evaluated each boy as a student and as a member of the community. Whether his grades were good or bad, a boy was considered worthy as long as he clearly applied himself. His relations with others were a more severe yardstick: if he was impertinent or unco-operative, if he seemed to shirk or dislike his chores, if he caused friction or enjoyed it, if he appeared to be too often distracted from his books or his prayers, he should be sent packing for his own good. If, though, the boy was bright and quick, willing, studious, obedient, respectful, cheerful, meek, pious, and humble at all times, the cunning rascal was undoubtedly up to some mischief he was too clever to be caught at and should be sent packing immediately for the good of everyone else. The best boy was the average boy who tried to keep the rules and do his best and failed occasionally but kept trying. Perfection was the last thing anybody expected in seminarians, but malleable boys could be encouraged to try for it, and in the effort was the making of saints. The Mill Hill Fathers spent two hundred dollars a year training each boy, but most families could afford to pay between fifty and seventy-five dollars of it. Each family was obliged to pay at least twenty-five dollars; it gave the boy a sense of responsibility.

Walsh and Price went next to France where they made similar studies at the Paris Foreign Mission Society. Paris was practically home for Walsh; Father André spent a few days with him and together they visited places made shrines for them by the presence of Théophane Vénard, who was now beatified. Walsh wrote to Lane:

> In Paris. Same old place—hardly stranger to me now than New York—except when it is up to me to do the *parlez* business—and then I have to pinch myself. Father Price is getting a new shock about every quarter of an hour although much escapes him—since he is not of this world—(not as much, I fear, as his companion). But someone has to be alive—and I seem destined to be the distracted one. We know not the future. At present I feel absolutely unworthy, not to say unfit, to go on with this great work—and that I can be no more than a passing agent through whom God will work. We are both depending almost entirely on prayer, and I on the prayers of others. As for Father Price, he seems to enjoy his prayers much more than any other exercise or recreation. We hardly have time to compare notes. Just now he is out buying a stock of necessaries—to be thrown away when used. His bag is full of manuscripts, but this is about all he carries with him.

In the Paris seminary they noted far greater austerity than the Mill Hill Fathers imposed. There were fewer privileges, no comforts, and less individuality. Spiritual books were read at meals by students whose voices sounded exactly alike: loud, high-pitched, fast, monotonous. It was difficult to understand what was being said and impossible to remain interested. Both Price and Walsh were experienced writers: they squirmed to hear the written word recited so meaninglessly. Price was reminded of his North Carolina home, and he said, "Sounds like they're auctioning tobacco." Walsh had to agree, but he suggested that the obvious effort at a mono-personality for the students probably accounted for their militant stability as isolated missionaries once they got out into the field. Walsh had to smile when he saw the students leave on their weekly hike at the tempo he had endured while studying under French priests: the brisk gait of silent men determined not to enjoy themselves.

"But they make good missionaries," Walsh said. "That you can't take away from them. I just hope our boys turn out as well."

Next they went to Milan via Switzerland, and again they studied seminarians. They finally arrived in Rome on the night of June 18 with their minds and notebooks crammed with more data on seminarians than anybody really had to know. They were tired. They went directly to the American College, where they were given the bad news that there was no room for them. At the Canadian College they had the same luck. It was now too late to knock on any more doors, so they took rooms at the Minerva Hotel. In the morning they found sleeping facilities at the rectory of St. Sylvester's Church which English priests ran on one of the hidden plazas that pop up so unexpectedly at the end of dark Rome streets.

Price was uneasy. June 20 would be the silver anniversary of his ordination, and he had hoped to spend the day at the Lourdes shrine of Bernadette Soubirous or at her tomb at Nevers. Now he saw there was small chance for this; he was disappointed and restless. On June 19, he and Walsh began their rounds of Church offices, presenting letters of introduction and explaining why they were in Rome. Some men had heard of them, others had not: it was extremely frustrating not to know exactly where they stood. Before leaving Boston, Walsh had prepared a special edition of *The Field Afar* in which news of Vatican approval of the new society was announced, and he told Lane to wait for a cable from Rome before going to press. They had arranged that if approval was not received in time, Lane was to make editorial changes. By the end of the first day in Rome, Walsh began to suspect that months, even years, might pass before any hint of approval was given. Slow Rome, oh slow Rome.

The next morning, the twentieth, Price disappeared. Having him disappear in America was bad enough, Walsh felt, but disappearing in a country where he did not know the language was serious. More serious, there were appointments that should be kept by both of them; now Walsh would have to go alone, hoping he would not be asked the whereabouts of his partner.

Up at dawn, Price had traveled clear across Italy to the village of Loreto, on the Adriatic. His goal was the Church of the Holy House, a magnificent structure containing a small house of plain stone which was purported to be the home of Nazareth where the Virgin Mary had been born and raised, where she received the Annunciation, and where she went to live after the Ascension of Jesus. In 336, Empress Helena had caused a basilica to be erected over the house in Nazareth and it was a shrine for Christians until the invasion of the Turks in 1291. Then, according to tradition and certain documentation, angels lifted the house from Nazareth, transporting it to Dalmatia, and the site became a place of miracles. Three years later, angels moved the house across the sea to Loreto. Another church was built over the house. It was there that Price went to celebrate his twenty-fifth year as a priest.

By now, Walsh knew better than to question Price about his disappearances because he never got any answers. When Price returned late that night, Walsh grimly told him the events of the day, informing him that the next morning they were to see Cardinal Gotti, the head of the Sacred Congregation of Propaganda, who would be the principal figure in the Vatican decision to be made regarding the society. Then Walsh went to bed.

Gotti was expecting them. He put aside the letters of introduction they offered, revealed that Archbishop Falconio had already sent him some general information, and now he asked for details. He was warm and friendly and interested. He thought they were wise in having inspected European societies on which their own would be modeled but he urged them to prepare to learn more from their own experiences than from the experience of others. He asked where they intended to locate and from the tone of their answers he perceived the reason for the evasions.

"This is Rome," he said. "We are very hierarchial here. The decision for approval is not mine alone. Therefore, I suggest that you write an outline about your society, saying in it that you will of course submit yourselves to the bishop in whose diocese you settle. It will make a difference to the other members of my board who must consider your request."

"We will be happy to do that," Walsh said.

"When will you take it up with the board?" Price asked.

"We have a meeting in three or four days," Gotti said.

"Will we know then?" Price pressed.

"I cannot say. We always have many things to discuss. Some-times these things take a long while."

Walsh asked, "When may we inquire of you?"

Gotti consulted his calendar. "Come back—let me see—come back on Thursday, the twenty-ninth. That is a holiday, the Feast of Saint Peter and Saint Paul; most people will be away. I will be free to see you then and we can chat."

They spent two days writing their outline and having it trans-lated into Latin and Italian, then they delivered it to Gotti's office. There were still courtesy calls to be made, so they occupied themselves with these. One day Price disappeared again, but this time he did not indicate even in his diary where he had gone. Time had the weight of granite. Walsh and Price agreed that if, when they saw Gotti again, there was no indication when the Propaganda board might consider their appeal they would return to Boston and await it there.

The morning of June 29 finally arrived. Walsh and Price made their way to Gotti's office: the holiday had emptied it and they were ushered quickly inside. They kissed the Cardinal's ring and took the nearby chairs he indicated.

"Have you been enjoying Rome?" Gotti asked and opened a folder on his desk.

"Very much," said Walsh, but with an uncertainty that made Gotti smile.

The Cardinal handed Walsh a document which he recognized as a Latin copy of the outline. He glanced at Gotti with an un-spoken question. Gotti asked, "Aren't you going to examine it?"

Walsh paged through the outline to the end and there he saw that a paragraph had been added. He read it quickly, then jumped to his feet and thrust the document at Price. Jolted, Price whipped his hand from his pocket so clumsily that his rosary dropped into his lap.

Walsh said, "Your Eminence, will you excuse me? I must send a cable to Boston." Gotti laughed and dismissed him. A few min-utes later the message was on the way to Lane:

"PRINT F A."

VI

THE approval was temporary, but it was an approval nevertheless. Walsh and Price were authorized to buy property, build a seminary, and accept students. They were to direct their project jointly with the bishop in whose diocese they settled, and they were to keep Propaganda informed of their developments. At a later date, to be set by the Propaganda board, they were to submit their rule, and a final decision about the new society would be made at that time.

After scurrying out of Gotti's office like schoolboys set free and after sending the cable, Walsh and Price hurried to St. Peter's. The basilica was crowded with pilgrims, there to honor Saint Peter on his feast day. Against one wall was an enormous statue of Peter enthroned, more than twice life-size, and for the occasion a jeweled tiara had been placed upon its head and a jeweled cope hung from its shoulders. Along the wall stretched a thick line of visitors, all the way to the doors, and one by one they approached the statue and, in humility and obedience, kissed its foot, now worn smooth from centuries of lips.

Walsh and Price could not contain themselves for the long wait to display their fealty to Peter and his Church. Instead they went forward to the crypt of Saint Peter and knelt there, looking down at the place where lay the remains of the Prince of the

74

Apostles who had himself been a missionary, and they stayed there a long time at their prayers.

When they returned to St. Sylvester's rectory they found a note awaiting them with news that Pope Pius X would receive them the next morning. The appointment was a complete surprise and they were both excited about it. They wondered why it had been arranged: certainly it was an honor, and they were not prepared for it. They thought perhaps the Pope wanted to question them about their plans, so they collected all their documents into a neat package to present to him. Price worried for a moment. He asked, "Do you think anything might have gone wrong?"

Walsh considered the suggestion, then shook it off uncomfortably. "I don't see what or how," he said. "Don't even think about it."

Next day, at the appointed hour, they made their way through the progression of anterooms to the Pope's office and at last they were ushered in. Protocol required them to genuflect three times, but as they were rising the second time the Pope extended his hands in gentle impatience and said, "No, no, no." And he motioned them to chairs. From the quizzical expression on his face they perceived that, like them, he was not sure why they were there.

Walsh handed over the packet of documents. The Pope adjusted his glasses and began to go over them. His expression turned serious. He looked up at them, evaluating. In Italian he said, "Americans in the missions? So soon?" He read some more, then still reading he said, "But maybe it will be good for the Church in America." Price began to squirm.

Then the Pope reached the page that bore the endorsement of the College of Propaganda. His face lit up. He put down the documents. "Why, it is all settled," he said, obviously relieved.

He smiled at them and they smiled at him. For all purposes, the interview was over but no one knew what to do next. Walsh had brought along a photograph of the Pope and he presented it to be autographed. In six tight lines, the Pope wrote that he gave Walsh and Price his blessing, that he blessed their society and all America. Then he came around from his desk, indicating that he was ready to give them a personal blessing. They knelt in front of him, and as the Pope pronounced the blessing he touched each man's head. They rose to depart, backing from the room. The Pope returned to his desk, watching them, lifting both hands to them in an *Addio*.

In a sense, the meeting had been anticlimactic, arranged solely as a favor on the basis that anybody able to have a few moments alone with the Pope would feel privileged. By its nature, the papacy contained the dignity of history, the grandeur of authority, and the nobility of Christian leadership, enhanced in this case by the personal sanctity of Pius X himself: awkward though the meeting had been simply because of unpreparedness, it nevertheless made a deep impression on Walsh and Price and once again they went into St. Peter's for prayers.

That night they wrote a report of all that had happened in Rome and sent it off to Cardinal Gibbons. When they finished, they sank back in their chairs exhausted.

"I have never been so tired," Walsh admitted.

"The tension," Price diagnosed. "I'm still all tied up inside."

"Do you want to head home right away?"

"Do you?"

"I thought," said Walsh, "I might make my retreat somewhere in Europe before going back. Once we get home we won't have a moment's rest."

"I'd like to go to Lourdes," Price revealed.

"Yes, I thought you would. How much time will you need?"

"A few weeks?"

Walsh nodded, agreeing. "Why don't we meet in England in September?" he said. "That will give us both plenty of time. I want to study all my notes and I'd like to go to Paris again. We can meet at the Mill Hill Fathers, in London."

"That's two months," Price pointed out. "But if you think we have the time—"

Walsh did. Privately, he was a little worried about his health and he wanted to rest as much as he could because he knew a long time might pass before he could rest again. Of late he had noticed an occasional difficulty in breathing; he was now in his mid-forties and naturally concerned a bit about his heart. Also, there had been sudden small stabs of pain in his hands and at his shoulders; he hoped he would not become a victim of the arthritis that plagued Father Lane. A rest—he needed a rest.

Price wrote in his diary:

A feeling of great responsibility has come over me, Mother, since
Cardinal Gotti gave the authorization—I have felt as if a terrific cross
were put upon my shoulders, which I have, however, with gladness and
love accepted in the manner Our Lord would wish. . . . There is no
elation in my heart, Mother; the crucifixion, with the nails and the
thorns, the cross doubly heavy, is before me.

Thus, despite the speed of their success in Rome, the emotions
of Walsh and Price were strangely leveled as they went their separate ways. Speed was perhaps the problem. Everything had happened so fast. In less than a year a dream had turned into a duty,
and the weight of it was that they were not alone in it. Others—
dozens, hundreds, maybe even thousands—would lean upon them
now, for guidance, training, leadership, even daily bread. They
were like new husbands who, when the honeymoon was over, saw
suddenly that romance was threatened by the blunt realities of
life and they were frightened by it. They both needed the solace
of love, and now they went looking for it.

They spent the Fourth of July in Rome with friends at the
American College and the embassy, then they took the train to-
gether as far as Genoa, where they parted. Walsh went on to the
Mill Hill mission house in the Tyrol, at Brixen, and began his
retreat. Price went directly to Lourdes. He stayed there almost
two weeks, dividing his time between the shrine and the home of
Bernadette Soubirous. Three or four times he spent the whole
night in prayer at the shrine. Using a brew of English, primitive
French, and Latin he managed to make himself understood at the
Soubirous home and was allowed to visit Bernadette's room whenever he wished. In view of his book about her, he had many questions to ask, and out of this grew a friendship with the family
that lasted the rest of his life.

Price, too, wanted to make a retreat. He knew that Jesuits conducted a house in Dublin where priests often went for a month's
retreat. With this in mind, he went north to Paris for a few days,
then on to England from where he intended to make his retreat
plans. He learned, however, that the retreat house was booked
long in advance and that there was room for him only for a brief

visit. He settled for this, then hurried back to France, going now to Nevers to visit the tomb of Bernadette in the Convent of St. Gildard, where she had spent thirteen years as a nurse and sacristan until her death at thirty-five on April 16, 1879. It was here, in 1909, when the process of her canonization was begun, that Bernadette's body was exhumed and found to be incorrupt.

Typically of him, Price arrived without notifying anyone and was discovered late in the afternoon making the Stations of the Cross in the convent chapel. The Soubirous family had written the Mother Superior about the American priest who had taken such an intense interest in Bernadette, and when she was told about the priest, obviously American, who was lost in deep prayer in the chapel she deduced that he must be the man. Later that day Price went to the Mother Superior with an unusual request. He asked for the key to the vault where Bernadette was entombed, explaining that he wished to make a night's vigil there. The Mother Superior was hesitant; nobody had ever asked such a thing before; she did not know what to do. Price did not plead, and yet there was an urgency about him that indicated the importance of the vigil to him. The nun finally gave him the key. His diary for the next few days hinted at a tremendous spiritual impact, but the full extent of it was not revealed for many years.

Revealed soon, on the other hand, was an idea that struck him for a new association to honor Mary and Bernadette. He outlined his plan in his diary:

Organize an association—The American Association of Our Lady of Lourdes—or The Immaculate Conception for the Conversion of America. Get out a magazine, *The Immaculate Conception,* and make it the organ—get those interested to get up a pilgrimage, at lowest to spend eighteen days, in honor of the eight apparitions, praying at Lourdes for the conversion of America—get out literature—get the pilgrims at Lourdes to pray for this—have an American headquarters at Lourdes— with literature, etc., spread all over—have those who could pray the way of incurables to Lourdes; get out well-selected books on Lourdes Grotto, advertisements, etc.

So he was off again. The depression that clung to him when he had left Rome was gone. Again he was raring to go, eager to organize, to lead, to guide, to mold. Under the caption "Reasons why America should be the Greatest Mission Country in the World," he wrote in his diary:

(1) It is the most powerful and influential country, and this ought to be turned to the glory of God; (2) it must become missionary or perish —the forces against the Church are so powerful that, if it does not become missionary and fight, it will cease to exist; (3) the older missionary countries are dying; (4) the American character is one of intelligent, restless, practical activity that must accomplish its end; (5) blessed by the Church with the Immaculate Conception—this means to fight sin in all its breadth among Catholics, heretics and pagans; (6) America is the only country that can successfully cope with the mission situation in activity, in modern methods, in material resources, and in influence; (7) the English-speaking world is, and will remain, in the ascendancy for a long time to come, but the U. S. is the bulk of that and must in the future more and more predominate.

I am thinking also, Mother, how to form a missionary band of lay people for the conversion of the country. What can a lay person do? (1) Try to help out the priests of the parish in every way; (2) try to repress all vice and moral evil as far as one's influence goes; (3) make a specialty of keeping Catholic books and papers around and rejecting all that are non-Catholic in their influence; (4) say some prayers every day, a decade of the rosary, for the conversion of America to the Catholic Faith and for the foreign missions; (5) promote the conversion of America and aid the foreign missions by work, contributions, etc.

What he was actually doing was expanding on his old ideas for North Carolina, bringing in the foreign missions because now he was involved in them himself. His personal attitude toward missionary work was clear in his new idea—the spiritual shoring up of a country that already called itself Christian: make it Catholic. As admirable as this was, as worthy as the whole idea was, it nevertheless intruded upon the project on which Price was already embarked. Either he could not foresee that his partnership with Walsh would occupy him full-time or he was not willing to let it. The sudden excited interest in a project quite apart from Walsh evidenced a divisiveness in Price that was to keep him unsettled all his life. This trait accounted further for the disarray at Nazareth and, in future years whenever anyone tried to determine which man was more responsible for the success of their joint effort, it gave additional proof that neither could have done it on his own; it was surprising that they managed to do it to-gether.

Walsh continued single-mindedly. After his retreat at Brixen, he worked on his notes about seminaries and seminarians, corre-lating them in the neat fashion that was typical of him. When he finished he had an effective handbook for seminary faculties, and the fact that he prepared the notes for his own use only was a loss for other men in the same position. The retreat brought him spiritual peace, the Swiss summer provided relaxation, his paper work sparked him, but, like Price, he needed something more. As Lourdes was the natural restoration for Price, Paris and the at-mosphere of Théophane Vénard was the place for Walsh. At Paris, Walsh saw Father Eusebius Vénard, the martyr's brother, and solidified a lifetime friendship with him. Théophane did for Walsh what Bernadette did for Price: each man found in his favorite saint the resources to rededicate his life to the purposes of his priesthood. For each man, love was the secret weapon, and, from the spiritual companionships of saints who had loved en-tirely, the two men were able to love more—to love God, the Church, souls, even to love the hardships they might have to en-dure for the sake of these things.

At the end of August, Walsh crossed over to England refreshed, restored, revitalized. There he stayed with the Mill Hill Fathers and he was able to solve another problem he had anticipated: a faculty for the forthcoming seminary. The Mill Hill Fathers prom-ised to send him professors if he could not get enough in Amer-ica. The promise held double importance for Walsh: it meant that his students would be trained by men with missionary ex-perience and it meant the professors would not be Sulpicians. In view of his own sad adventures with a bishop who had aversions to the Frenchmen, Walsh considered the second point to be of substantial value.

There was no news from Price. But Walsh had grown used to this. He went ahead and bought tickets for the trip back to Bos-ton, packed his things, and prepared to leave for Liverpool to catch the ship. Some of the Mill Hill Fathers were distressed over Price's silence, but Walsh comforted them: "Never mind. He will show up. If he comes racing in here after I've gone to Liverpool, just send him on to me."

Walsh went to Liverpool. He boarded the ship, found his state-room, unpacked, and made himself at home. A half-hour before departure time, he went out on deck to watch the crowds. Ten minutes later he saw Price scurrying up the gangplank and went to greet him.

"I made it," Price said triumphantly.

"So you did," said Walsh, "but I didn't expect you so early."

The issue of *The Field Afar* that announced the formation of the Catholic Foreign Mission Society of America also contained this paragraph:

Youths or young men who feel a strong desire to toil for the souls of heathen people and who are willing to go afar with no hope of earthly recompense and with no guarantee of a return to their native land are encouraged to write, marking their letter personal, to the Editor of Field Afar, Station A., P. O. Box 98, Boston, Mass.

It was an invitation to martyrdom.

VII

THEY decided against locating their seminary in the Boston arch-diocese. They also decided against North Carolina, Washington, or Philadelphia. Walsh was partial to New York for several rea-sons: it was centrally located, it had a large Catholic population, there was money available, Archbishop Farley had just been named a cardinal, and this had stirred Catholic life in the city. Walsh listed these points to Price during their discussion and Price agreed that New York had its advantages. On October 13, a month after their return from Europe, Walsh and Price went to visit Farley and they put the question to him. He was delighted.

"Will you want to settle in the city itself?" he asked.

"We'd prefer a country place," said Walsh.

"Then why don't you look around Westchester County? The Dominicans and the Salesians have houses near Hawthorne. Maybe you can find something near them."

Walsh already knew Father Bertrand Cothonay, superior of the Dominicans. A former missionary to Tonkin, Cothonay had vis-ited Walsh in Boston and had supplied him with many details of the country where both he and Théophane Vénard had once worked. When Walsh wrote Cothonay that his new society might locate near Hawthorne, the Dominican invited him and Price to stay with him while they shopped around. Hawthorne was about

thirty miles north of New York City. In addition to the Dominicans and the Salesians, the Christian Brothers had a training center at Pocantico Hills, adjacent to the country estate of John D.
Rockefeller, and in the village of Hawthorne, Mother Rose Hawthorne, converted daughter of Nathaniel Hawthorne, had organized a new congregation of nuns and built a hospital for the
care of incurable cancer patients. A few miles away was St.
Joseph's Seminary, training school for the archdiocesan priests of
New York. Hawthorne was an unusually Catholic community indeed.

Walsh and Price were impatient to get started. Walsh's main
concern was *The Field Afar;* he realized he could not edit it very
well from Hawthorne as long as its offices remained in Boston.
Furthermore, Walsh and Price were already acquiring a family.
Walsh had indicated in *The Field Afar* that his new society would
be poor and therefore needed some volunteers to help get it
started. Four young women immediately volunteered. One was
Mary Josephine Rogers, a Boston schoolteacher who had known
Walsh for several years and had previously helped get the magazine into the mail by addressing envelopes; the other three—
Mary Louise Wholean, a recent Wellesley graduate; Sara Sullivan,
a secretary at the Harvard Medical School, and Mary Dwyer, who
worked in a Boston office—offered their services without salary
anywhere and for as long as Walsh wanted them. Also on hand
were Ernst Hollger, an Austrian farmer Walsh had met in Europe, and Thomas McCann, a skilled mechanic from Brooklyn,
both of whom said that although they did not wish to become
priests they were ready to do any manual labor necessary in the
capacity of lay Brothers. Mary Rogers told Walsh she could not
join him until the end of the school term, but the other three
women were eager to get to work at once. So were Hollger and
McCann, and so was Father Lane, Walsh's seminary comrade and
cofounder of *The Field Afar.* Unable to do parish work because
of his arthritis, Lane was then chaplain at a Boston trade school;
he had obtained his release and permission to help Walsh on a
temporary basis. He wrote Walsh almost daily, pleading, "When
shall I come down?"

Goaded by these unexpected pressures, Walsh recognized that
he could not delay too long if he wanted to hold on to the vol-

unteers he had. For days, he and Price hiked the snow-bound, un-named streets of Hawthorne, inspecting available houses and driving by carriage through the countryside to look at farms. The offers they liked they could not afford; the offers they could afford they did not like. And they were running out of offers.

The severe winter chilled Price's Southern temperament. One night when he and Walsh returned to the Dominican priory after another futile day, Price threw his hat at a chair and demanded, "Let's take one of them—any one of them. I can't stand much more of this."

"Very well, then." Walsh removed his coat with outrageous care. "We'll have to make a decision."

"I wish we would."

"I mean about other things." He sat down and watched Price pace the room. "Will you agree that, right now, the first importance is the magazine?"

"I'll agree to anything," Price said testily.

Walsh pursed his lips. He hoped they were not going to have an argument. "Then we must first find a home for the magazine?"

"Yes."

"And the secretaries?"

"Yes, yes."

"You know how little money we have?"

"Of course I do."

"If we buy one house for the magazine and the secretaries, we won't have enough money to buy a second house for the men, for us."

"We can worry about that later."

"I don't think we should proceed that way."

Price stopped in front of Walsh. "Then what do you suggest?"

"Since we obviously must get started on this thing soon, I suggest," said Walsh, "that we rent a couple of houses until we can find what we want or raise more money."

"Paying rent would be throwing the money down the drain," Price said.

"Then what do you suggest?"

Price's mind went blank with frustration. "Nothing," he said. "All right, let's rent."

"It's settled, then?"

"It's settled."

"Very well. We'll look for houses tomorrow."

"Good night." Price left the room.

Walsh sat a long time. He was distressed by the clash that had just occurred. It was not serious, but if they could be so terse with each other over the first problem that faced them what would happen when some crucial decision came along? Compromise was the only solution, but surely there would come times when compromise would be impossible. What then? Sooner or later, Walsh reflected, they would have to reach some understanding about authority. If they were to share it, as the Rome approval indicated, they would have to divide it into zones of activity so that one man would be free to pursue certain aspects of the work without constantly fretting about the reactions of the other. The present arrangement, Walsh felt, could lead only to repeated tension and uncertainty. He felt, in fact, uncertain about the whole thing. Sitting there alone at midnight in the Dominican parlor, he felt like a guest who knew he had overstayed his welcome but had nowhere else to go, and he was suddenly homesick and blue and downhearted. If it had been possible to pack and go back to Boston on the first train, he would have done so, if only for the comfort of a friendly face and a familiar surrounding. But he knew it was impossible: he was committed now and must go on, at least until failure, utter failure, could not be denied. He just wished he could go through the ordeal ahead with someone toward whom he felt closer.

He stood up. He put out the lone lamp and went upstairs. A small night light in the second-floor corridor sent his shadow looming across the hall. As he passed Price's room he heard the hoarse whispers of prayer. He went to his own room and softly closed the door behind him.

Next morning he rose early and went to the chapel to say his Mass. The heaviness had left him, but the uneasiness remained. He wondered what the night had done for Price. He was surprised to see Price's door open and the room empty. Price was nowhere to be seen in the chapel or in the sacristy. As Walsh was vesting, a young Dominican came in to be his server. Ordinarily they would not have talked, but Walsh was curious about Price. He asked softly, "Has Father Price said Mass?"

"Yes. He went out."

Ah, so. Gone again.

As he followed the server to a side altar, Walsh decided to offer his Mass for the new society, asking not for the miracle of a smooth road but merely the blessing of a smooth partnership.

He was at breakfast with Father Bertrand when Price came in. He said, "Father, tell Father Price what you were just telling me."

The Dominican waited until Price said grace and sat down, then he said, "If you're going to rent for a while, I think I know just the place."

"Actually two places," Walsh put in. He tried not to study Price's face too obviously.

"The Klinger property," Cothonay went on, "scarcely a stone's throw from here; I can see it from my office window. We used it ourselves when we first came here. Both good houses; no electricity, but you won't mind that. There's a well, and the pipes are in if you want to get a pump for running water. And the big house has a furnace."

"Sounds good," Price said.

"Yes, it's very nice, especially since it's only temporary," Cothonay said.

Price looked at Walsh for the first time. "What do you think?"

"We ought to look at it."

"All right. And if we decide no, we can start our search again. It's not as cold this morning as it was yesterday; I won't mind the walk." That was his apology and explanation; the previous night's scene was forgotten.

They took the houses. True, the houses were sparsely furnished; true, the hand pump at the well was frozen; true, long vacancy had coated the rooms with heavy dust; true, the furnace looked beyond repair; true, the two buildings were as inviting as tombs. But they were home.

Walsh wired the secretaries in Boston to come along as quickly as possible, then he went to Boston himself to supervise the packing of *The Field Afar* for shipment to Hawthorne. Price went to New York to buy additional furniture for the houses, office equipment, food, and household supplies, then he went on to Nazareth

to arrange for the shipment of his own things. The three secretaries—Mary Louise Wholean, Mary Dwyer and Sara Sullivan—
arrived at Hawthorne on January 6, the Feast of the Epiphany,
commemorating the arrival of the Magi at Bethlehem; Father
Cothonay greeted them as "The Three Wise Women." A week
later Price was back from North Carolina and Walsh came down
from Boston with Lane. Thomas McCann was summoned from
Brooklyn, and Ernst Hollger was on his way from Europe.

They were a going concern.

By the end of February, they had thirty applicants for the seminary—but they still had no seminary.

Money was the desperate need. In *The Field Afar* they openly
begged for money to buy land. Readers who had followed the
progress of the society from the magazine's first edition had a
possessive interest in its future, but most of the readers were poor
and the donations they sent in came mostly in coins wrapped in
cotton. To raise more money, Price went on the road, visiting
cities and towns along the Eastern seaboard, preaching in churches
and soliciting subscriptions. The day's mail determined everybody's mood: days when the mail was unusually light put everyone on edge and sent them slipping one by one into the room
they used as a chapel to ask God to ease their poverty. Price continued his old habit of disappearing for weeks at a time; Walsh
remarked in the community's diary: "My Martha seems to be
lost again somewhere out in the vineyards while his Mary worries
here at home at prayers."

Walsh had much more than the prayers to occupy him. In addition to editing the magazine, handling the mail, and searching
for suitable property for the seminary, he was also the cook for
the men's house. He observed in the diary that others in the house
yearned for the times they were invited for meals by the secretaries or the Dominicans. He wrote of this bachelorhood ordeal in
the magazine and occasionally some woman reader from a nearby
community volunteered her services, but such cooks rarely stayed
long. Often there was no water for cooking or cleaning, sometimes there was no food, and at other times visitors piled in without warning. The men soon got used to waking up in the morn-

ing to discover that their cook had vanished in the night, then Walsh would have to go heavy-heartedly to the kitchen to take up the pots and pans himself.

At the peak of these bleak hours, two events occurred that provided hope when it was most desolately needed. On Good Friday, a check for five thousand dollars arrived from Cardinal Farley, an event that immediately inspired everyone to a hearty *Te Deum*. Then, when Walsh went into town to thank Farley, he stopped to visit the young priest he had recommended for the directorship of the New York office of the Society for the Propagation of the Faith.

Now a monsignor, Dunn said, "There's a woman in New York you should meet. I think she'd be willing to help you from time to time."

The woman was Julia Ward, who had built a job as seamstress into a career as a designer of women's clothes. She was indeed willing to help, and for years she was referred to, both in the diary and the magazine, as the Lady Bountiful. With the help provided by her, the Cardinal, Price's travels, and subscribers, Walsh found, late that spring, that he had ten thousand dollars he could use as a down payment on property for the seminary site. His plan was to buy a farm that already had buildings which could be used as a temporary seminary until he had enough money for a proper structure, and with this in mind he scoured Westchester County. He located such a farm at Pocantico Hills, near the Rockefeller estate and convenient to the Christian Brothers school.

When all the preliminaries were out of the way, Walsh gave his check to the real estate agent handling the transaction. It was a Saturday afternoon; Walsh was to return on Monday to sign the legal documents. On Monday, the agent told him that the deal was off.

"But why?" Walsh asked.

"I found another buyer," the agent said.

"But you had a buyer," Walsh insisted. "Me."

"This person offered to pay much more," said the agent.

"That's immaterial," said Walsh. "You accepted my check on Saturday. You are legally bound to let me have the farm."

"I don't think so," said the man. "I have the right to change my mind. Besides, I have already turned the property over to the other man."

"Who is he?" Walsh asked.

"I'm not at liberty to reveal that."

"You can reveal it to me now or later in court," Walsh threatened.

"Mr. Rockefeller."

"John D.?"

"Yes."

Walsh was furious. "What does John D. Rockefeller want with that farm?" he stormed. "He owns enough property around here as it is."

"He wanted it, so I sold it to him," the agent said flatly.

"When did he decide that?"

"I don't know. His lawyers were here Saturday after you left; they made a good offer, so I let them have the farm."

"Well," said Walsh, "you can tell Mr. Rockefeller's lawyers that they will hear from mine."

He did not have a lawyer, but he decided it was high time that he got one. For that matter, the state laws required that the Catholic Foreign Mission Society be incorporated; in complying, Walsh felt he would come upon a lawyer to represent him. In addition to himself, Price, Farley, and Dunn, the corporation members were Monsignor Patrick J. Hayes, then rector of Cathedral College, the archdiocesan minor seminary, and later to be cardinal-archbishop of the city; Victor J. Dowling, Justice of the Appellate Division of New York; Major John F. O'Rourke, and Michael Maginnis.

At the conference creating the corporation, Cardinal Farley asked, "Which of you is going to be superior of the society?"

This was the question Walsh and Price had skirted for over a year. Now they could no longer avoid it. They looked at each other, each waiting for the other to speak.

Farley said, "Good heavens, you mean you haven't thought about it as yet?"

Price said to Walsh, "You be the superior."

"All right," Walsh said quietly.

That was that.

In the pretrial discussions of the property suit, Rockefeller claimed that he had no knowledge of Walsh's down payment, but now that he had the estate he had no intentions of giving it up. It was well known in Westchester County that Rockefeller disliked close neighbors. He had tried repeatedly to buy out the Christian Brothers, whose land overlooked his, and years later he succeeded in doing so. On another occasion, he managed to have a railroad moved because its nearness annoyed him. He was not, however, to get rid of Walsh that easily.

The case dragged on for three years and involved several appeals to high courts. If anything, it was a nuisance to Rockefeller, who had not expected Walsh to put up such a fight. Periodically, Walsh printed progress reports in *The Field Afar,* which delighted his readers. If too much time passed without news of the suit, the readers inquired how the battle was going. For them, victory was no longer a matter of money but of triumph over the multimillionaire who, they felt, had tried to pull a fast one. In the end, Rockefeller settled out of court for eight thousand dollars damages. Legal fees had eaten deeply into the payment, but the mere fact that Rockefeller was defeated brought great cheers from the subscribers.

Within the first weeks of the suit, Walsh realized that he would never get the property. He had his ten-thousand-dollar check back; he resumed his search for the society's permanent home. He found it in August, a ninety-three-acre farm on Pines Bridge Road overlooking the town of Ossining and the Hudson River. It was situated on what was known as Sunset Hill, the highest elevation in the vicinity, and it offered a beautiful sweeping view of the countryside. On the farm were two large houses, both in good condition, and a big barn. There was a well and a creek. The air was clear and cool, and the area boasted that it was free of mosquitoes. The property was for sale.

Rather than take any chances that anyone's desire for privacy might really mean a privacy from Catholics, Walsh decided against attempting to buy the farm himself. Mary Rogers, the Boston schoolteacher, was now at Hawthorne. It was she who made inquiries of the property owners, she who dealt with real estate agents; the down-payment check was in her name. Once the transaction was complete and there was no possibility of trouble, she deeded the farm to the society for the sum of one dollar. At last the society had a home.

Walsh already had a name for it. The new property was on a hilltop—a knoll; it seemed proper to Walsh that the property, the work itself, and everyone involved in it would be especially blessed if all were dedicated to the Mother of Jesus, to whom he had a deep devotion. Sunset Hill therefore became Maryknoll, and to be a Maryknoller thereafter became a special blessing.

VIII

By AUGUST, the society had over fifty applicants. As consoling as this was, it also presented problems. In the first place, there was neither the money nor the facilities to accommodate that many students at the new property. Secondly, there was no way of knowing which of the applicants were sincere and which had applied for any number of personal reasons, few of which added up to a true vocation. Most Catholic boys considered the priesthood at some time in their lives, just as most Catholic girls gave thought to becoming nuns. It was a normal reaction to the Catholic environment in their homes. Many would do more than think about it, which accounted for the crowds in most training centers. If ten per cent of the boys who entered a specific seminary actually survived to ordination, the school could feel that it was more than holding its own. In a larger and older institution, there might be safety in numbers, but at Maryknoll there simply was no room. Walsh was faced with the responsibility of choosing, say, a half-dozen young men who, mostly through letters, had indicated clues of a true vocation for the priesthood—for the missions. At this stage, a misjudgment could mean that some other youth, perhaps worthier, would be denied entrance and might as a result abandon his vocation. This was a risk every vocation director faced; Walsh approached it cautiously.

He was sure of one boy. In appraising vocations, both Walsh

and Price agreed that their safest bet was to approach youngsters who were already in seminaries. On his travels, Price visited all seminaries on his route and talked to the students about the missions. He was not always welcomed by the faculty for the simple reason that nobody wanted to lose any good students to the adventurous appeal of the missions. Aware of this, Walsh paved the way by articles in *The Field Afar* in which he acknowledged the need for diocesan vocations but stressed that for every young man who went to the missions there would be five more who would, because of him, be inspired to enter the priesthood at home. Carrying out this idea himself, Walsh went one day to speak to the students at Cathedral College in Manhattan. Finished, he was about to leave when he was approached by one of the students, a short boy, with smooth dark hair, large serious eyes and a sober mien.

"That was an interesting talk, Father," he said.

"Thank you, my boy," said Walsh, "And what's your name?"

"Ford. Francis Ford."

"You from Manhattan, Francis?"

"Brooklyn. My father edits the paper there."

"Oh, yes," Walsh said. "I know his work." He waited.

"Father," young Ford said, "I think I'd like to join your society. I've always been interested in the missions."

"That's fine, Francis. I'm very glad to hear that. Why don't you write me a letter all about yourself. Later on when we're ready for students I'll get in touch with you."

"All right, Father," said Ford. "And maybe I'll come up to Hawthorne for a visit some day."

"Do that," Walsh encouraged. "And talk to your father about the idea. Tell him to let me know how he feels about it. And tell him I'd like to meet him some day."

"All right, Father. You'll hear from me."

Walsh knew that he would. In his own mind, he marked Francis Xavier Ford down as his first seminarian.

Price, too, met a young man he was convinced was mission material. His travels had taken him into western Maryland, and in the town of Cumberland he encountered a Catholic lawyer who told him, "I think my son has a vocation. Maybe you should talk to him."

"I'd be glad to," said Price.

At the first meeting, Price was not too sure about James Edward Walsh. "How old are you?" he asked.

"Twenty-one," Walsh said.

"That's a little old to be starting out for the priesthood," Price said.

"I've already finished college."

"Your father told me. Did you study Latin?"

"No, but I can learn it."

"Yes, I suppose so. What makes you think you want to be a missionary?"

The young man smiled. "A few years ago a priest suggested it to me and I laughed, but now I've changed my mind. Maybe somebody's been praying for me. I just know now that I want to be a missionary and that I'm going to become one."

As they talked on, Price's doubts fell away. He was most impressed by Walsh's determination: an older seminarian would need that. The studies might be more difficult for an older student, personal habits would be harder to change, the companionship of younger men would require greater patience and understanding. They discussed Walsh's spiritual life: Price was convinced that Walsh's vocation decision had not been a sudden thing, that he had been thinking about it and praying about it for a long time.

Price wrote to Hawthorne: "You will be hearing from James Edward Walsh, an admirable young man I have met here and who I feel is destined to become one of us. I wonder only how we are all going to get along in the same house with two men who have practically the same names."

Lawyer Walsh wrote to Father Walsh: "I feel you should know that right now things are not too good for me financially. Jim knows this, and his only reason for not joining you might be his reluctance to become a burden to me. Therefore, if there are any expenses involved in his training I wish you would not mention them to him but let me know them privately. I'm sure I can find some way to meet them."

Father Walsh replied: "Do not worry about expenses. If you can keep your son in spending money, we should be able to find a way to take care of the rest. I will let you know when to send him on to us."

In the first week of September, he sent for young Walsh, for Francis Ford, and for William F. O'Shea, of Hoboken, New Jersey. If the three students expected to dive immediately into their studies they were dismally mistaken. Starting the ninth of September, they made several trips each day by horsecart between Hawthorne and Maryknoll, lugging boxes of records, files, furniture, and office equipment. On the cold, rainy night of September 18, they made the last trip, crammed into the cart with the driver, Father Walsh, and the two lay Brothers. Fainter hearts would have required more reward than the joy of knowing that the job was over and they were ready to settle down.

It took a month to settle down. The main house had to be converted into classrooms, dormitories, and quarters for priests. A structure attached to the barn was made into living quarters for the Brothers now increased to three by the arrival of a Boston printer. The house formerly used by a tenant family became headquarters for *The Field Afar* and quarters for the secretaries. It was dedicated on October 15, the Feast of St. Teresa of Avila and was called St. Teresa's Lodge; the secretaries called themselves Teresians. They let Walsh know that they hoped eventually to form themselves into a religious congregation of Sisters who would not only assist the society in office work but go to the missions themselves. As a step in that direction they adopted a religious garb of a full-length gray dress and short cape; the veils and vows would have to wait almost five years.

In early November, Walsh accepted three more students: Daniel McShane, of Columbus, Indiana, who was already well advanced in his seminary studies; William E. Lambert, of Buffalo, and Alphonse S. Vogel, of New York. On November 21, the birthday of Théophane Vénard, the entire community gathered at St. Augustine's Church in Ossining, where cassocks and cinctures were given the six students and the establishment of the society was formally proclaimed.

Two students—McShane and Walsh—were ready to study theology, which the new seminary was not ready to teach, so they commuted daily to the archdiocesan seminary about twenty miles away. The remaining four were instructed at Maryknoll by the faculty Father Walsh managed to collect: two Dominicans, a Mill Hill Father, Lane, and himself. Dr. Paluel Flagg, of Yonkers, taught mission medicine twice a week, treating any Maryknoll illnesses on the same occasions. At frequent intervals, classes were interrupted to allow everybody to go out and help unpack crates that continually arrived or to assist in emergency repairs or to aid Father Walsh in the kitchen upon the sudden departure of another cook.

Nevertheless, by the time Christmas came, some semblance of order had been achieved and spirits were high. After a Christmas banquet at the main house, made gayer by the efforts of a professional cook, the priests, students, and Brothers went to pay a holiday call on the Teresians. A Christmas tree stood in the reception room, bright with decorations the women had made themselves. A rectangular piece of paper caught Father Walsh's eye and he went to examine it closely. It was a home-made check, designed by one of the Teresians. It was made out for the sum of a million dollars, payable to the Catholic Foreign Mission Society of America. It was signed John D. Rockefeller.

In January, 1913, *The Field Afar,* now with a circulation of twelve thousand, went monthly. At the same time Father Walsh reported to Rome:

1. We have a permanent location, excellent and quite ample in view of further development.

2. On the property, which cost us (for ninety-three acres of land of all buildings) $45,000, we have paid $15,000, leaving a mortgage of $30,000, of which we shall be free, and, we believe, prepared to cancel in three years.

3. Our official organ, *The Field Afar,* has proved profitable, not only as a direct investment but indirectly by securing for us a steady stream of gifts.

4. The work has been welcomed by a very satisfactory proportion of the bishops, priests, and laity throughout the country, and new friends are being added daily to our lists.

5. We have reason to believe that within a year we shall be in possession of at least twelve foundations ($5,000 each), and we shall have

accumulated, in addition, a substantial portion of the full amount necessary to pay for our property, besides meeting all current expenses. We
have already three complete burses, including one from His Eminence
Cardinal Farley, who has shown his constant interest in our work.

6. Finally, in view of the number of students (six) with whom we
begin and of the encouragement given by religious teachers in various
parts of the country, we have strong hope of a steady flow of vocations.

But the vocations were slow to come. In all of 1913, not another
student entered the seminary. One, Lambert, left. This was
strange, considering the fifty that had applied the previous year.
Foreigners who had charged that luxury had softened Americans
too much for the challenges of mission life pointed to the vocation shortage as proof of their convictions. But Walsh felt there
was more involved. He began to suspect that maybe he and Price
had erred in preferring applicants with seminary experience or
at least a solid Catholic education. After all, neither of them had
seen the inside of a Catholic school until they entered seminaries.
As a solution they dug up Price's early idea of establishing branch
schools for younger boys from which students could be drawn for
the major seminary, which he had expected would be affiliated
with the Catholic University. Bishop Edward F. Hoban, of Scranton, had in many ways proved his interest in the society; now Price
approached him with the idea of opening a minor seminary in his
diocese to train boys for Maryknoll. The Bishop immediately approved and arranged the rental on a big frame house near his
cathedral. The new plan was that boys of early high school age
would live in the house to get used to a seminary atmosphere
while taking classes at the nearby Christian Brothers school.

The new institution was named after Théophane Vénard, and
Lane was put in charge. The first term, twelve boys entered. This
was most encouraging, but it was also the cause of premature optimism. The boys were young. At their ages, it was impossible to
determine whether they actually had the vocation or their mothers did. Most of them lived within a few miles of the Vénard, but
they were always homesick, frequently ill out of loneliness, and
the confusion of trying to lead a seminary life while attending a
day school with regular students brought on countless distractions. Furthermore, the house itself was a financial dead weight.
Not only did none of the boys pay enough tuition to cover their

upkeep, but the building itself provided no income. At Maryknoll, at least, the fields gave fruits and vegetables and fire fuel. It became necessary to send trucks of food and wood to the Vénard each week to cut down expenses. After a few months, the Vénard turnover proved most disheartening, but this was the risk of working with teen-agers.

In the end it was decided that, however worthy the idea was, the present operation was impractical; the Vénard closed after fifteen months. The following year Bishop Hoban informed Walsh that a suitable farm was available at Clarks Summit, a dozen miles out of Scranton, and he said that if money was the only reason Walsh might be reluctant to try a minor seminary again surely some assistance could be arranged by the diocese. Walsh was willing to try: this time the result was quite different. Rural life seemed more conductive to the longevity of teen-age vocations, for even though boys left at the normal rate there were enough others with the spiritual tenacity to survive their boyish woes to give evidence that the Vénard was permanent. Adding to the school's stability was Price's appointment as its superior. His travels kept him away much of the time, but his personal piety and the understanding of boys which he had acquired at the Nazareth orphanage made sufficient impression on the students while he was home to endure during his absences. In time, the Vénard became the model for half a dozen similar preparatory seminaries the society opened across the country.

The years began to move swiftly. In 1914, the number of students at Maryknoll doubled. Equally important, young men who wished to join the group that now called itself the Auxiliary Brothers of St. Michael arrived in a steady flow. Across the lawn, the Teresians also attracted regular recruits. Eager to begin their lives as Sisters, three of them obtained permission from Cardinal Farley to go to Scranton to make their novitiate with the Sisters of the Immaculate Heart. Their hope was to affiliate themselves eventually directly with the society, but when this proved to be beyond the scope of canon law they set up a new congregation within the Dominican Order, with the provision that allowed them always to consider themselves Maryknollers.

On November 10, 1914, Daniel McShane was ordained at St. Patrick's Cathedral—the first student to become a priest in the

Catholic Foreign Mission Society of America. At first, Walsh thought of sending him overseas to get some missionary experience from members of the Paris Foreign Mission Society in Indo-China, but on reconsideration he decided to wait until more Americans were ready so that they could arrive in the missions as a unit of their own society.

The hope of obtaining such men without the long delay of seminary studies began to appear when diocesan priests across the country started to apply for membership in the society. The first such man to join was Father Patrick J. Byrne, of Washington, D. C., who arrived at Maryknoll a week after his ordination in June, 1915. Walsh had to fight the urge to send Byrne straight off to the missions; like others who followed him, Byrne was assigned, in turn, to teaching at Maryknoll and the Vénard, to soliciting magazine subscriptions, to hunting for further vocations, and to outright begging for donations. It was frustrating, to be sure, but it was all part of the job that had to be done.

By the summer of 1917, five of the six original students had been ordained and joined the society. In all, the society had ten priests, a dozen Auxiliaries, and sixty students. Also, the Sacred Congregation of the Propagation of the Faith approved the society's provisional statutes and placed the society under the Congregation's immediate jurisdiction, acts which gave the society full stature within the Church. It was ready now to fulfill its purpose.

IX

JUST when everything was going so well, Walsh got the shock of his life. One evening Price came to him and announced, "I think I want to quit."

"Quit? Quit what?" Walsh asked.

"The society."

"The society? Why? What's the matter?"

"Nothing's the matter," said Price. "I just want to do other things. I feel I've done all I can here."

"That's ridiculous," Walsh said fiercely. "We haven't even started here."

"Perhaps, but you don't need me any more."

"What's behind this?" Walsh demanded. "What's going on that you don't like?"

"I've told you: nothing. But I have other interests, and you know it. Even before I met you I was interested in starting a society to do missionary work in North Carolina, and you know that lately I've been trying to organize an American Association for Lourdes. I want to give these things more of my time."

So that was it: Price's habitual divisiveness, his old habit of trying to do a dozen things at once at the risk of doing all of them half measure.

Walsh said, "Would you be willing to agree that our society is an important project?"

"Certainly."

"And do you realize it is as much yours as it is mine?"

"I would never think of that."

"I know you wouldn't and neither would I, but I mention it to prove a point." Walsh leaned forward on his desk. "From the beginning I have respected your desire to remain in the background, but I can assure you that everybody who knows Maryknoll also knows that you and I have been in this together from the first day. If you leave now, for any reason whatsoever, you will create the public impression that you are dissatisfied with something here and you want to get out."

Price brushed the argument aside. "You're exaggerating."

"I am not," said Walsh firmly. "If you quit, you will destroy the morale here at Maryknoll and among all the people who have been helping us."

"I don't believe that, and besides nobody would have to know."

"Just how could anybody be kept from knowing?" Walsh shook his head. "You must not do this. I beg you not to, as your friend, your partner and—since you force me to it—your superior. I know I can't make you stay, but I beg you not to go."

Price thought about it. "You put me in an awkward position."

"I'm sorry, but it can't be helped. I can only ask you to reconsider."

"I will, of course."

"And let's talk about it again after you've made up your mind."

"Yes."

Walsh said, "Don't quit, Fred. I need you."

This was true for more reasons than the risk of bad public relations. Whatever the difference between them, Walsh had a sincere respect and affection for Price, and he was particularly struck by Price's piety. One afternoon while giving the students a lecture on spiritual formation, Walsh pointed to the chapel and said, "I can assure you that what you need most to be successful missionaries is in there." Everybody knew Price was in the chapel at that moment and they understood what Walsh meant. As often as possible Walsh asked Price to supervise the spiritual formation of the students. When retreats were held, especially at the Vénard, it was Price who was assigned to preach them. He was not a dra-

matic speaker, his sermons were never well prepared, he lacked
the gift for a phrase, but he was direct, simple, and when he
spoke of the Virgin Mary or Bernadette he could stir the spirituality in a student no matter how dormant it was. Many students
chose him as their personal confessor—evidence of the willingness
with which they entrusted their souls to him. Despite his whims
and eccentricities, he provided, Walsh knew, the spiritual stability
of the society, and to be deprived of him at the time the society
was developing its character would be an irreplaceable loss.

Price was unaware of this influence, and if anyone had commented on it to him he would have scoffed. On the contrary, he
often doubted that he was making much of an impression on the
students. At one Vénard retreat, a teen-age boy fell asleep the
moment Price began each of his three one-hour talks the first day.
Price finally said to him, "All I can say is that you must have a
clear conscience." Price himself did not. He filled his diary letters
to Mary with self-deprecation, bemoaning what he considered his
spiritual shortcomings. Probably had he known how others at
Maryknoll felt about him he would have spent even more time
on the road in order to escape the embarrassment of it.

His decision, then, to leave the society stemmed solely from his
impatience to get on with other things. Surely the fact that Walsh
was the superior was no issue. In addition to suggesting Walsh
publicly at the time of the incorporation, Price later wrote to him:

It is my desire that you should be and act as Superior of the Catholic
Foreign Mission Society of America in every way that is compatible
with the mutual obligations and responsibilities which we assumed in
reference to it, and in so far as I can I do for my part hereby authorize
you so to be Superior and so to act, with the understanding that the duties
of office of Superior, as the duties of other offices, are to be determined
and regulated according to the plan of organization to be drawn up.
And that you may have no hesitancy in assuming the office of Superior
so far as I am concerned, I will add that it is a great happiness for me
to have you do so and that I urgently request you to do it.

Nevertheless, Walsh was extremely disturbed. His concern was
deeper because of his plans to leave soon on a tour of the Orient
to make arrangements for the missionaries he hoped to send to the
East as soon as possible. Now he had to worry that during his

absence Price might take off, creating internal and external situa-
tions that could be seriously damaging. Walsh understood Price
well enough to know he might never again mention leaving, but
on the other hand he might be gone in the morning. Something
had to be done to resolve the issue.

He announced that he would leave for the Orient on September
3. His departure, he said, would mark the actual beginning of
the society's mission work, and he felt it would be a fitting time
for the priests to make their *Propositum*—their pledges to remain
in the society for life if so they desired, as the statutes prescribed.
Also, he said, during his absence the society's affairs would be
conducted by Father Byrne. If anybody thought Price should have
taken over, nobody mentioned it.

The night before his departure, Walsh had still heard no further word from Price regarding his resignation. As planned, the
entire community filed into the chapel to hear Walsh's farewell
address. He spoke very carefully:

"This little ceremony here today marks a striking event in the
history of our young society—an event of twofold import. It com-
memorates the eve of the first departure from Maryknoll for fields
afar and it is the occasion of the first making of the *Propositum*,
the purpose to remain in the society during life by the priests of
the society. It is thus a truly historic event, the significance of
which we can only begin to appreciate now.

"In the last few weeks I have been asked many times who will
guide Maryknoll while I am absent. This was a very natural question for the people outside to ask, and there was only one answer
to it—God. God has guided Maryknoll so far. The work is His.
Daily we have here the opportunity of seeing His Providence, His
hand directing the work. The consciousness of this is enough to
make a man realize that he is nothing but an instrument—and
often he fears lest he prove an unworthy one.

"God has indeed been lavish, giving what was needed and that
so generously that we have had to realize it is evidently His will
to push this work. This is why, as I look forward to the absence
to begin tomorrow, I feel no hesitation. I have no misgivings. I
have only a supreme confidence in God's watchful care over Maryknoll and the Vénard.

"Any work of God can get along with any man, and God will

show how well our society can prosper without the extra effort of any individual. The sooner we who aspire to the life of the missioner realize the wonderful Providence of God the better it will be for all of us. Many of our solicitudes will be removed and our work will go faster than it would otherwise. I voice your faith in Providence as I acknowledge here on the eve of departure God's lavish generosity, and I thank Him in your name and in mine and in that of this young society.

"So much for the eve of what may be looked upon as the first Maryknoll departure. Now there is this other event—significant, portentous—the making of the *Propositum*. We have been here, shaping the one course. We have all had our eyes on the great mission which is before us. We have been personally interested in the formation of the society. Within the experience of several here we have received from Rome the Decree of Praise, officially approving the efforts already made. And yet we know that each of us in his heart has been looking foward to the time when this body would be developed to the point where we could feel that it was vigorous—though young—and solidly established and that its members were confirmed in the splendid resolution they had taken to enter upon and continue the work.

"Now we witness the flowering of that resolution in the *Propositum*, which several of us are going to make. To continue to death in the service of the society, that is the purpose which will be expressed today. The strength of this society is not based on a vow. It is grounded solely on fidelity of the individual members. The *Propositum* calls for a supreme confidence in the society itself, in its purpose, in its constitution. It calls for the faculty of adjusting oneself to the dispositions of others. And it calls for control of self.

"In these things lies the strength of the society, and as you witness the offering of some of us today keep these ideas before your minds. You are to be members of the body of this work. First of all, then, you must have a confidence that is unshakable, a confidence in the purpose of the work, a confidence in the constitution which has been framed not by tyros but by the experience of three hundred years, a confidence in those who guide the society, a confidence in your fellow members that they will work shoulder to shoulder with you for the common end. Such is the confidence that must be cultivated in those who would become and remain members of this society.

"Then there is that little delightful characteristic of fitting into the dispositions of others that makes for so much of our happiness, not only here and at the Vénard but later when we shall gather from time to time after months of fatigue, trial, loneliness, and desolation to meet one another in the perfect union of brother-hood. In this unity of spirit we are going to be strengthened—or lacking it we are going to fail. God's grace will be given to us in proportion as we cling together, meet one another's defects, and exercise a mutual Christ-like charity.

"Finally, we must have not only this supreme confidence, this regard for one another, but also the element of self-control. We have taken 'Restraint' as one of the watchwords of our life here. The man who can restrain himself for God, he is the man through whom God is going to work wonders in this world. That element of self-control must be exercised particularly in a work of this kind and in a society not bound by vows. We must learn how to control ourselves in little things so that we may be able to practice control later on in the great crises which we must expect in our lives.

"If this is our spirit we need have no fear that God's grace will be withheld. This is the spirit which is characteristic of the soldier of Christ, the spirit which Christ our King expects of His followers. We are seeking His Kingdom and if we keep this idea before our minds all things else will be added to us, as is so beautifully expressed in the Gospel of the day. As the *Propositum* is made by some let all renew their purpose to reach the height of the ideals which they formed on entering this work and which have been recalled to them today.

"I have one request to make—and I feel it is hardly necessary to make it: that you will remember me in your prayers. I want to feel that you are praying that God, the Father of my heart, will guide me, that my Elder Brother Jesus Christ will nourish me as often as it is possible for me to arrange for that Visitation, that I shall have the strength and the light of the Holy Ghost, that tre-mendous Engine, eternal, infinite, that Power awful in Its Strength. I do not know just what will be the result of my journey —I simply have this confidence, and I do not believe that it is presumptuous, that God is going to bring me to the right place in view of our future work. We know that God works through human means, and I want the strength and light to represent you, the body of which I am privileged to be the head, and I want you to co-operate with me that I might secure this strength and light.

"And when you speak to our Blessed Mother, put me in her keeping, that I may come back safely to you."

Finished, he looked at the men in the chapel, his eyes moving from one to the other. Then he went to the altar, removed from the tabernacle the lunette containing the Blessed Sacrament, and placed It in a monstrance. He then knelt and pronounced the *Propositum*.

"I, James Anthony Walsh, son of James and Hannah Walsh, of the archdiocese of Boston, member of the Catholic Foreign Mission Society of America, in the presence of Almighty God, of the Immaculate Virgin Mary, Mother of God and Queen of Apostles, and of the Holy Apostles Peter and Paul, on bended knee promise and swear that I will consecrate my whole life to the work of the missions committed, or to be committed in the future, to this society and that I will observe the constitutions of the society and obey my legitimate superiors. So help me God and these His Holy Gospels."

He stood up and faced the men, indicating that others who wished to should now come forward and take the lifelong pledge. The first man to make his way down the aisle was Fred Price.

X

WALSH's trip through the Orient lasted almost six months. He went first to Japan, then to Korea and Manchuria, then by train and coastal ships southward through China to Hong Kong. Every stop was a little homecoming: he met men he had known for years through correspondence, many of whom had received checks from him or via him through the pages of *The Field Afar*. It was therefore a trip among strangers who were already friends. Walsh sent back lengthy letters that provided a travelogue for the magazine and the basis for a future book. He loved the Orient; even the noise, the filth, the disease, and poverty failed to depress him. He saw in them, actually, a challenge for the missionaries he hoped soon to be sending to the countries he visited—Japan, Korea, Manchuria, China, and Tonkin.

But this was not a pleasure trip and Walsh had much to think about. On the boat out of San Francisco he got into conversations with several Orientals and they were surprised to learn of his long-range plans. American Catholic missionaries to the Orient? Were there that many Catholics in America that they could send out missionaries? Weren't Catholic missionaries all Europeans? The Church in America didn't amount to much, did it? America was a Protestant country, wasn't it? Just look at the facts: there he was, one Catholic missionary aboard a ship that had twenty-five Protestant missionaries among its passengers.

The facts were not actually that disheartening. True, Protestant missionaries in China outnumbered the Catholic ones by five to one, and the ratio among the Americans was far greater. Also, the Protestants had almost twenty thousand Chinese missionaries working with them, while there were only six hundred Chinese priests. But in Church membership the figures were quite reversed. There were almost two million Chinese Catholics compared to two hundred and forty thousand Chinese Protestants. The difference was a matter of training. Chinese Catholic converts had to undergo a long period of preparation, in some areas as long as four years, before baptism, and thus when they came into the Church they understood what they believed and why, and they stayed. Most Protestant missionaries, on the other hand, baptized as soon as a willingness was displayed, with the result that they amassed little more than large numbers of Christians who, attesting that they belonged to several Protestant denominations, could not be claimed by any of them.

Despite this, Walsh disliked the attitude that the Church in America was ineffectual and could not produce missionaries. He was especially dismayed to find a similar attitude among many Catholic leaders he met in the Orient. They pointed out that missionary life in the Orient was rugged and they wondered if Americans, softened by the comforts of luxury, could make the grade. All Walsh asked was the chance to show them.

With each bishop and archbishop along his route, Walsh hinted for invitations to send in Maryknollers, but the invitations did not come in Japan, Korea, Manchuria, or as Walsh traveled southward in China. Few prelates brought up the subject; some indicated their doubts that Americans could do the job, while others said they were not ready as yet to relinquish parts of their territories to newcomers.

Walsh continued down the China coast. At Hong Kong he learned that Bishop de Guébriant of Canton was in the city. Sometime previous, in acknowledging a gift, the Bishop had indicated to Walsh that he hoped Americans would soon be at work in China. Encouraged, Walsh tried to see the Bishop but was told he had a full schedule and would see Walsh in Canton if he could go there. It was the afternoon of Christmas Day when Walsh arrived in Canton and made his way to the Bishop's office.

After greeting him and thanking him for countless gifts, Bishop de Guébriant asked, "Well, now, when are the Americans coming?"

"We are ready now," Walsh said.

"Where will you go?"

"Would you like us to come here?"

"Most certainly," said the Bishop. He led Walsh to a wall map and pointed to a large area on the coast of the South China Sea. "This is the district of Yeungkong. Do you know it?"

"No, I don't."

"Well, you are going to. It is yours if you want."

"We want it," said Walsh.

"Then let us prepare the papers for Rome." The Bishop sent for his secretary.

They began their transaction with a prayer to the Holy Ghost, then they prepared a document which consigned to Maryknoll the old mission station at Yeungkong, on the coast southwest of Hong Kong, and at Loting, about a hundred miles inland, plus the area in between, and they agreed that when sufficient Americans were available the area would be extended to the West River, about fifty miles deeper into the country. In church terms, the whole area was regarded as one mission, but actually it would include some thirty mission stations. At one time, priests of the Paris Foreign Mission Society served the mission, but most of them had been recalled to France for military service in World War I and now the vast territory of over a million people was without regular religious facilities. Occasionally a French priest was able to travel through, and at the time a Mill Hill Father was on temporary duty but that was all. The mission had about five thousand Catholics, scattered over a wide area; in these times most of them were lucky to see a priest once a year.

Now the Americans would solve that. After the document was signed, Walsh cabled Maryknoll: "MISSION FOUND." The news arrived the day after Christmas and another holiday was proclaimed.

Walsh didn't want to leave China without at least a look at the area where his men would work. Early in January, accompanied by Father Auguste Gauthier, the French priest who had been covering the territory alone, he left Canton and, by train and boat, toured the area. Most of the villages had no Catholics and few Christians, but in the places where they came upon some of their own they were greeted like royal visitors. In the eyes of the isolated Chinese Catholics, Walsh might as well have come from another planet. They had heard about America but had never met an American, and to learn now that American priests were coming to live among them was amazing news indeed. They studied Walsh awesomely from a distance; he could not converse with them, but when he tried to show his friendliness with smiles and a few remarks in English they beheld him intently, assured that he must be saying something important. By the time he returned to Canton Walsh felt like a seasoned missionary, the first of his society to travel into the zone where Americans would set up their first Orient mission. He wrote Maryknoll that those chosen to start the actual work should consider themselves blessed.

There were two more places Walsh wanted to see before going back to the United States. Fulfilling his wish, he went first to Tonkin and toured the section where Théophane Vénard had worked and died. Returning to Hong Kong some weeks later, he sailed out to Sancian Island, a few miles offshore from the new Maryknoll mission, and visited what had become a shrine to all Catholic missionaries in the Orient. In August, 1552, Saint Francis Xavier, the great Spanish Jesuit missionary, had died on the Sancian shores, his arms outstretched toward the mainland. He had been the first missionary of the era to bring the faith to the East, converting thousands from India to Japan. His dream was to work in China, but China was then virtually a walled country: foreigners were restricted to a small number—and foreigners who intended to turn the people into Christians were strictly prohibited. Determined, Saint Francis made arrangements to enter the country at Canton under the cover of night, willing to risk his life to reach the people. Bad weather held back his ship at Sancian Island, then illness struck him and he was put ashore. He died on the sands, looking across to China, his feverish eyes

on the very hills where the Maryknollers were soon to begin their
history.

Walsh was back at Maryknoll in April, at Easter, and he had
many stories to tell. Everyone had read his letters, but hearing the
stories again from his own lips made them fresh and new. His
return also meant that soon appointments would be made for
the missions and there was a great deal of conjecture about them.

When he was settled and again at work, Walsh felt ready to
make the decisions but he felt he should not make them alone.
He asked Price, "Who do you think should go?"

"I, for one," said Price.

"You really want to go?"

"Yes, very much."

"You're certainly the best qualified," Walsh said. "I'd feel better
if you were there to run things. But I've been wondering about
your health."

"It's fine. I know I'm fifty-seven years old and haven't many
years left in me," said Price, "but I feel fine, and I want to go.
I should be able to be of some help for a while before I die."

"You've got years in you," Walsh said. "Good, then. Who else?
They ought to be men who've been with us a while."

"What about Frank Ford? He was the first boy we had."

"Yes, he should go."

"And Jim Walsh?"

"I had Jim in mind. He's older and very stable. How about
Bernie Meyer?"

"Very good. He's an Iowa farmer and a man like that is important in the missions."

"I think so, too."

"Who else?"

"Well, that's four. That's enough for a start, isn't it? If we pick
any more we might be short-handed here at home, and more than
four might be a bit unmanageable over there at this stage. You
four go over and get things started, then we'll try to send another
group each year."

Price nodded. "When do we leave?"

"September, I thought."

"Fine."

It was a busy time for everyone. The three young priests were allowed to go home and visit their families, aware they might never see them again. Money had to be raised to pay the fares to China and equip the pioneers for their work; Walsh made appeals in *The Field Afar* while Price went back on the road with similar requests to people he had met on his previous solicitations. Walsh and Price both believed that the departure of the society's first group would stir broader interest and result in more vocations: a larger seminary would be needed, one especially designed so that it could be expanded over the years without getting to look like a labyrinth. Walsh's brother was by now an important church architect and he was summoned for conferences. Price meanwhile withdrew from the association he had begun for Lourdes devotees and turned it over to others. In addition, there were medical preparations to be taken by the four missionaries, passports and visas to obtain, passages to book and, for each of them, years of accumulated personal effects to dispose of because they could not possibly take everything they had to China.

Walsh had brought back from the Orient a large, highly decorated Buddhist temple bell. On the night of September 7, the bell was struck: a signal to the community that the first actual departure of a Maryknoll mission band was about to occur. Few outsiders were present: Monsignor Dunn, from the New York Propagation Society; Father Bruneau, Walsh's old Sulpician friend, Doctor Flagg, who taught the students mission medicine, the chaplain from Sing Sing where students gave catechism lessons to prisoners. But the small chapel which the Lady Bountiful had built was crowded with students, the Teresians, Auxiliaries, farmhands. Cardinal Farley was ill, but he sent word through Dunn: "Tell them that I bless them."

The four to depart were in the sanctuary, each at a *prie-dieu*. Walsh rose and read his instructions to them to their new assignments. Everyone present recited the canticle of Zachary. "Blessed be the Lord of Israel, for He has visited us and wrought the redemption of His people, for they shall go before the face of the Lord to prepare His way, to give knowledge of salvation to His people unto the remission of their sins, to enlighten those who sit in the darkness and the shadow of death." Then each of the four made his *Propositum* anew, restrengthening his position in the society, and Walsh gave each man a crucifix to wear at his cincture. Together, all in the chapel sang the *Veni Creator,* calling upon the Holy Ghost to guide them, then Walsh gave his blessing and the Departure Hymn was sung by those to remain. Walsh had translated the song from French; for years it had been the Departure Hymn of the Paris Foreign Mission Society, and its chorus heralded,

> *Go forth, farewell for life, O dearest brothers;*
> *Proclaim afar the sweetest Name of God.*
> *We meet again one day in Heaven's land of blessing.*
> *Farewell, brothers, farewell.*

Sooner than anyone expected, the hymn proved to be prophetic. Almost a year to the day, word arrived from China that Price had died.

XI

THE night of departure Price had broken a standing rule for himself by posing for photographs with Ford, Jim Walsh, and Meyer. The four then packed their cassocks and appeared on the seminary porch in their traveling clothes. It was late evening now; flash pictures were taken. With effort Price was able to tolerate further photographs without instinctively turning away. Then the four priests got into cars for the drive to New York City and the train to the West Coast. As they drove along, Price asked Jim Walsh, "Do you know what day tomorrow is?"

Walsh considered, then said, "The eighth?"

"Yes, but what feast day?"

Walsh remembered the prayers of his breviary he had read that afternoon. "The Feast of Our Lady."

"Yes. Her birthday. Isn't it wonderful?"

Walsh had to smile. Price's love for Mary touched all men who also loved her. It was strange, Walsh thought, that after knowing Price eight years and yet not really knowing him they should be together on this first trip abroad for Maryknoll missionaries. Like most people, Walsh had looked upon Price as somewhat of a puzzle. As a student, Walsh had, like others, been amused by Price's many eccentricities. Price's comic unconcern for clothes had once inspired Jim Walsh to write of him:

114

I know it is a sin
For me to sit and grin
At him here.
But the old three-cornered hat
And the breeches and all that
Are so queer.

But the years spent in the spiritual self-examination of seminary
life and the studies of theology and philosophy that can supply an
insight into piety had given Walsh an understanding of the man.
Regardless of how much Price might know about running a
mission, most important to young Walsh was the spiritual influence the older priest would be upon both priests and the people.
It was an influence that achieved good without effort; it achieved
good simply because it was present. It was like grace, given by
God out of love and having an effect upon all responsive to it.
Walsh was glad to be with Price.

The issue of *The Field Afar* after the departure carried this
article:

Father Price has been associated with the work of Maryknoll from the
beginning and is in fact one of its two organizers. At his repeated and
urgent request—not to say threat—we have until now done our best to
satisfy him by keeping his name and photograph out of *The Field Afar,*
but we feel that once he has turned his back on this land of his birth
he will not object—certainly not too strenuously—to the appearance of
both—at least occasionally. For one so closely connected with *The Field
Afar* his modesty will not allow the paper to refer any longer to itself
as PRICELESS.

Now Price felt the complete missionary. Even aboard the ship
across the Pacific he took steps to work at it. Gone was his old
hesitance with strangers. Each morning he called his three young
assistants together to discuss ways to approach other passengers.
"The purpose of these meetings," he said, "is to plan what work
we can do for souls during the day." He divided the ship into
four parts, assigning a priest to each, then gave instructions on
how to gain attention and perform missionary duties. Jim Walsh
later wrote:

He was full of plans, some practical, some perhaps impractical, but
all were the emanation of an ardent spirit filled with love for souls. It

was noteworthy also to what extent he himself attracted people. The humble and self-effacing old man, a complete picture of other-worldliness, gathered people around him everywhere he went, people who hung on his kindly words and loved his genial manners. And among these it was not the young or the devout who were attracted to him the most; as a rule it was the case-hardened businessman and the ordinary American pagan of any religion or no religion at all.

At Japan, the four priests broke up into two teams. Price and Ford took the long tour through Korea, Manchuria, and North China; Walsh and Meyer went to Shanghai to await them. From Peking, Price wrote to Maryknoll:

The more I see of the Chinese, the more I love them. I cannot but feel the deepest and the most unspeakable pity when I see a people so industrious and peaceful and amicable dying by the millions without the Catholic Faith, simply for want of missionaries. May God speed the work not only of Maryknoll but of all mission societies of the world in sending missionaries to this field where the harvest is ripe unto whiteness.

It was also in Peking that he received his government papers to remain in the country. In trying to give his name a Chinese equivalent, the government agents pronounced it Pou-ri-ce, and in Chinese that meant "Universal Jewel is here."

He and Ford rejoined Walsh and Meyer at Shanghai and together they all went on to Hong Kong, then to Canton. Bishop de Guébriant assigned Father Gauthier to go to Yeungkong with them to get the first American effort on its feet.

"I understand there is already a church at Yeungkong," Price said.

"Oh, yes," the Bishop said, "but more of a chapel."

"What is it called?"

"Our Lady of Lourdes."

Price beamed. "Oh, really? How wonderful."

The Americans arrived at Yeungkong on December 21, a double occasion for celebration since it was the Feast of St. Thomas—Price's name day. They had traveled by Chinese junk to a place twenty-five miles offshore and because the captain felt he could not reach port before nightfall he refused to go any further until morning. Rather than wait, Price hailed a small sailing vessel of fishermen and transferred his party to it. They reached the city at eleven o'clock and it was too dark for them to see where they were.

In the morning they looked around.

The walled city of Yeungkong was on the Yeungkong River, about twelve miles inland. On the coast were three or four little fishing villages, but Yeungkong itself had fishermen who each day made the long journey to and from the sea. Yeungkong, with an estimated population of several thousand, was a poor city, having been stripped often by the opposing armies of the political factions which had been trying to set up a government for China since the overthrow of the emperor at the turn of the century. In the wake of the armies came bandits—indeed, some of the military battalions were little more than that—and so there had been constant strife in the area for twenty years.

The basic problem was that China could not decide whether or not it wanted to be part of this world. For centuries it had remained isolated, under the domination of emperors and war lords who managed to acquire enormous personal wealth while keeping the people in dire poverty. The surge of European expansion in the early eighteen hundreds made China a precious goal. The disunity of the country, meanwhile, made it a helpless victim. There was, however, a strong majority feeling to keep the foreigners out. Great Britain took the aggression against this sentiment. In 1839, the Chinese government denounced British efforts to bring large amounts of opium into the country and either burned or threw into the sea huge supplies of opium which British merchant ships had dumped on the wharves at Canton. The British used this as grounds for a war that lasted four years, which they won. As a result, Chinese ports were opened to British trade and residence, and Hong Kong became a British colony. Opium addiction thereafter proved to be a serious Chinese problem which other countries subsequently used as a weapon.

The antiforeign feeling of China never fully disappeared, and out of it came intermittent battles for many years, not only against the invading foreigners but also between opposing factions within the country. European countries proposed a familiar idea: chop China up into zones of European commercial influence which the Chinese, in the face of European power, would be forced to accept in the name of peace. The United States disliked the plan because it meant that a nation would be dismembered against its will and substituted instead what became known as the Open Door policy —all nations would have equal rights to do business competitively in China, with the Chinese themselves deciding which offers seemed most attractive. China agreed. In 1900, Chinese conservatism took its last firm stand against foreigners in the Boxer Rebellion, the failure of which led to internal uprisings headed by Sun Yat-sen, a physician who became the central figure in a socialistic movement called the Kuomintang. His closest aide was Chiang Kai-shek. Within the Kuomintang was a radical group that evolved into the Chinese Communist Party.

When the Maryknollers arrived in China there were two governments. The Kuomintang ruled the south, with headquarters at Canton; the conservatives—the war lords—held the north and had a loose confederation at Peking. The mandarin (local governor) at Yeungkong was a Kuomintang army officer. Armies of both sides roamed the country, often supporting themselves by ransacking towns and cities and stripping farms. Meantime, the Communists in Russia had overthrown the czarist government and, eager from the start to expand their influence, were already making contact with Chinese Communists, preparing them for another civil war that would erupt some fifteen years later. Included in the Communist plans from the very beginning was the extermination of the Catholic Church.

Price gave little thought to the political atmosphere of the country when he settled his group at Yeungkong. He knew that the fighting and the soldiers-turned-bandits might endanger the priests when they began their travels inland, but that was one of the risks of missionary work and everyone had to be ready for it. The Yeungkong mission station, located within the city, was, like most homes of any value, walled in and included a half-dozen brick buildings. The main house had two floors, with two rooms on each. Price took one of the second-floor rooms for himself, designating the other as the dining and recreation room. The three young priests shared one of the lower rooms, with the other used as an office. The church was small—sixty feet by twenty by twelve. Rarely used since the French priests had been called into service, the building was dirty and damp, about as cheery as the catacombs. The other buildings in the compound were more like huts. A few old people were living in them, having been driven from their own homes by marauding soldiers and bandits. There was no electricity or running water. In the city were only seven other white people, all of them Protestant missionaries who worked either at the Protestant hospital outside the city walls or on the Protestant newspaper that was the only paper the city had.

The first Catholic priest of the period to enter China itself was a Jesuit missionary named Matteo Ricci, who arrived about thirty years after the death of Saint Francis Xavier. By 1700, there were some forty thousand Catholics in Kwangtung Province, of which Yeungkong was the south coastal district. Then persecution by the pagan and antiforeign groups broke out, taking the lives of many of the Catholics and sending the rest fleeing to the Portuguese colony at Macao. A century later Protestant missionaries were arriving, first from England and then from the United States. Gradually, too, priests returned, but singly and almost secretly. One priest who stayed at Yeungkong for a while was forbidden to take water from the well because he was suspected of poisoning it. To get water, he had to pay an opium addict to fetch it for him. One day he received a supply of Mass wine in a keg that people believed contained gun powder. He was forced to open it; when the people saw it was full of liquid they ordered the addict to sample it to determine if it was poison. The addict ended by drinking the entire keg of wine and was drunk for a week.

Priests of the Paris Foreign Mission Society began to arrive in numbers in 1849, and they discovered that the missionaries who had dared enter the country during the severe hundred and fifty years since the first outbursts had built up a church in Kwangtung Province of some eight thousand Catholics. By proceeding slowly, cautiously, and wisely, the Frenchmen were able to add to that number over the next sixty years so that, despite persecutions and setbacks, when the Americans came on the scene there were five thousand Catholics in the Yeungkong district itself—gratifying in view of the conditions but sad in view of the million in population.

On Christmas Day, Price baptized two adults whom Gauthier had prepared on his previous visits and two children whose parents brought them to the church. It was a noisy occasion. Most of the Yeungkong Catholics were from the rural areas, and when they poured into town for the unexpected joy of having priests present to celebrate Christmas Masses they brought along their entire families plus the live chickens, ducks and geese they intended to slaughter at the mission compound for their Christmas dinner. In addition, they were all well armed with fireworks which they began to set off on Christmas Eve and continued exploding all Christmas Day. Price wrote to Maryknoll later that enemy armies could have bombarded the city and nobody would have known it. It was, nevertheless, a glorious day. Price preached his first sermon to the people, which Gauthier translated, and he promised that in a short time he would be able to speak to them directly.

But he never kept the promise. Although Gauthier found a language instructor to teach Chinese to the Americans, Price had the most trouble with it. Study was difficult for him. He was much older than the others and could not absorb as quickly as they. The thousands of written characters of the Chinese language made little sense to him; the five hundred and eighty words which took on different meanings through tonal qualities were beyond him. Weeks later when the younger men were able to stumble through conversations with the Chinese, Price at best was restricted to a bright *"Tin chew po yao!*—God protect you!" And when the people grinned back at him Price couldn't be sure whether they appreciated the greeting or he had made a mistake and said something entirely different, something utterly ridiculous.

He had, moreover, many distractions. He was in charge, which meant he had to approve everything. He turned one of the compound buildings into a school and another into an old people's home, both of which required planning, reconstruction, and much red tape. He wanted also to do something about two other local problems. There were over twenty thousand lepers in the province, without medical care, hospitalization, or a comfortable place to die. And every day, babies, mostly girls, were being abandoned by their mothers, often just a few hours after birth. Frequently the babies were left to die at the roadside or in a field, but now from time to time they were found early in the morning at the gate of the mission compound. Something had to be done. Price wrote Walsh at Maryknoll for special funds to open an orphanage and a leprosarium. The money was months in coming, but by early summer of 1919 both institutions were in operation and were quickly filled.

And there was the Yeungkong district itself, sprawling inland over mountains and across rivers, encompassing hidden villages, towns, sizable cities, and thousands of tiny farms. It was necessary to survey the district in order to determine where assignments of priests would prove most advantageous both for the Catholics who lived there and for the promise of converts. Price made a few short trips, but they proved far too arduous for him and thereafter he left them to the younger men. The climate was bothering him: subtropical, humid, hot, rainy, it ate into his bones and caused him a constant pain, a condition he aggravated by refusing to rest.

By Easter, the three young priests knew enough Chinese to be able to travel without Gauthier as an interpreter. Price therefore felt they were ready to go out on their own. He assigned Jim Walsh to the mission station at Loting, northwest of Yeungkong, and Meyer to Tungchen, farther to the north. Ford stayed at Yeungkong to supervise at the local level and to act as procurator for the entire district. The assignments meant more work for everyone—a joy to the younger men and a burden to Price.

In May, Price was forced to go to a Hong Kong hospital for treatment of rheumatism and nerves. The doctors warned him that he needed a long rest, but in ten days he was back at Yeungkong. Ford met him at the dock, and as they walked back to the mission a Chinese coolie tried to take Price's suitcase but he refused.

Ford said, "But, Father, he is supposed to carry it."

Price said, "I would rather carry the man myself than let him carry my luggage."

The severe summer days were a torment for Price. In early August he developed an ulcerated tooth. He also became aware of abdominal pains which he attributed to stomach trouble. When he could stand the discomfort no longer, he went back to St. Paul's Hospital in Hong Kong. The tooth was treated without difficulty, but the abdominal condition was difficult to diagnose until a blood analysis was made. It was appendicitis. Because of his weakened condition, the doctors were reluctant to operate until he acquired some strength. They watched him carefully, but he did not respond to their medications. His pain increased, and there were hours when he seemed unconscious. At last, the operation was performed on September 8, the Feast of the Nativity of the Blessed Virgin—a year to the day after Price's departure from Maryknoll.

It was hopeless. The entire abdominal cavity was gangrenous; antiseptics and serums were of no use. It was only a matter of time.

Price knew it. He wrote a letter and marked it: "To be opened after my death." And he gave it to one of the Sisters nursing at the hospital.

She chided him. "Father, what a silly thing to do. You're not going to die. You can't. There is so much work to be done here."

"I want to work," he said, "but I am old—too old for work. All I can do is pray, and surely I can pray better in heaven."

For three days his pain increased. On the evening of September 11, he told his nurse, "Tell Father Tours I want to receive Extreme Unction in the morning."

"You are in too big a hurry to go to heaven," the Sister said.

"Tomorrow is the Feast of the Holy Name of Mary," he said. "It would be a perfect day to make my trip to see her."

Father Jean Tours, a member of the Paris Foreign Mission Society, went to Price at seven in the morning, giving him Holy Viaticum, Extreme Unction, and a plenary indulgence. Tours said later that the manner in which Price accepted the last rites was the most inspiring event of his priesthood. He returned to Price at nine. Price's hands and forehead were cold.

Price said, "The time is coming. I am finished. I am going."

"Father Price," said Tours, "will you kindly bless your friend, Father Tours, and in his person bless dear Father Walsh and all Maryknollers?"

"Most certainly," said Price, "and from the depth of my heart."

Tours said, "You offer now your sufferings and even your life for the prosperity of your beloved society? You pray that they all may do the work of God in a truly apostolic spirit?"

"Oh, yes." Price breathed with difficulty, then added, "Tell Father Walsh my last thoughts were for them all and that I die in the love of Jesus, Mary, and Joseph and of Maryknoll."

He closed his eyes and began muttering. Tours leaned close and heard over and over: "Jesus, Mary, and Joseph, I give you my heart and my soul."

Then he went silent. At ten o'clock, the Sister came in to see how he was. He whispered, "I suffer so."

The Sister said, "Soon it will be all right, Father. Soon you will be with the Blessed Mother and your beloved Bernadette."

He stirred. "Do you think so? Oh, what happiness!" His eyes closed again. A few minutes later his eyes opened and there was a wild expression in them. Then he sank back. He breathed heavily once or twice, and then he was gone.

Then people began to find out things about him. His diary was discovered in his room and the spiritual secrets in its were overwhelming. The devotion he expressed toward the Virgin Mary and Bernadette was almost poetic; he measured all things in terms of them. He noted: "I do not eat apples because Bernadette expressed a dislike for them on account of their association with original sin." He had privately taken a vow of poverty, carrying it to such an extent that he would not even allow himself the luxury of personal comfort. In November of 1917, when he was suffering a severe attack of rheumatism, he noted: "Slept in bed, first time in a long time." This supported remarks housekeepers had made, both at Maryknoll and in China, that they could tell from the condition of his bed that he had not slept in it but merely ruffled the sheets to give others the impression that he had. Usually he permitted no one into his room, but one housekeeper entered to clean it one day and found that he had removed the mattress from his bed and was sleeping on boards.

He considered humility the basis of all virtues and commented in his diary: "How sweet I find it that nobody pays the least attention to me." A story of this came to light when a nun later revealed how he had come to the back door of a Catholic school in 1911 on a rainy day. The nun had answered the knock, aware that tramps usually knocked on the door for a free meal. Opening the door, the nun saw a drenched man, his collar up, his hat brim down. "Go to the kitchen and Sister will give you something," she said. The man muttered his gratitude and left. It was that night, when the Sisters were called together to hear Price speak, that the nun realized who the man was. He never mentioned it to anyone.

At Yeungkong, instruments of mortification were found in his room—another surprise. At Hong Kong, the Sister who helped him prepare for surgery noticed a chain wrapped around his left leg and held in place by a small lock. "Father," she said, "don't you think you ought to remove that. The Protestant surgeon may not understand."

"I can't remove it," he said. "I threw the key away years ago."

The diary revealed he had acquired the chain in Rome in 1911. For over eight years he had worn it as a painful reminder of the virtues he was struggling to develop in himself.

For almost the same length of time he had worn a wedding ring on the third finger of his left hand. The diary observed: "I thought of covering the ring with a piece of black glove kid—so that it is little noticeable, and if one asks what it is I will tell him it is a means to remember certain things—which is true."

He did cover it, but it was still noticed. A student questioned him about it, and Price asked, "Can you keep a secret?"

"Yes, I can," the boy said.

"So can I," said Price. Nobody asked about the ring again.

He had appeared with the ring after his second visit to France, in 1913, and Walsh presumed that Price had somehow convinced the nuns at the Nevers convent to let him have the ring Bernadette wore as a nun, signifying her mystical marriage to Christ. This was the general deduction for almost fifteen years after Price died, until Walsh visited the convent and was told he was wrong. A study was made of the lengthy diary (when transcribed later it ran over fifteen hundred typewritten pages) and hints of the meaning of the ring began to appear.

The principal marking on the outer side of the ring was the IHS —the first three letters of the name of Jesus in Greek. Next to it was a lily marked MB to MB. Enclosed in brackets were DM April 7, 1915; SM March 25, 1917; ND Aug. 15, 1918. Crosswise was July 2, 1917. Engraved inside the ring was MB+ to MB 4:17:13 7:16:13.

Of the initials, only the MB could be interpreted from diary comments. In one sense, the letters indicated Mary and Bernadette. In another, they indicated Marie Bernadette, a name Price adopted for himself. The preface of the book Price wrote about Bernadette was signed with those initials. At one time, Price had asked the Teresians to address him as Father Bernadette. Thus it would appear that the ring symbolized a pact between Mary, Bernadette, and Price. And yet it was more than a pact, as the diary entries substantiated.

The diary revealed that Price had entered a relationship with Bernadette that was as beautiful and binding as marriage vows. His love for her and the holy life she had led and his desire to emulate her sanctity amounted to a kind of marriage in his mind. On April 7, 1915, at Maryknoll, Price recorded: "We made our vows at Holy Communion of our Mass. In the afternoon, we made a pilgrimage to our shrine and renewed our vows—sang Magnificat."

The other dates on the ring also referred to the mystical marriage, all of them serving to remind Price of the unique union into which he had entered. It was a marriage of spiritual dedication, a holy thing in itself—unusual, to be sure. But then Price was an unusual man.

As a priest, Price should not have worn the ring, regardless of the importance of the mystical marriage to him. He knew this, but nevertheless wore the ring several years before he took steps to obtain permission. According to the diary, he visited the Apostolic Delegate—Giovanni Cardinal Bonzano—in Washington on August 18, 1918, and requested the permission. The nature of the request was such that Bonzano passed it on to Rome. By the time the answer came, Price was in China. Walsh wrote him from Maryknoll, saying that the decision from Rome was enclosed. By oversight, Walsh then forgot to enclose the decision. Price thus wore the ring to his death without knowing that permission had been refused.

The letter which Price had marked to be opened after his death revealed equally unusual news. On his second trip to Nevers he had asked the Sisters if he could be buried in Bernadette's tomb but they felt this would not be proper. He then pointed out that in the tomb chapel was a niche in the wall near Bernadette's remains and he asked if it would be possible for his heart to be placed there. The Sisters felt this would be all right, and it was done.

Price's sudden death shocked everyone. None of the priests with him realized how ill he was, so none had accompanied him to the hospital. Father Tours notified the three priests by telegram and then he sent a cable to America. When Walsh opened it at Maryknoll he doubled sharply as if he had been struck. Then he said:

"Summon everyone to the chapel. We now have a dear friend in heaven and we must ask him to help us."

The

Second

Decade

The Maryknoll Fathers Seminary, Maryknoll, N. Y.

In this building, which was the first seminary, Maryknoll began in 1911.

Maryknoll's first missionaries: Fathers Price, Ford, James Anthony Walsh, Meyer, and James Edward Walsh.

James Anthony Walsh,
Maryknoll's co-founder.

The interior of
Maryknoll's chapel.

Ordination Day at Maryknoll.

Maryknoll missionaries on
Departure Day.

Francis Cardinal Spellman during ceremony at Maryknoll.

Bishop Raymond Lane of Maryknoll and Cardinal Aganagianian with a group of seminarians.

A Maryknoll classroom.

Maryknoll Sisters outside their mother house and novitiate at Maryknoll, N. Y.

Father Peter Reilly gives a catechism lesson on a street in Hong Kong.

Father Hugh Craig visits his parishioners at work in a rice paddy in Korea.

Father J. E. McClear
baptizes in Guatemala.

Father Francis Assenmacher offers Mass in Bolivia.

Father Jacob Esselborn teaches the Indians of Bolivia via the air waves.

At a trade school in Molina, Chile, Father William Coleman teaches the use of industrial tools and equipment.

Fathers Kuhn and Schiff sing with their Wa'Chaga parishioners.

Maryknoll Brother Damian
with two pagan
Wakeneye warriors.

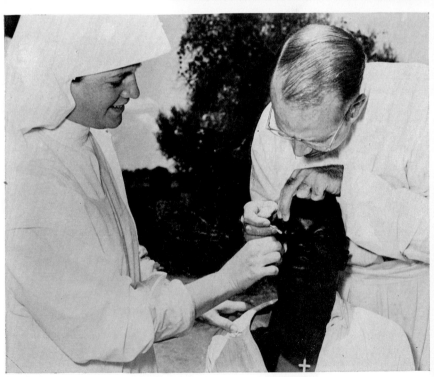

Sister Agnes Jude Mitchell and Father Baskerville give some
timely medical help.

XII

SUDDENLY friends in heaven began to accumulate at a shocking rate. Cardinal Farley died. So did Walsh's seminary comrades Stanton and Lane. Marie Louise Wholean, one of the first Teresians, died of cancer. In the influenza epidemic at the turn of the decade, a priest and a student at the Vénard died. Despite the glory in a good Catholic death and Walsh's confidence that his friends indeed were in heaven, he grew aware of a certain loneliness. All those with whom he had started out were gone now. Old friends whose memories, with his, could have served as yardsticks of progress were gone. He felt his years.

Now everything depended on him. He could, of course, delegate some of his responsibilities to the younger men who surrounded him, and he did. But it was not the same. Although he had been superior general and final authority of the society for ten years, he had looked upon men like Price and Lane and Farley as partners in his leadership. Now he was on his own. He could appoint assistants, but they were precisely that. Everything was up to him.

Growth was essential in two spheres—at home and in China. At home the society needed more vocations and better facilities for them. Both required sending men on the road to do the kind of promotion work Price had done. But doing so meant that men were not going to China where they were desperately needed.

129

There were only three there now—not counting Gauthier: so few to do so much.

There seemed only one way to proceed and that was to try everything at once. Walsh's brother designed a new four-story seminary building that could be enlarged with wings as demands required and funds allowed. To raise money, Walsh resorted again to the pages of *The Field Afar*, asking readers to buy bricks for the new building as once he had asked them to buy square-foot plots of the property when it was acquired. This was a slow process but, given time, it worked; in fifteen years the completed building stood on a hilltop at Maryknoll exactly as Walsh had envisioned it, its Chinese pagoda-type tower piercing the sky like an Oriental cathedral.

The promotion work had to be done in shifts. Most of the Maryknoll priests were busy teaching, but on their free days, their holidays, and their vacations they made quick trips to solicit funds by preaching in churches and to search out new vocations. A New York house was purchased on East Fifty-seventh Street to serve both as a contact center and overnight accommodations for Maryknollers caught in the city too late to catch the last train to Ossining. The parlor was turned into a mission museum and visitors could be depended upon either to buy some trinket or make a small donation. Since San Francisco was apparently to be the embarkation city for the society, a house was also purchased there to serve as a contact center, a shipping office, and a stopover for Maryknollers traveling to or from the Orient. Both Los Angeles and Seattle had large Japanese settlements; the Teresians, who were becoming known as the Maryknoll Sisters, opened houses in both cities as social centers and kindergartens. Here again the society found helpful outlets to the public. Through them and others that were established over the years, the men in promotion work served a purpose as vital in its own way as the actual mission effort abroad, for it was through these men that the society obtained the money and the vocations to keep the missions alive.

Even so, Walsh realized it was important to continue sending men to China. That, after all, was the reason for the society. Furthermore, the hope of going to the missions was what had attracted vocations in the first place and what had stirred the students and the priests at home to give themselves so completely to whatever was asked of them. In the autumn of 1919, while Maryknoll was still stunned by Price's death, Walsh sent three more men to China. They were Daniel McShane, Alphonse S. Vogel, and William F. O'Shea who, like Ford and Walsh, were among the five of the original six Maryknoll students to reach the priesthood. Now they would all be in China together. Of the five, three were destined to be martyrs.

The letter from Maryknoll shocked young Jim Walsh. "I hereby," the superior general wrote, "appoint you superior of our Yeungkong district mission. You will in general be subject to Bishop de Guébriant, but in Maryknoll matters you will be responsible directly to me. I pray that God will guide you in the decisions and assignments you will have to make. You know you have only to ask for my help in any of the problems that face you."

Holding the letter, Jim Walsh reflected seriously on what it meant. He suspected he had been appointed merely because he was the oldest of the three Maryknoll priests remaining in China and had been ordained ahead of the others. Seniority might be a satisfactory way to determine leadership in other fields but Walsh wondered if it was proper in the missions. Frank Ford would have been a better choice, he felt. Ford was in the town of Yeungkong, where the men and supplies entered the district, he was already serving as procurator and he had been the closest to Price, thus in a better position to assimilate the old man's ideas and spirit. That, Walsh believed, was what was needed: another Price. He did not hope to become one himself. But he had become the superior, and out of obedience he had to accept the position.

What would it mean? At the moment, not very much. He was, in effect, the commanding officer of an army of two. The letter had disclosed that three more were on the way, but they would not be much help for a while, what with a language and a new way of life to learn. Then when they were ready it would be up to him to make the best use of them. Five priests among a million pagans could scarcely scratch the surface. Very well, if that was all they could do that was what they would do: scratch.

For months, that was all they did. The new men learned quickly

and were eager to get to work, but Walsh restrained them until
he felt confident that, isolated in a remote mission station, they
would not find themselves helpless because of the language. In
two years, Meyer had become skilled at Chinese and quizzed the
newcomers after their daily instructions from laymen. On his inland trips, he took the new men with him, one at a time, and he
would speak only Chinese to them to get them used to it.

The trips were always exciting and they were always difficult.
Torrential rains fell most of the year; the fact that the priests
seldom arrived at a village in dry clothes became a joke among
them. When packing for a trek, they took as many changes as the
number of towns they would visit. In the mountains away from
the sea the nights were often cold. There were few trees, which
made kindling a luxury, and there were thus many nights when
the only heat the travelers had came from the brief fires over
which they cooked their meals. When they were new in a place,
they could expect some measure of hostility from the people. In
the hidden villages, all strangers were suspect, especially when
they were quite plainly foreigners. As a safeguard, the missionaries
tried to arrive at a new town during the afternoon so that they
could be seen and evaluated from a distance. If necessary, they
slept outdoors at night rather than arrive at a suspicious hour. On
entering, they asked to meet the village leader or the mandarin, if
there was one. Often village leaders would be waiting for them
on the road as they approached, but mandarins considered such
curiosity beneath their station and frequently kept the priests in
an outer room for hours before receiving them. To grow impatient
or indignant on such occasions would be extremely bad manners,
so the priests could do nothing but wait until the mandarin felt
his importance had been sufficiently impressed upon them.

It was impossible to foretell what kind of reception they would
get. If the mandarin belonged to the radical faction of the Kuomintang he was almost sure to be a Communist and would have
no use for priests. If, on the other hand, there was illness in the
town, then politics and religion were put aside for the sake of
the medicines the priests always carried. The duration of the
hospitality then depended on the mandarin's gratitude, which was
fleeting, or on the people's concern which, once the priests had

proved their friendliness, could be enduring and very touching.

In a dozen places ranging from sizable cities to clusters of shacks, the priests located secret chapels that Paris Foreign Mission pioneers had established years earlier. They were more like dungeons —small, dark buildings at the end of a gloomy street or at the edge of a swamp. People who remembered the Frenchmen told how they would remain hidden in the chapels for weeks at a time, performing their ministry like spiritual bandits, opening the door only to passwords, creeping out at night to attend the dying, then finally disguising themselves as peasants in order to leave town without being arrested. Wherever the Frenchmen had been and regardless of how long they had been away, the Maryknollers found people—sometimes only three or four—who had kept the faith and now provided a nucleus for the revival of it.

Jim Walsh was anxious for the revival—for the expansion—of the faith. It would come, he knew, only when there were more missionaries to promote it, so he urged Maryknoll to send on all who could be spared at home. In 1920, six priests came. In 1921, there were five priests, a lay Brother, and six Maryknoll Sisters. The following year brought three more priests, another Brother, and five more Sisters. The Sisters went directly to Yeungkong where Ford had built a convent for them. Those who were nurses could go quickly to work with the aid of laymen who translated their patients' complaints for them; those who were teachers concentrated on the language so that they could communicate with the children. The Brothers unpacked their tools and began to put the time-battered mission stations into shape. The number of stations increased each year, from the original three to nine in less than four years. Under Price, Yeungkong had been headquarters, but Jim Walsh found the coastal town somewhat inaccessible on his constant travels. In 1924, Rome allocated to Maryknoll the territory to the north of Yeungkong, an area the size of Ohio, which included Kongmoon City. Walsh moved his headquarters there and now had far better transportation and communication with his stations than Yeungkong provided. At the same time, the Maryknollers were invited to take over an even larger area to the north of the West River in the Kwangsi Province; Meyer was sent there as superior. The burst of expansion was

climaxed by the news from Rome that the southern area had
been made into a prefecture and that Walsh was named prefect
with the title of monsignor.

The increased activity meant increased travel for everyone, and
this involved increased dangers on the road. The civil war was
again picking up speed. Armies of mercenaries roamed the high-
ways, their generals encouraged greater banditry than before, and
in the vast area where the Maryknollers worked there was scarcely
a village that escaped attacks and lootings of one kind or another.
And there was this problem: the Kwangtung Province, where the
Maryknollers had begun their work, sided with the republic
forces of Sun Yat-sen, but the Kwangsi Province where the missionaries were beginning to extend was under the domination of
local war lords. Thus there was constant fighting between the two
provinces, with the missionaries caught in the middle.

In June of 1921, Meyer and O'Shea were working with Father
George F. Wiseman, of Arlington, Massachusetts, at the Kochow
mission on the western borders of Yeungkong district. The town
was in republic hands and was considered safe from attack. Then
word arrived that republic mercenaries to the south had mutinied
and deserted, leaving a broad gap in the Kuomintang defense
line. An army swept around from the west into the breech, cutting
off Kochow. The attack came at a bad time: General Foo, in
command at Kochow, confident of southern support, had just
returned from the tour of northern battle stations along the
Kwangsi border and had left most of his soldiers there. When the
invaders attacked from the south, Foo had only a handful of
soldiers to defend the town.

The invading army, under the joint command of Generals
Wong and So, began its attack early on a Sunday morning, and by
noon it was evident that Kochow would not last long. General
Foo sent for Meyer and O'Shea and told them, "I will have to
surrender. Will one of you go to General Wong and ask him what
terms he will accept?"

It was sad news. Meyer said, "Then Kochow will become an
enemy stronghold."

"I cannot worry about that now," Foo said. "Will you perform
this task for me?"

"Yes."

"Do you have an American flag?"

O'Shea was surprised. "Yes, we do. Why?"

"It may be wise to carry it," said the General. "That way they will know you are not one of us and will listen to you."

O'Shea considered this, then commented to Meyer: "Maybe we shouldn't be mixed up in this. We really aren't, you know."

Foo said, "You are mixed up in it simply because you are here."

"I'll go," Meyer said.

Foo said, "Good. I'll have a truce flag made for you. Be ready in an hour."

The fighting was still heavy when Meyer approached the South Gate, the truce flag in one hand and the American flag in the other. "Open the gate," he told the officer there.

"I can't. They'll all rush in."

"I have to get out," said Meyer. "I am on a mission for General Foo."

"Then you will have to get out some other way. I am not opening this gate."

"All right. I'll go over the wall."

He went to the southeast corner, climbed to the catwalk, then jumped over the wall to the ground, the flags waving. Snipers in the outer buildings sent bullets at his feet. He held up the flags as he made his way through the fringe of the houses to the fields beyond. Inside the wall, O'Shea hurried back and forth among the Kochow soldiers telling that a truce had been called. He was amazed to see that as the shooting stopped the attacking soldiers came from their hiding places, went to the wall, and began chatting with the Kochow soldiers as if they were old friends. They were, actually, all mercenaries, fighting and killing each other merely because they were paid for it. There was a bakery outside the wall which the northerners had looted, and now they passed cakes up to the Kochow soldiers.

Meyer advanced across the fields. A couple of shells burst near him, then all went quiet. An officer stopped him. Meyer said, "I have a message for General Wong." The officer led him to a small house where the two generals were waiting.

Meyer said, "General Foo has instructed me to tell you he is ready to surrender, depending on your terms."

Wong said, "We have already sent two officers to tell him our terms. Why did he send you?"

"Maybe he didn't have time to tell me. What are your terms?"

General So said, "General Foo's men must leave the town by the North Gate by four o'clock. Is that an American flag?"

"Yes, it is."

"How many Americans are in the town?"

"Three of us."

"You are soldiers?"

"We are missionaries."

"Then why did you carry your flag? Did you think the sight of it would frighten us?"

"If the sight of it prevented you from shooting at me I am glad I carried it."

"It won't do you much good after four o'clock," said Wong. "We are coming in then."

Meyer returned to the town. The south gate was opened for him; inside he found O'Shea and told him what happened. They went together to Foo's headquarters, arriving in time to see the two enemy officers depart.

Foo said, "They give us until four o'clock."

"General Wong told me," said Meyer.

"It is almost four now," O'Shea said. "Did you accept?"

"What else could I do?" asked Foo. "But there still is a chance. This morning I sent messengers to recall the troops I left in the north. If they arrive in time we may be able to hold."

Meyer pointed out, "But you have already accepted the terms. Shouldn't you be moving your men out?"

The General frowned. "You don't understand war. If I feel, even at the last moment, that I can win I will throw their terms back at them."

Meyer and O'Shea exchanged an unhappy glance. O'Shea asked, "Well, what do you suggest we do in the meantime?"

"I suggest you get ready for anything."

When they got back to the mission compound they found it crowded with people—refugees from the town toting their few possessions, frightened soldiers seeking sanctuary, looters after what they could carry away. The two priests hurried into the church. The looters were already there, dumping the sacristy drawers in search of things of value.

"The altar," Meyer said. He led O'Shea to it. They opened the tabernacle, removed the Blessed Sacrament, and consumed the Hosts to prevent further desecration. "Now let's get them out of here," Meyer said.

In the yard, Wiseman was struggling in pidgin Chinese with the soldiers. "No guns," he said, "you stay, but guns go."

They went to aid him. As Wiseman had perceived, armed men in the mission compound gave the invaders an excuse to shoot up the place. The men could stay, but they would have to be disarmed. Meyer explained this to the Kochow officers, who understood, and the men were disarmed and put in a roped area. It was also important to remove the belongings of the refugees. Undoubtedly the invaders would loot the town, and if they discovered that the refugees had carried everything to the mission they would come after it. Meyer and O'Shea gave the refugees a choice of putting their possessions outside the mission gates or going out with them. Meanwhile, Wiseman rounded up the mission women and locked them in a room to protect them from rape.

Four o'clock passed. The Kochow soldiers were still in town, most of them at the mission. Suddenly invaders' shells bombarded the east gate, and soon there was a roar of terror in the streets as the invaders rushed into the town.

Meyer was caught at the mission gate putting out luggage. The invaders pushed him aside and stalked in. When they saw the soldiers there was a burst of gunfire, until O'Shea convinced them that the soldiers were unarmed. Then the invaders went to work. The soldiers' weapons were gathered up and the men were searched. Officers were disarmed, searched and stripped. The refugees were also searched; anything of value was taken from them. The mission buildings were ransacked. Sacred vestments were dumped on the floor, files were thrown about, pictures were torn down, and statues overturned. By accident the marauders overlooked the small cabinet where the gold and silver chalices were kept. And they had no time to break down the locked door where the women were. On the way out, they stopped at the barn and took O'Shea's white horse.

The mission raid lasted only twenty minutes, but it took the rest of the day to clean up after it. Some things could never be repaired: no amount of laundering, for example, would ever remove the footprints from the vestments and altar linens. It was almost midnight when the priests finally sat down to a bit of supper. They could still hear the rumblings of panic on the streets beyond the mission walls.

The looting continued all Monday. A steady stream of Kochow people wandered into the mission to have their bruises and cuts treated or merely to bemoan their fate. Actually they had got off rather easy: only six people had been killed during the raid, surprisingly few in terms of raids. Tuesday afternoon O'Shea was summoned by General Wong.

"I understand your horse was taken," the General said.

"It was."

Wong pointed to a small herd collected from the town. "Identify it and take it back."

"It's the white one."

"Take it."

"Thank you," said O'Shea. "Is the raid over now?"

"Yes. We will be pushing on tonight."

"And General Foo?"

"He is going with us."

"You are taking him prisoner?"

"No. He has joined us." The General lighted a cigarette. "Foo is a good man. He has won many victories. Losing this town was no discredit to him. When we are ready to leave we will return his men and his weapons to him. He will make a good ally."

Wiseman was astonished to learn of Foo's flexible loyalty. "Does everybody around here switch sides so fast?" he asked.

"These people have always had so little that you can't blame them for wanting to ride with the winners," Meyer said. "What scares me is that some day the winners might be the bad guys. Then what will happen to all of us?"

XIII

AMONG those who switched sides frequently were the soldiers who had deserted from the armies of mercenaries and formed themselves into bandit gangs. As far as the war was concerned, they did not care who won, and in years to come this trait was to put them into the hands of China's worst enemy. Usually the soldiers deserted because they were tired of fighting, but frequently they deserted simply because they felt they could do better apart from the competition of full-army looting. Also, they disliked the discipline of armies, and they deplored having to give up their booty to officers who claimed the right of confiscation. In most cases, the gangs were small—ranging from perhaps six to twenty men. Occasionally, however, there might be as many as a hundred. These were the serious threats, the real dangers. Whereas the small gangs would attack travelers or hold up a farm, the big gangs could ransack a village as thoroughly as ants. The gangs, small or big, were everywhere. A Maryknoller did not consider himself a full-fledged missionary until he had been robbed at least once.

The bandits were interested only in money. If it was handed over to them without resistance they went quickly on their way. They would take horses or food or ammunition if these things were in special need, but most of all they wanted money. Traveling merchants were therefore their favorite prey. Such a man on his way home after selling his merchandise to farmers and villagers would be sure to have a good amount on him. In defense, merchants often took armed servants on their sales trips, but the bandits were fast and clever, and they could be ruthless when it was necessary. Their attacks succeeded more often than not.

They knew, too, that a rich merchant undoubtedly had more money at home than he carried with him. Thus they frequently held the man for ransom. If they could not get him, they took his eldest son. In either case they were confident they would be paid off, and they were. They seldom kidnaped a girl or a woman, regardless of her relationship to the merchant: a man would give his fortune for the return of the son who would carry on his name but he would think twice about the value of a woman who could easily be replaced for the same purpose.

The influx of foreign travelers—missionary or commercial—provided the bandits with a fresh market. A European or American company readily paid a ransom for one of its representatives, if only out of a sense of obligation. But the thing soon got out of hand. Instructions came from head offices that foreign salesmen should confine themselves to the big towns and cities where they had police protection, hiring Chinese to cover the remote areas. This unnerved the Chinese salesmen, who feared that their chances of being ransomed depended entirely on their sales records.

With missionaries the situation was more complex. Protestant or Catholic, they wanted to get to the remote people. Doing so, however, proved to be expensive because of the ransoms. Most Protestants solved the problem by settling at a centralized, walled community, offering their services to all who came by, proselytizing among the isolated people by giving them religious tracts to read at home whenever they came in for medical care. With Catholics, the problem was different. It was the duty of Catholics to receive the sacraments regularly and if for any reason they could not it was the duty of priests to take the sacraments to them. This meant travel; it also meant the risks of kidnapings. For a while the ransoms were paid. But Catholics were always poorer than Protestants and each ransom meant that the work of the mission was seriously curtailed. Furthermore, the missionaries realized that when the ransom was paid for one, the safety of all others was greatly jeopardized because of the temptation they offered to the bandits. More soberly, the priests had gone to China prepared to die for their faith: if they were kidnaped because they were priests and killed or left to die because the ransom was not or could not be paid, then they were martyrs. It was therefore decided that ransoms would no longer be paid, regardless of the situation. Gradually the bandits realized this, and the kidnapings of priests sharply decreased. When they occurred it was because the bandits did not know they had taken a priest or because they hoped for a weakness in policy or because they were desperate.

But the robberies were common. A traveling priest usually had money with him for his board and room, to provide for the extremely poor, to pay his carriers and catechists, and to use any ferries or steamers along his route. If he had any experience, he carried only part of his money on himself, hiding the rest among his packages that he knew would not interest bandits, and with luck he could complete his trek with a little something for the final bandit attack on his last miles. It was important always to have something; the bandits did not believe that a priest would have nothing. When there was nothing, they could be mean. Usually they looked rougher than they were: their life in their mountain hideouts left them so unkempt. But even the mildest were not beyond pistol-whipping a victim who resisted them. Many were trigger happy and delighted in frightening their victims with a wild barrage as they attacked. If by accident—and it was usually accident—a bullet struck the victim, it was his bad luck and the bandits were unperturbed.

The worst of it was the incident itself. One never knew what might happen. A disgruntled bandit in a foul mood might become vicious and violent, and an event that would otherwise pass quickly could well end in a battered face or a broken limb for a victim who made the slightest wrong move. No matter how often a man was robbed he never got used to it. A man who would be brave in any other circumstance—on a battlefield, before wild animals, against the elements—would be justifiably frightened during the few minutes in the presence of unpredictable bandits. And yet a man who showed his fear was worse off: the bandits took advantage of fear. A victim therefore had to be submissive but stoic, co-operative without being compromising. The missionaries often said they felt safest when they were wearing their cassocks during robberies because the bandits couldn't see their knees knocking.

The Maryknollers wrote home of their encounters with bandits, and if at times hindsight provided more adventure than the incident actually had, it nevertheless produced some exciting reading in *The Field Afar*. In 1921, Father General Walsh accompanied the fourth group of Maryknollers to go to China in order to make a firsthand estimate of future needs. On part of the trip he traveled with Frank Ford on a small motor-driven houseboat up a quiet river. One day he commented, "You know, I've been thinking how fortunate we've been not to run into any bandits."

Ford thought he detected a tone of disappointment. "Be happy," he said. "It isn't very pleasant."

That night they tied up at a little village and Ford went ashore for an hour. The next morning they had traveled about thirty minutes when a cluster of sampans darted out from the banks and surrounded the boat: bandits came aboard. They dug through suitcases, dumping most of them on deck, they bullied the crew, they pushed the priests around and frisked them. After ten minutes they left, empty-handed and complaining.

The craft moved on. Walsh said, "Well, that was certainly something!"

"We were lucky," said Ford. "It's usually much worse, especially when they don't find any money."

Walsh thought about that for several moments, then, "It's odd that they didn't order us to empty our pockets. They must have known we'd have some money with us, if only to buy fuel."

"Maybe they didn't think about it," Ford said. He settled in his chair and looked away.

Walsh let a little time pass, then, "Father, what did you do when you went ashore last night?"

"Why?"

"I'm curious."

"I visited some friends."

"But you told me you'd never been around here before. What friends?"

"Oh, after you're in China for a while you get to know a lot of people."

The craft puttered on. Finally Walsh said, "I've got the sneakiest suspicion that you went ashore last night and arranged all this just so that when I get home I can brag that I had an adventure with Chinese bandits."

"Why, Father General," Ford said, his handsome face bright with astonishment, "how could you accuse me of such a ridiculous thing!" He sank low in his chair and pushed his hat over his eyes. In a moment a soft murmur came from him that sounded distinctly like muffled laughter.

It was a time for growing. Both in China and at home, the society won new friends each year. The old accusation that Americans lacked the stamina to make good missionaries had faded: now the problem was to find enough Americans to do the job that other missionaries in China eagerly offered them. For a couple of years the problem had been a very serious one, but it turned out to be a problem of publicity. Despite all efforts by Father Superior to make the society known, its horizons for the most part remained within the sphere of Catholics specifically interested in the missions. Thus the scope for reaching new vocations was limited. Walsh's practice of appealing for Maryknoll vocations among men already in seminaries had brought results, but it was also true that the decision to become a priest was a sudden thing that often struck men who previously had never given the matter a thought. The idea that all priests were saints from infancy was an exaggeration promulgated by well-meaning nuns in elementary schools, but it had the result of frequently discouraging older men from at least giving the priesthood a try because they felt they had not accumulated enough piety over the years. Actually these men made excellent priests because they had more maturity and confidence than others who had been in seminaries since the age of twelve and dropped out in such large numbers when the time came for the final step. So it was urgent to reach the older men who never read Catholic magazines or books, who seldom spoke to their priests outside the confessional, and who always rejected the idea of the priesthood whenever God put it into their minds.

Price's death helped toward that end because of the reports of it in the daily press: many men learned of the society for the first time. World War I helped in that it took men away from their old environments and showed that they could indeed adjust to a new way of life. And the fighting in China and the attacks of bandits and pirates upon the mission stations helped because all this also got into the newspapers and made men think. The Twenties helped: the country plunged into a wild party and after a taste of it some men found it shallow, empty, unrewarding, and they sought some way to put meaning into their lives. Whatever the incident of decision, an increasing number of older men began to apply to Maryknoll. Most of them lacked a sufficient knowledge of Latin for their studies, so Walsh initiated an accelerated course for them that subsequently became common practice in other societies.

To promote further contact with such prospects, Walsh opened offices in cities across the country where Maryknollers did public relations work to make the society known outside the usual mission channels. They preached in various churches on Sundays, but more than that they went out of their way to contact prospects on their jobs, in their clubs, at their homes. Uncovering a latent vocation and cultivating it to a reality was as important to the promotion workers as the conversion of a pagan Chinese—more so, since without the vocation the number of conversions would remain restricted for years. The method was highly successful and accounted for Maryknoll's rapid growth in the Twenties. Within five years after the first four missionaries set foot in China, the society had twenty-five priests in the Orient, another twenty-five teaching in Maryknoll schools, and others roaming the country in search of those who had yet to realize that they were numbered among God's marked men.

The Bishop raised his hands and said helplessly, "China is getting out of control."

Frank Ford nodded, not sure whether he understood or agreed. He remembered that many years ago Napoleon had said, "China is a sleeping beast. God help the world when she begins to stir." Now she was stirring; the Bishop did not like it.

They were at Swatow, a city of almost two hundred thousand, on the China coast northeast of Hong Kong. Ford had been summoned to start a new Maryknoll mission at the inland town of

Kaying. With him was Father James M. Drought of New York
City, a young Maryknoller finishing his first year in China. It
was October, 1925.

Leaving Yeungkong had been like leaving home for Ford. Although Price in his few months there had made most of the plans
for the mission station, it was Ford who had carried them out—the
schools for boys and girls, the orphanage, the home for aged
women, the home for blind children, the three-story building—
the largest in town—which was now the convent of the Maryknoll
Sisters.

Ford said, "The place has become like Vatican City. I will be
glad to get back into the bush."

The day he left, the people threw a big party for him: an
enormous banquet, fireworks, a parade through the streets. He was
deeply touched. He was about to start his mission life again in
a new place for Maryknoll, and he was excited about it. But he
knew it would not be like Yeungkong. Yeungkong was home.

At Yeungkong he had written a prayer:

Grant us, Lord, to be the doorstep by which the multitudes may
come to worship Thee. And if, in the saving of their souls, we are
ground underfoot and spat upon and worn out, at least we shall have
served Thee in some small way in helping pagan souls and we shall
have become the King's Highway in pathless China.

At Kaying, the highway was to be rocky, dangerous, fatal.

The assignment put Ford in the same administrative position
as Jim Walsh at Kongmoon. He would be in charge of a large
area with a population of over two and a half million, of whom
some five thousand were Catholics. The people were Hakkas.
Three centuries before Christ, they had lived in the north, in
the Shantung and Shansi provinces. Wars then forced them south
to the Honan and Anhwei provinces, where they lived for another
six centuries. Again, fighting sent them on the move, again south,
this time into Kiangsi and Fukien provinces, and they had just
about settled when, in 618, further revolutions pushed them over
the mountains into Kwangtung. The Cantonese did not want them
and would not let them occupy the broad fields that swept to the

sea. They therefore settled on the mountainsides where, for over a thousand years, they had managed to scrape a living out of the dry soil. In the past hundred years, many of them had emigrated to the Pacific islands, then on to South America, leaving behind what they considered a worthless, hopeless fatherland. Then Nature stepped in: coal was discovered in the mountains. The Hakkas became rich. Being rich, they became powerful. They fought their way out of the hills, across the fields to the sea, and now they claimed the area as their own.

The first priests, members of the Paris Foreign Mission Society, had entered Hakkaland, as it was called, in 1849. Their progress was slow. The Hakkas were proud, history-bound to their own language and customs, and they were difficult to convert. In seventy-five years the missionaries had not produced a single Chinese priest in the area; the growth of the native clergy was the best yardstick of mission achievement.

Ford was anxious for a native clergy. He said:

"They are the backbone of the local Church and will guarantee its permanency; they are the pledge by which the native Christians are bound to the eternal Church. A country without a native clergy, or having an insufficient native priesthood, is always in danger of being stranded for lack of a pilot. In time of persecution, the first to be wiped out or driven out is the foreigner."

The observation was prophetic. Also, it reflected the opinions uttered at the same time by Pope Benedict XV when, by wise indirection, he pointed out in a general statement on mission affairs that the French in China had not done enough to foster a native clergy, particularly a native hierarchy. Ford's first act, then, on arriving at Kaying was to open a seminary. The front porch of his house served as dormitory for a dozen boys; his dining room served as the classroom; he served as the professor. Within two years, Ford erected a new structure as a seminary for forty boys, again with himself as the lone professor.

An incident occurred which almost ruined the work. Ford's first student had been a thirteen-year-old boy named John Yap, who came from one of the best Hakka families. He was a good catch for a special reason: his position in Hakka society encouraged other boys to emulate him. Ford knew most of the boys would drop out, but as long as they kept coming he hoped that a few of them would reach the priesthood. John Yap was a model student, pious, studious, a willing worker. The new seminary had just opened when John was stricken with a serious lung infection which rapidly grew worse. The pagan method of deduction—that there was an immediate cause-and-effect relation in all things—stirred talk in Kaying that the boy was dying because he was at the seminary. Other parents, even though they were Catholics, were inclined to suspect there was something to the talk and gave signs of withdrawing their sons from the school. The danger was familiar to Ford: in the past he had seen that when death came quickly to a newly baptized baby or an old man given the last rites the pagans blamed death on the sacraments and stubbornly refused them for a long time.

Now Ford's entire native clergy program faced the same danger. It might have come had John Yap been a different kind of boy. When he realized his death was near, John sent for his father and said, "I want you to accept that my death is God's will."

"How can that be?" asked the man. "Why should God want you to die?"

"It is not our place to question Him," the boy said. "I believe it. I want you to believe it."

The man studied his son. "You are close to God now and must know what you are saying. I believe you."

With that the boy closed his eyes and died.

After the funeral John's father was besieged by his neighbors to admit that the boy had died because he was at the seminary, that the seminary must therefore be an evil place, but he said over and over, "It was God's will. John believed it; I believe it."

The conviction saved the seminary, for had the man felt otherwise the parents of the other students would quickly have called their sons home. Among those who remained were many who, in the years ahead, were to pay the price of martyrdom for their priesthood.

Situated about two hundred miles north of the Maryknollers at Kongmoon, Ford's district was subject to steadily increasing attacks by the growing Chinese Communist element. As with most Chinese military contingents, the ordinary soldiers with the Communists were mercenaries, but their leaders were Russian-trained and Russian-supported, their top men had either gone to Russia or attended training centers maintained by Russians in the northern provinces. They roamed through the country like bandits, attacking villages and towns, and mission stations were their special prey. Usually there was little at a mission for them to steal, but that was not the point. They attacked missions to destroy them.

The Communist expansion in China had followed a familiar pattern. As soon as Communism was established in Russia, its leaders went to work on their plan to bring the rest of the world into their political scheme one way or another. In neighboring China, the Kuomintang government was struggling for existence: a perfect victim. As early as 1919, Russia was inviting young Chinese to its universities; Communist organizers were already at work among Chinese youths and laborers; there were Communist leaders in the Kuomintang army. In 1923, Sun Yat-sen realized he would need outside help if he was to hold his government together against the Chinese Old Guard in the north. He appealed to the United States, Canada, Great Britain, and Germany for military and financial assistance; they all refused him. There was no place left for him to turn except Russia, and the Russians quickly responded. Appointed as his special advisor was Michael Borodin. In the process of bringing in equipment and personnel, Borodin put Russian and Chinese Communists into every important job and in two years he was practically dictator of the country. The rise of Chiang Kai-shek among the Kuomintang conservatives brought an end to the outward Communist influence. Borodin was sent out of the country and Communism was outlawed. But the Communist Party had taken root and could not be eradicated. In an enormous country with poor communications and poor transportation, with already two governments in civil war, with great poverty and wide disease, with no friends in the Western world, there was only weak defense against the Communist elements that roamed the land like a brushfire of little wars. Their attacks on missions were a calculated part of a plan to rid China of its freedoms—most important, the freedom of religion. As long as people refused to give up that freedom they would be less willing to give up others for the sake of the Communist-promised peace and prosperity. Thus, years before Communism was the dominant influence in China its pioneers were putting the Communist antireligion precept to work.

Ford got the worst of it. Twice the Communists took Kaying, holding it once for several weeks before the Nationalists won it back. At Shakchin, about twenty miles north, Father Patrick F. Malone, of Brooklyn, was shot at by Communists as he tried to escape across rice paddies. When they could not find him, the Communists shot his dog.

XIV

AND yet Maryknoll continued to grow. A dramatic example of it occurred at Wuchow, a city of seventy thousand on the banks of the West River in the Kwangsi Province opposite Maryknoll missions to the south in Kwangtung Province. A Protestant missionary who became a Catholic priest reported to Maryknoll: "This is the neglected province. There are multitudes who have never heard the Gospel. I have preached to thousands who have never heard the name of Jesus, and in all my travels I have never met a Catholic priest."

In 1920, the French bishop of Nanking asked Maryknoll to take over part of his vicariate—the part in Kwangsi. Jim Walsh and Father Frederick C. Dietz, of Oberlin, Ohio, went there to survey the area and become acquainted with the language. A French priest told them: "You'll have to hire a pagan to be your altar boy."

In Wuchow there were no Catholics at all; in the province of six million people there were about one hundred and fifty Catholics. Kwangsi was incredibly poor. The hills of Kwangtung erupted into mountains in Kwangsi; there were no roads outside the city area, the soil was worthless. Kwangsi produced only mercenary soldiers and bandits.

150

Walsh and Dietz achieved little. On the advice of the bishop, they settled at Pingnam, a hundred miles west of Wuchow, but this was a mistake. It was impossible for them to make effective contact with the people; they even had trouble hiring someone to teach them the language. Before they could get started they were both recalled to Kwangtung, Walsh to become superior at Kongmoon and Dietz to direct the Loting language school. For three more years Kwangsi went untouched. Then Bernard Meyer was appointed to the province with instructions to take steps to set up Kwangsi as an independent mission district. He knew he would need money, so he returned to the United States where he spent over a year raising funds.

In 1927, Meyer moved into the quarters Walsh and Dietz had abandoned at Pingnam. He soon discovered, however, that although Pingnam had a few Catholics, Wuchow offered more opportunities. Protestants had made a little headway there; the city had more contact with the outside world, the province's few roads led from it. Meyer moved to Wuchow. At home, he had convinced Father General Walsh that if he was to make any progress he must have men: most of the 1927 departure group was assigned to him. In a year Kwangsi was a different place. There were five hundred new Catholics in the province; Wuchow, which never had one before, now had twenty-five. Nine Maryknollers were conducting three different mission stations, a dispensary, a student hostel, and thirteen village schools. Moreover, there were eight hundred Chinese under instruction, a number that doubled the following year. A seminary opened near Pingnam attracted thirty-five students, the first of which was ordained in 1933. Meyer sent for Maryknoll Sisters to assist him in the dispensary and schools. At the same time the Sisters organized a new congregation for Chinese girls who became the first in Kwangsi to enter the religious life.

It was at this time that a special honor came to Maryknoll. The prefecture of Kongmoon had grown to such size in the number of priests, Catholics, and mission stations that Rome decided it should be elevated to a vicariate. The news was sent to Maryknoll and Kongmoon simultaneously: Jim Walsh was to be Kongmoon's first bishop. The choice also made him Maryknoll's first bishop. The announcement stirred great excitement in China and America: there could be no more vivid evidence of Rome's approval of Maryknoll than this.

Only Jim Walsh remained unmoved. "This is a wild note," he said. "If there's one thing I won't be able to stand it's having people drop to their knees and kiss my hand every time I walk into a room."

To Father General Walsh he wrote: "The responsibility is mine, but the honor is Maryknoll's. I will never forget that."

It was honor indeed. Consecration made a man spiritual heir to the Apostles, a selected instrument of the Holy Ghost. Through a bishop passed the sacramental treasure of the Church: he became living evidence of its lineage to Peter. He was, wherever he ruled, a new Peter—a rock on which the Church relied for leadership and guidance. In a sense, consecration made Walsh more of Rome than of Maryknoll, for now he was more responsible to Rome than to Maryknoll. But he remembered his *Propositum,* by which he had pledged himself to Maryknoll for life. As bishop, he was the autonomous spiritual ruler of Kongmoon, subject only to Rome, but he knew that Kongmoon was Maryknoll in China, and although by tradition and law he would be the deciding factor at Kongmoon he assured Father General Walsh that whatever happened in Kongmoon would reflect the attitudes and ideas of the Maryknoll superiors.

If he wished, Walsh could have gone home to Maryland to have his relatives and old friends present on the occasion of his consecration, so rare an honor that the time and expense of the journey to Cumberland would not have been considered extravagant. But he did not go. Instead, he sent for Father Sandy Cairns and asked him to make the arrangements for the ceremony.

Cairns asked, "Where will it be?"

"Sancian Island," Walsh said.

The choice was typical of Walsh. The island, made holy by the work and death of Saint Francis Xavier there, had become a Catholic shrine and—more important to Walsh—a Chinese Catholic shrine. It was for the Chinese that he had become a missionary, to them that he had dedicated his life. The high honor, he felt, was not for him, the first American to become a bishop in China, but for China itself, for having grown so in the faith that

another bishop, who happened to be an American, was required
to carry on the work.

He chose May 22 as the day. He invited all the missionaries and
laymen he knew to be witnesses and he asked the bishops of
Hong Kong, Macao, and Fukien to be his coconsecrators.

Walsh arrived at Sancian a week early to have time for a retreat.
Three or four days before the event, the laymen began to arrive,
crossing over from the mainland on junks and large sampans.
The housing shortage was severe; people slept on floors in private
houses in order to have a place indoors. The day before the ceremony the bishops arrived to study together the ritual they were
to perform. That night a steamer left Hong Kong crammed with
more than five hundred guests.

It rained the morning of the twenty-second. The steamer had to
anchor in deep water; passengers were transported to shore in
small sampans. The tide was running high and when the boats
reached the beach the passengers—Sisters, old men and women,
youngsters in long colored robes—had to gauge the waves so that
they could hop ashore without getting drenched. Then they made
their way across a precarious foot bridge to the church. Bernard
Meyer noticed that white ants had eaten the church beams to
hollow shells and he wondered if it was wise to let so many people
inside. But they would not be kept out and those who could not
fit into the small church stood outside in the rain, listening to the
choir and the prayers, waiting for their bishop to come out and
give his first blessing.

The ceremony lasted three hours, all of it centered on Walsh.
The humidity and body heat inside the church produced a stifling
discomfort that weakened Walsh. After the recitation of a litany
during which he had stretched prone at the foot of the altar he
could not get up without help. At last it was over. Dressed in full
vestments, wearing his miter and ring and carrying his crosier,
Walsh went down the aisle and outside to give his blessing to the
people waiting there. A great cheer went up, fireworks exploded,
the people sang hymns at the tops of their voices. They had
a bishop!

Across the bay was the chapel where Xavier had reposed after
death until his body was removed to India. If the presence of a

holy man made a place holy, then surely the chapel was a treasure of grace. Walsh led the procession of bishops and priests and Sisters and laymen across the beach in the pouring rain to the chapel and he knelt there to pray, praying that China's first missionary would guide and bless her newest bishop.

The steamer was to leave at three o'clock, taking most of the party back to their mainland homes. Because there was an indulgence attached to the act of kissing a bishop's ring, all those who had attended the consecration wanted to receive it, at the same time wishing to display their affection and respect for Walsh. He was therefore asked if, as they made their way to the steamer, he would receive those who wished to kiss his ring. He looked at the great crowd and pursed his lips, then said, "O.K."

A line formed and the procession began, Maryknoll priests, Brothers, and Sisters, others of the clergy who had come, men, women, children, each approaching, genuflecting, taking his right hand, and buzzing a kiss at his ring. After several minutes of it, the endless stream of obeisance unnerved Walsh.

"Aw, come on," he muttered, "why don't we cut this out?"

Daniel McShane was not there; Walsh was disappointed. McShane had been among the original six students and was the first of them to be ordained. He had taught at the Vénard for a while, then directed the house in San Francisco. In 1919, he headed the second group of Maryknollers to go to China. He was assigned to Tungchen where he studied Chinese for a year under Bernard Meyer and then he was appointed pastor of Loting. It was not an easy job. The town was in the No Man's Land of the civil war and frequently changed hands, so there was continual havoc at the mission compound. The Loting people, furthermore, were hostile toward foreigners; co-operation was slim and conversions were slow.

Extreme poverty and the chaos of war compelled the Loting families to abandon their infant daughters in great numbers. In an effort to save the girls, McShane opened an orphanage, filling it with the babies he found at roadsides and in fields. When the people realized what he was doing they began depositing their daughters at his doorsteps. For many months, the children were the only ones he baptized. Most of them died; the Chinese felt that a house where anyone died was cursed, and this kept them away from McShane. When he tried to obtain a house in the market town of Lintaan to open another orphanage he had trouble finding anyone who would rent to him because they did not want their property to be cursed. He was traveling when he received news that the first death had occurred at Lintaan and that the Sisters had been put out of the building. He hurried there, and his argument for the right to retain the building became the talk of the town. It was the town that decided: since McShane had revealed his purpose for the building before obtaining the lease, the owners had no right to evict him just because a death had occurred in it. The orphanage remained.

Aiding orphans proved to be McShane's biggest job and expense. In five years, he took in over two thousand of them. In the middle of May, 1927, he prepared to make the trip to Sancian Island for Walsh's consecration. One morning he found another baby on his doorstep, took it in, baptized it, and turned it over to the Chinese girls who assisted in the orphanage. That night he was not feeling well. The next day word came from other Maryknollers in the area that they were awaiting him for the journey to Hong Kong and he sent them a note to start out, that he would catch up with them in a day or so when he felt better.

But he did not improve. His body was hot, he felt nauseous, and he could not hold down food. He summoned the doctor from the Presbyterian mission. After examining him, the doctor said, "You've got smallpox."

McShane was surprised. "How did I get that?"

"I've seen several cases in the past week or so," Doctor Dickson said. "I hope it's not an epidemic. Have you been with anyone who has it?"

"Not to my knowledge."

"Did you see any strangers the day you got sick?"

"Just the baby I found on the doorstep."

"I'd better look at her."

The doctor was back in a few minutes. "Yes," he said, "she has it. I've removed her from the others; they seem to be all right. Now let's take care of you."

He did not respond to treatment. Each day he grew weaker. For hours at a time he was unconscious. On June 2 he managed to write a note to Father William Downs, of Erie, Pennsylvania, assigned to Hong Kong. Apparently sensing that he would not recover, he wrote:

> I'm over a week on my back with smallpox. Thank God I did not go down to spread it to the others.
>
> Please tell Bishop Walsh I'm trying so hard to offer my sufferings for his many new responsibilities. I give him everything I have. God love him and dear Father Superior, my mother and brothers and sisters. Tell them I'm praying for them. I hold no grudge against anybody. I am thinking of the Sisters and Brothers also. Dr. Dickson has been especially kind to me. Can't retain the least food and the heat is intense.
>
> God's blessed will be done. No mail seems to be coming this way. Pray for me.
>
> McShane

Dickson did not think the note would reach Hong Kong in time, so he sent a telegram that McShane was very ill and would not live much longer. The Maryknoll priests and Sisters of the Loting district were already on their way back; telegraphers along the wire heard Dickson's message and gave it to them. Father Otto A. Rauschenbach, of St. Louis, feeling he could travel faster alone, left the other priests to proceed with the nuns, and hurried ahead on his own. He reached Loting the next day.

McShane was extremely weak, but he was able to go to confession and respond to the prayers of the last rites. Unable to swallow, he did not receive Communion.

He managed, "How was the consecration?"

"Just fine. Very beautiful."

"I wanted to go so badly," he said. "I've never been to Sancian. Xavier is one of my favorite saints. I would have liked seeing the place where he was." He looked blankly around the room. "Well, maybe soon I will see the place where he *is.*"

He closed his eyes and did not open them again. He died the next morning just as the other Maryknollers who had followed him into the society hurried over the last hill to him.

XV

PATRICK J. BYRNE was unhappy. He had joined Maryknoll in 1915, a week after his ordination in Washington, D. C. He had been born in Washington in 1888 in a house that stood where the U. S. Supreme Court was later erected. This accident of his personal history always amused him: he invariably referred to the Supreme Court as "my family homestead." He had first heard of Maryknoll when he was a student at St. Mary's Seminary in Baltimore on the day Walsh and Price came to speak about their new society. Also in the auditorium was Daniel McShane, who transferred to Maryknoll immediately. Byrne waited until after his ordination to join the society and became the first priest to enter Maryknoll in this way.

McShane and Byrne were good friends. One of Byrne's duties was to travel to nearby churches on weekends to preach about Maryknoll in order to raise funds and sell subscriptions to *The Field Afar*. He did not consider himself a good speaker and dreaded the chore. After preaching at a Brooklyn church he received a letter signed by what appeared to be a very old woman. She praised his talk and said, "If I know when you are coming again, even if I have to crawl on my hands and knees, I shall go to hear you."

Byrne was impressed. He passed the letter around the Maryknoll recreation room and said, "See what an orator I am." He began to

157

give more care to his talks and actually improved greatly. Then the other Maryknollers could hide their secret no longer and revealed that McShane had written the letter. Byrne laughed; he did not care: the trick had worked.

When Walsh left to seek a mission field in China he appointed Byrne to be his vicar-general. Byrne knew he had been chosen because of Price's idea of leaving Maryknoll, and he was uneasy about it. He had a great affection and respect for Price; passing over him in the society was unpleasant. On Walsh's return, Byrne expected to be relieved of his position, but Walsh kept him on. Each year Byrne watched others leave for the missions—another source of distress. He found some consolation in the teaching he was required to do at the Vénard; it got him away from exercising the authority he disliked.

Walsh was aware of Byrne's sentiments. In November of 1922 he wired him at Scranton and instructed him to report to Maryknoll for a conference. Traveling north, he ran into snow at New York. It slowed down his train to Ossining, and his taxi to Maryknoll had to be dug out of drifts repeatedly. He was late arriving for the meeting and when he entered the conference room he found it already in progress.

Walsh greeted him with a gesture toward a window. "Are you responsible for this?"

"I hope not," said Byrne. "I always like to think I bring sunshine wherever I go."

"Do you, now?" Walsh asked, his arched brows soaring. "How apt."

Puzzled, Byrne took a seat.

Walsh arranged papers in front of him. "And now," he said, "let's get to the primary reason for this meeting. I have received instructions from Propaganda in Rome to accept consignment of a new mission territory. It is in Korea."

An eager buzz passed around the table.

Walsh went on: "The territory is in the north, along the Yalu River, and includes the two provinces of North and South Heiando. From the information I have, it seems to be a large area, about the size of New Jersey, Maryland, and Delaware combined. There is a population of about two and a half million people; according to the report, about four thousand of them are

Catholics, thanks to the grace of God and the Paris Foreign Mission Society. I have no idea what else is there—how many stations, what facilities, any schools. But I imagine some of us will find out sooner or later."

He looked around the room, his face blank but his eyes amused. "I haven't been able to make up my mind who should go—until now. This morning I was reading that this particular area suffers the worst winters in the world and I suppose it would be plain charity to choose a man who has his own built-in heating system. Now that I've learned that one of our confreres thinks he spreads sunshine wherever he goes I've decided, Father Byrne, that you're it."

There was a stunned pause, then applause broke out. Byrne beamed at Walsh, sensing that the decision had been made long before he entered the room and grateful that Walsh had chosen this way to have those dearest to him share the news.

Korea was the only country in the world where Catholicism had firm roots years before any priest showed up. For centuries, Korea had been a battlefield for China and Japan, each country demanding tribute from the peninsula while ruling it. At the time George Washington was being inaugurated, China held Korea; each year a Korean embassy traveled to Peking with the payment. There existed in Korea at this time seven young men, all rich, all intelligent, all cultured. Eager to learn more of the world from which they were cut off, they always asked the tribute bearers to bring back books for them. Catholic missionaries were already in China, so among the books that were brought back were those which the priests had translated or written. They became keenly interested in Christianity. One year a friend of the group, by name Ri Syeng Huni, disclosed that he was going to Peking with his father to make the annual payment; they asked him to look up the missionaries in the Chinese capital and find out as much as he could about the religion. Ri Syeng Huni remained in Peking for several months, and in carrying out his friends' request he became so impressed by what he learned that he asked to be baptized and he took the name of Peter.

When Peter returned to Korea and told his friends what he had learned, four of them decided that they wanted to be Christians.

Since Peter was the only Christian in the country it became his duty to baptize his friends. From this small group evolved a team of lay missionaries that roamed the country teaching others what they had learned, and in eleven years they brought more than four thousand Koreans into the Church.

It was then that the first priest arrived, a Chinese named Tjyou. In five years he raised the number of Catholics to ten thousand. Gradually the government, most often a puppet government under China or Japan, grew aware of what was considered a foreign influence in the country. Persecutions began. Tjyou was killed in a massacre that took three hundred lives.

The first Korean priest was ordained in 1846 in Shanghai. He returned to his country, was discovered after fifteen days, and was killed. More to attend the Catholics who were there than to seek further converts, French priests realized they had to get into the country. They had no trouble landing, but the towns and cities were walled and to enter them the priests had to crawl through sewerage ducts. They lived in disguise, moving about only at night, and when they were discovered they were killed. Others replaced them. For the next thirty years the persecutions were so severe that the number of people who died for their faith was inestimable but numbered into the thousands.

In 1876, Japan retook Korea. Having opened its own doors to the world, Japan was less concerned about the so-called foreign influence of Catholicism and the persecution waned. What continued was the work of fanatics and it was serious enough for priests and laymen to prolong their caution. The trouble ended in 1885 when the puppet government signed treaties with the United States and several European powers, and on the heels of this, American Protestant missionaries began to arrive. Between that time and the arrival of Maryknollers, some two hundred and fifty thousand Koreans had joined the Church, of whom some ninety thousand were still alive. There were also some three hundred thousand Protestant Koreans in the country.

Byrne went to Korea via Rome, where he had an audience with Pope Pius XI. He wrote to Maryknoll:

It's a strange feeling that comes over one, seeing for the first time the successor of St. Peter, who is the Spiritual Head of many millions and

who, in speaking officially, can make no mistakes in dogma or morals.
It is a sentiment of reverence, of course, but there is a sort of logical
consequence: "Well, the earth has nothing higher. The next thing to see
is an angel!"

In Korea he was not prepared for the angels he encountered.
Like China, Korea was predominantly pagan, which meant that
Sunday was just another day. So that Catholics could keep their
Sunday duty, Mass had to be held as early as three o'clock in the
morning, ending in time for the people to go to work. Byrne noted
in his diary:

> No matter how cold the day nor how early the Mass, the village com-
> munity turns out. One of the Fathers here has christened the churches
> "holy refrigerators"—but the Christians will come before Mass, to re-
> main after, and should there be more Masses, remain for all. At times
> the Sacred Species will freeze in the chalice before Communion and
> must be thawed by holding the cup in the hands and breathing upon it.

Byrne was a builder in the most practical sense. When he took
over the territory from the French in 1923 there were five missions
with sixty outstations with three dilapidated schools. In four
years, the stations were up to eleven, there were eleven excellent
schools, three dispensaries, and a home for the aged. From Byrne
alone, the number of Maryknollers had grown to sixteen priests,
two Brothers, nine Maryknoll Sisters, and six Korean Sisters.
Brother William, a master carpenter, was closest to Byrne; together late at night they would work over their blueprints, arguing
the best way to do the job facing them. When Brother Joseph,
Byrne's secretary, needed him to sign official papers he usually had
to hunt him out atop ladders or behind brick-making machines.
Byrne was sometimes impatient with slow-working Koreans. On
one construction he groaned for a week as he watched a work
gang pick away at a foundation pit. Then the workers took a
day off, a national holiday, and in their absence Byrne and Brother
William took over. When the Koreans returned they found the
pit dug and half the concrete poured. They were not impressed
either way and Byrne was not concerned about their reaction:
the job was getting done and that was all he cared about.

He built with an unusual purpose in mind. He wanted his con-

structions, particularly the rectories, to be as American in stand-
ard as possible, not only for durability but for comfort. He knew
what the long Korean winters could be like, and he felt that when
a missionary returned home at night, tired, hungry, cold, the
slightest convenience available to him could be enough to restore
him for the next day's ordeal. This was not meant to pamper the
missionaries. Byrne had a deep respect for the Frenchmen who
had pioneered the bleak north country and called them "unknown
saints," but at the same time he understood the black moods that
could strike a man when all his plans fell through or his potential
converts fell away. A hot shower, a decent meal, a comfortable
reading chair in a house that had a touch of home could take a
man's mind off his woes and convince him that tomorrow would
be a better day—and he would make it so. For the same reason,
he once bought a spacious house on the eastern shore for his
priests to use on vacations and retreats. He was criticized for this,
particularly by the French whose exaggerated standards of humility and poverty often made them look upon fresh bread as an
occasion of sin. But in later years, under the hardships of Communism, civil war, and pagan resurgence, many a priest, including
the French, were glad of the chance to get away for a few days
of rest and prayer in the house Byrne offered to all.

His health was not good. Soon after arriving in Korea he was
struck with severe dysentery that left him so weak that for two
months he had to say his Mass sitting down. He reported: "At
least I succeeded in getting rid of some of that superfluous flesh
that has been making life a burden for me in recent years." This
was a joke; he had always been underweight. He joked too about
a more serious condition. After a year in Korea he developed
sharp abdominal pains that were diagnosed locally as a hernia
and he went to Shanghai for surgery. By this time, appendicitis
was almost an occupational disease for Maryknollers in China,
and just before the operation Byrne told the doctor to take a look
at his appendix. The appendix proved to be his trouble: it was
on the verge of bursting. The doctor showed it to Byrne after the
operation, and Byrne said: "Too bad I'm not a saint. That would
make an unusual relic."

He made a joke out of everything. Once a Maryknoll Sister
broke her denture and had to go to Antung, across the Yalu in

Manchuria, to have it fixed. The repairs took several days; Byrne suggested that the nun return to her mission, that he would see that the denture was sent on to her later. Days passed, then two weeks, with no sign of the denture. Then one day a cart driver arrived at the mission with an enormous wooden crate for the Sisters. Unpacking, they found another box inside, then a box inside that, then another—they unpacked a score of boxes before they reached the contents: the teeth, biting into a big red apple.

When next they saw Byrne, the Sisters told him what a laugh he had given them, and he explained, "I wanted to be sure they worked before I sent the teeth back. Anyway, that cart driver needed a job."

From the start, Byrne sought some way to escape his own job as superior of the Korean mission. This was not shirking, it was not false humility, nor was it a distrust of his own decisions; he simply did not like giving people orders. As soon as the mission was running smoothly he wrote Father General Walsh that he felt someone else should be made superior, someone younger, fitter, with more of a mind for paper work. Walsh replied that he did not think a change should be made at the time. In 1927, letters from Maryknoll bore rumors that Rome was about to elevate the mission to a prefecture, with Byrne as superior with the title of Monsignor. He squirmed, he tried to elude the appointment but he couldn't. It came through; he accepted it uneasily. That year he spent much time at the Hiken mission station on a building program, and in the annual register of personnel he recorded: "HIKEN—Fr. Stephen Hannon, pastor; Msgr. P. J. Byrne, curate (retired)."

In 1929, he received orders to return to Maryknoll to attend the society's first general chapter—a conference at which superiors would be elected and a program planned for the next ten years. It was the first general chapter the society held. Although both the society's rule and Rome required a chapter every ten years, rapid growth and heavy work had resulted in repeated postponements. Now Rome insisted on it. Father General Walsh wanted it, too. He was now sixty-three years old; since Price's death he had led the society alone, filling all the major offices. He felt he had not long to go and wanted to prepare other men to take over.

Counting travel time, Byrne expected to be away from Korea

about four months. Therefore, he packed only a few of his be-longings, he left enough building plans for his absence to keep a construction battalion busy for a year, and his parting conversa-tions always began with: "When I get back—"

He did not return to Korea for almost twenty years, and when he did it was to become a martyr.

The
Third
Decade

XVI

THE chapter unanimously elected James Anthony Walsh to continue as superior general of the society. Pat Byrne was elected the first assistant—vicar-general—and it was necessary for him to remain at Maryknoll.

The chapter also made a significant change in the society's name. It was, officially, the Catholic Foreign Missionary Society of America, and its members put the initials A.F.M. (American Foreign Missions) after their names. In their discussion, the chapter representatives recalled how, in China especially, the Church had been given nationalistic identification by the people, a situation which undoubtedly grew out of the other societies already there—the Paris Foreign Mission Society, the Milan Foreign Mission Society, the Portuguese Foreign Mission Society. There was danger in this, particularly in view of the Chinese suspicion of foreigners. Furthermore, the Church belonged to no nation but to all nations: it was universal. It was Chinese as well as it was French or Italian or Portuguese or American. It was therefore decided at the chapter that henceforth A.F.M. would be replaced by M. M.—Maryknoll Missioner. Maryknoll was home; anywhere Maryknollers worked was another Maryknoll. Maryknoll it would be. The change was carried over to the society's major publication. The magazine continued to be called *The Field Afar,* but the word Maryknoll was added as a subtitle. As the years passed, the title diminished into smaller type and the subtitle grew into larger type, until at last the two were reversed. Maryknoll it was.

And Maryknoll was James Anthony Walsh.

For twenty years he had carried the responsibility of the society on his own shoulders. He had selected the students, deciding which to reject and which to dismiss later on, preferring quality to quantity. He made all the assignments and transfers, both in the United States and in the Orient. He kept up a heavy correspondence with all his men, aware that those in the field could provide ideas for better training of the students. At the chapter, he disclosed that several of the men had mentioned to him in their letters that they would have benefited from a novitiate during which they could have undergone intensive spiritual formation and he announced that henceforth students finishing the philosophy courses would spend a year in novitiate at a farm he was purchasing near Bedford, Massachusetts, before going into the studies of theology.

Despite the steadily growing society—there were now about a hundred and twenty-five priests—Walsh knew each man intimately. Anyone who managed, because of a rush of work, to get out into the missions without breaking through the formality of the superior-student relationship did so soon after going to work through letters. Men who at school did not feel close to Walsh lost the feeling once they were working, and they wondered how he had come to know so much about them, how he found time to display deep concern for them, for each of them.

He was, Walsh felt, what his position indicated: their father. When they were boys and young men he shaped them into what they became: priests and missionaries. They were the product of him, and if anything went wrong the blame could be his as well as theirs. He was indeed a father to them: interested, loving, guiding, sacrificing, but firm. One day he happened to be passing a room where a student was on the telephone with friends in New York. The youth had apparently left a valise in town and was making arrangements for its return.

He said, "Father General is going to be in New York tonight. I'll give him your address and he can pick the valise up for me."

The student turned around and found Walsh glaring at him. Walsh said, "Don't you ever tell anybody what *I* shall do. You are here for *me* to tell *you* what to do."

But that evening in the city Walsh went around and picked up the valise and took it back to the startled student.

As he grew older Walsh lost the air of levity that had been an early trademark. It would be difficult for any man to remain a jokester when every mail from China brought requests from Bishop Walsh or Ford or Meyer for five thousand dollars to build a church or two hundred dollars to build a school or merely twenty dollars to pay catechists. There were other men on the road at promotion and fund-rasing, but when the demand was quick and large the task was Walsh's. Time and again he borrowed money on the Maryknoll property or equipment, realizing that if he failed to meet at least the interest payments he could lose everything; this was a sobering realization for a man to carry around. The hierarchy had been generous to him and he squirmed at the times he had to go back to ask for more: it was not that he lacked the humility to beg; he lacked the heart to be refused because it meant he in turn must refuse others. After the stock market crash of 1929 he was never free of financial worries. He, of course, had no stock to lose, but many of his benefactors did. After the crash the Lady Bountiful was penniless and now, after years of her help, Walsh had to find some way to help her. Belts had to be tightened all along the line, and it was getting to be a very big belt.

The major seminary at Maryknoll was half finished and overcrowded. New buildings had gone up at the Vénard and the new preparatory seminary at Los Altos, near San Francisco. The society now had over fifty Auxiliary Brothers; they needed a house and training center. The Maryknoll Sisters outnumbered the priests and Brothers combined, and they were growing fast. They also needed a place of their own. Across the road from Maryknoll was property available to the Sisters; although they were independent of the society, Walsh guided them through the labyrinthine legal complexities and the ordeals of building.

He was a stickler on buildings. His brother Timothy designed those of the society, but Walsh did not hesitate to make changes in the architect's plans, inside or out. He believed that the decoration of a house could affect the mood of people who lived there. Once he went to the Vénard to iron out some financial and administrative difficulties and, while there, was discovered one afternoon up on a chair rearranging pictures. He insisted on seeing the blueprints for buildings to be constructed in the missions and often made changes that not only cut down expense but improved the design and practicality. He wanted the China constructions to reflect the Oriental style, which might always appear well on paper but sometimes resulted in a structure that looked like a hybrid of a pagoda and a bungalow. It was not unusual of him, months—even years—after visiting a mission rectory, to write and suggest painting a room a different color or knocking down a wall to provide more space. Quite possibly he did these things to stir his men to write him about more than their routine life, for if it became routine to them they would leave out things that might be important to others. He wanted to know about them. When Byrne went through another of his illnesses, Walsh wrote him: "You joke so much that I worry how you really are."

The years made him America's Grand Old Man of the missions, but he was not carried away by it. There was nothing chauvinistic about him. *The Field Afar,* which he still edited and wrote, continued to carry stories about other mission societies; he was pleased that Americans were joining them and going abroad for them. Also, the country was now donating over two million dollars a year to the Society for the Propagation of the Faith, and he was proud of this. At mission conferences he was the star attraction; he knew how to play the role graciously but he never overplayed it. On the contrary, he wrote his priests:

No one of us stands alone. We are interdependent, and the success of Maryknoll missions is measured by the perfection of each individual member. We are thought to be generous—more so even than the average priest in the homeland—and it can be presumed that no Maryknoller entered on what he considered his lifework who was not actuated by a fine spirit of generosity. But with the passing of time the soul of a priest experiences change, for better or for worse, and generous hearts, even those of missioners, can contract. To be safe, we must cultivate detachment because it is the sure way to real love for God. If we grow attached to anything created, to our own comfort, to time-wasting and useless recreation, to natural occupations, to food, to drink, to money or to social pleasures, we shall find ourselves drawing away from God and His consolations. The grace of God is surely at our hand in abundant measure because thousands are praying and making sacrifices for us. May we each and all—above all, myself—prove praiseworthy.

In a New Year's letter he wrote:

My prayer for you is the prayer that I will ask of you for myself, that during this year I may strive to know myself better, more as God knows me, that I may note the failings in myself and what is best in others, that as a consequence I may think less about myself and more about God and others, keeping close to all with whom I am associated in His glorious work.

His personal adherence to these ideas grew clearer over the years. He seemed to try less to amuse and more to serve. Strangers who met him could never be certain what he thought of them but they were sure he had listened to them. His attentive eyes seemed to take hold of a visitor and one suspected that he would not flinch if a bomb exploded under him, but when the business was done his averted eyes had the finality of a shut door. When visitors would not leave, he took out a large pocket watch and wound it with consuming concern. Actually the watch was broken, but in this instance it always worked.

This frugality with his time gave him more time for more things. When *The Commonweal,* a Catholic weekly, was about to fail, he campaigned for it in his own publications and in letters to Catholic groups. He was an active patron of the St. Paul's Guild for converts; he worked regularly with *Liturgical Arts Magazine.* Among his voluminous correspondence were frequent letters to the families of Maryknollers, usually in his own hand-writing, sending on bits of news the missionaries had sent him, and when he traveled he made a point of calling on the families however heavy his schedule: the families had given their sons to him; he preferred to feel that the entire family had joined Maryknoll and warranted his time as much as the priests.

In 1926 he made another trip to the Orient. In 1928 he went to Rome with Father James Keller, a Maryknoller who later founded *The Christophers.* Already in Rome as superior of the Maryknoll house for students attending the Gregorian University for higher studies was Father John Considine, who also founded the *Fides News Service* by which the Vatican provided background material to the world press on mission affairs in the news. Years later when Pope John XXIII asked the American hierarchy to co-operate in the development of the Church in Latin America, Considine was put in charge of the enormous project.

The purpose of the Rome trip was to discuss with the Sacred Congregation of Propaganda the final approval of the Maryknoll rules and constitutions. Ford came in from Kaying to evaluate them from the point of view of men in the field. In early December, the Vatican advised the calling of the general chapter; after the constitutions were approved by the chapter they would be approved by Rome. On December 4, Walsh and the other Maryknollers in Rome were received by Pope Pius XI.

The Pope, who had seen *The Field Afar,* told Walsh, "We are acquainted with your society and with what it is doing. It has expanded well and wherever it is it is working hard. For your society, then, all the blessings that you desire. We are following it with great interest and with joy."

He then said to the students, "And for your students a very special blessing because when we speak of novices and students we are speaking of the future. Really they *are* the future. We say *few* and *good;* not quantity, but quality, *n'cest-ce pas?*"

To Walsh he added in a low voice, "And then we also say *good* and *many.* For you may it be so."

The chapter approved the constitutions the following August and a year later final approval came from Rome. In sending the news to the missionaries, Walsh said:

May each of us accept these constitutions, their interpretations and any insistence on their observance as God's will in our regard and as a blessed means to a strong union of hearts, minds and wills. All for Christ! I wish here and now to include my own act of thanksgiving and acknowledgment to you and to all Maryknollers who have made possible this spiritual development of our society during this period of test—and have succeeded in drawing from our superiors this supreme manifestation of their confidence and good will.

The assistants in addition to Byrne were Raymond A. Lane, of Lawrence, Massachusetts, James M. Drought, of New York City, and William F. O'Shea, of Hoboken. All had experience in the missions; O'Shea had been one of the six original students of Maryknoll. They were more than mere advisors. Final decisions still rested with Walsh, but the four assistants had their own authority. They took over the directorship of seminaries and the training of students, budgetary affairs, the supply and maintenance of missions, promotion, and publications. Walsh's special values were his experience and the wisdom that evolved from them. The assistants consulted with him daily, but they knew his best service to the society in future years would be on the outside, making Maryknoll better known by his presence at conferences and rallies, so they relieved him of as much paper work as possible.

In 1931 he made his last trip to the Orient. The Depression that had followed the stock market crash and permeated every corner of the world caught several of the mission areas in serious financial straits. Walsh went to China to devise methods of paring costs without diminishing service. It was odd, he commented, how constructive experience remained fruitful: as a boy, after the death of his mother, he had run the family household during his father's period of financial setback; here he was, over fifty years later, faced with the same problem, but in a score of households in a foreign land.

He worried less about the hardships of poverty than he did about the change of values the Depression had stirred in people: their crass determination to recover what they had lost for the sake of possession itself. In *The Field Afar* he wrote:

I am well aware that we have a growing number of pagans in this country and that if they can be won from a worship of material things to serve the living God a mighty task will have been accomplished. The Christian has a duty towards these people, but not the exclusion of those who have never had the advantage of contact with the Spirit of Christ.

For the Awakened Orient this is the hour when ageless culture is disintegrating and nations suffering the pangs of rebirth need all that we can give to counteract the deadening poison of Sovietism and the flippant sophistication of the Western World.

Perhaps God expects more from us—more real patience, purer motives, more charity, greater forbearance, more thoughtfulness, less striving after natural satisfaction, less complaint about our conditions, less insistence on material means. Our riches are the riches of faith. These, with the love of God, a spirit of sacrifice and earnest prayer, will attract souls though we lack in material help what we think is needful. We can only do our best with what we have and leave the results to God.

To all I reiterate—more strongly than ever—that God's arm is not shortened. So far, He has made it possible for the society to provide every missioner with food and shelter, travel and other necessary expenses, and to secure occasional substantial help for the missions besides sustaining in large measure the several student bodies in this country and meeting heavy interest obligations.

We are often asked how we can do it, and the only answer is found in God's Providence, responding to man's activity.

The key word was activity. When he returned from China late in 1931 he began to show his age and years of heavy responsibility. His assistants took on more of his duties until they reached the point where he asked them if they weren't in too big a hurry to get rid of him. But he understood their motives and was touched by them. Throughout 1932 he spent more and more time away from Maryknoll to work for Maryknoll elsewhere. He found travel restful: it freed him of his tight office schedule, it allowed him to nap on trains, it provided the refreshment of change.

In April of 1933 he was at Bedford, enjoying himself at his favorite pastime of building: a barn on the farm he had purchased for the novitiate was being remade into a dormitory. While there, he received a telephone call from Father James F. Kelly, an old friend who had accompanied him to China in 1921 and who was now pastor of Our Lady of Lourdes parish at Jamaica Plain, near Boston. Kelly explained that his parish was greatly in need of a new church and the moment had arrived when a decision must be made one way or the other; would Walsh come to Jamaica Plain to discuss it. Walsh was there the next day, April 24.

"You know what financial shape the country is in," Kelly said. "I desperately need a new church, but I'm afraid to start on it."

"I know exactly how you feel," Walsh said. "My motto in these cases has always been: go slowly but go forward. You must trust to God, James. You're building the church for Him, not for yourself, and He knows. If God wants this church, He will provide the means to pay for it; if He doesn't, you'll find out soon enough."

"Then you suggest I go ahead with it?" Kelly asked.

"Definitely," said Walsh. "You can't discover God's will by doing nothing. Get started, then God will do the rest."

Kelly looked away. "I feel a little foolish, asking you to come 'way over here to discuss this when I guess I already knew what you would say."

"I have to say it to myself every day," Walsh said. "If I didn't believe in God's Providence with all my heart I'd be too scared to get out of bed in the morning."

Kelly smiled, his curates beamed; they would go ahead.

They had dinner, then went into the living room for cigars and coffee, all determined not to discuss money, not to mention their worries, but to relax in the comfort that God would provide. They were just getting comfortable when the doorbell rang and Pat Byrne was ushered in.

Walsh was surprised to see him, then distressed. "Father Pat, what are you doing up here? I thought you were at Maryknoll."

"I came to see you, Father General," Byrne said.

Walsh knew only the greatest urgency would have prompted the two-hundred-mile trip. He grew serious. "What's wrong, Pat?"

The doorbell rang again. Raymond Lane came in with Drought and O'Shea. "Hello, Father General," Lane said soberly.

"You, too?" Walsh said. "What's gone wrong?

Byrne glanced at Kelly and the curates, then at Walsh, indicating whatever had gone wrong was a family matter and ought not be discussed in the presence of outsiders.

Walsh asked, "Pat, did somebody die? What burned down? Is there a war in China?"

All four assistants were there. Only a tragic crisis could have brought them. "I can't stand this another minute," Walsh almost shouted. "Pat, what's going on? Is something wrong?"

"Well, yes, Father General, I'm afraid something is very much wrong." Byrne took a cable out of his pocket. "It appears we are making a mistake, a very grave mistake. We have received advice from Rome, and we realize now the mistake is—" he paused and tears seemed to fill his eyes—"that we've been standing here calling you Father General when we should be saying Bishop General."

Walsh's arched brows plunged into a frown. "What are you talking about?"

"This arrived from Rome this morning," Byrne said, handing the cable to Walsh. "You've been appointed a bishop."

The fact sank in and Walsh fell back in his chair. "You fools!" he said. They all rushed forward to congratulate him.

When calm came and they had opened a bottle of wine, Walsh said, "A bishop. I have never cared for these things. I have never had any particular taste for rings or miters or crosiers or purple robes or flowing vestments. I honor these things in others and I know that they hold a sacred place in the hierarchy and in the work of the Church, but I have never cared for them for myself because I always feared they would interfere with and hamper my lifework. But of course I am getting to be an old man now and perhaps it won't matter."

"It will matter for Maryknoll," Byrne said.

"Of course," said Walsh, "and it is for Maryknoll that this has been done."

Because of his position in mission work, it was decided that he would be consecrated in Rome in the chapel of the Sacred College of Propaganda. Cardinal Fumasoni-Biondi, head of the college, would consecrate him; as coconsecrators, Walsh chose Archbishop John T. McNicholas of Cincinnati, an old friend of Maryknoll, and Bishop Dunn of New York, the man Walsh had brought into mission work by suggesting him to the the first director of the Society for the Propagation of the Faith in New York. Walsh asked that the consecration take place on June 29, the twenty-second anniversary of the day in Rome when he and Price had received first approval to start Maryknoll.

One of the people who traveled to Rome to witness the ceremony was Father Bruneau, the Sulpician whom Walsh had known at the Boston seminary and who was one of the cofounders of *The Field Afar.* Now an old man living in retirement in a French monastery, Bruneau took Walsh aside after the ceremony

and said, "Well, my friend, I remember the day when you were
looking for a job."

When he returned to Maryknoll a month later the seminary
band greeted him on the front steps with a jazzy and ragged rendi-
tion of the only song it knew: "Chinatown, My Chinatown."

XVII

Now there were jobs for everyone.

At the time Pat Byrne was setting up Maryknoll's first mission in Korea, Raymond Lane was occupied with the same work just to the west in Manchuria. Ordained in 1920, Lane had been assigned to Maryknoll for office work. This was a disappointment, but Lane knew somebody had to remain at home to do the paper work and he resigned himself to it. The years passed quickly.

One morning in the late summer of 1923, Lane encountered Walsh as they both were on their way to their offices. Walsh took Lane by the arm and asked, "Father Raymond, how would you like to go to China?"

Lane spun around. "Are you serious?"

"Yes. Are you?"

"You know how badly I want to go."

"Very well. You shall." They resumed walking, Lane's feet somewhat off the ground. Walsh said, "I want you to go to Hong Kong and take over our business office there. It isn't exactly missionary work, but I think you'll enjoy it more than what you're doing now. Learn Cantonese, help out at the St. Louis Industrial School; with luck, one of these days we'll send you into the bush."

Lane left Maryknoll in October. He and Father John Morris,

of Fall River, Massachusetts, were the only members of the 1923 departure group. Morris was on his way to Korea to join Byrne.

It was a rainy night that dampened spirits as well. When the ceremony was over and the priests lined up for a farewell hand-shake, Lane wondered if he would get through it without break-ing down. Walsh approached and put both hands on Lane's shoulders. "Good-by, old man," he said softly.

Lane felt old indeed. "Good-by," he managed. "Good-by."

Lane's aging mother was waiting for her farewell in an adjoin-ing room. She was losing her sight, and when she heard him enter she brushed against chairs as she went to him. This was too much for Lane. He burst into tears and was unable to speak.

"Don't worry about me, son," the woman said. "I'll be all right."

Lane was sure of it, he was sure he would be all right, he was sure everyone would be all right, but the farewell was more than he could bear and he hurried outside, letting the rain mingle with the tears on his face. Every young man departing from Mary-knoll experienced the same pain of love. Most of them were lucky enough to have a moment alone when the tears came, and come they did. They could be away from their families through all their study years; with their *Propositum,* they put Maryknoll ahead of their families, but when the time came to say good-by to family and old friends and Maryknoll itself, even though good-by meant the beginning of fulfillment of a long dream, there were always the tears, always the pain. And yet it was a good thing: it showed that the young men had hearts. Where they were going they would need them.

Lane was in Hong Kong two years, busy mostly as procurator for the China missions. Kongmoon, Kaying, and Wuchow kept bank accounts in Hong Kong; Lane used them to buy supplies and ship them on. Supplies also came regularly from Maryknoll— medicines, canned food, clothes, books, school equipment. Lane forwarded them wherever he felt they were needed. In addition to his daily studies of Cantonese and Portuguese, he taught at the industrial school, preached on Sundays at Holy Rosary Church, and made a trip each week to the Maryknoll Sisters convent at Kowloon on the mainland to give a spiritual conference.

His life was far from routine. Word came one day that two

Maryknollers on Sancian Island—Tom O'Melia and Otto Rauschenbach—had been kidnaped and were being held for ransom. Lane rushed to the U. S. Consulate in Hong Kong for help. There was a great deal of red tape, and days passed before the cruiser *Sacramento* was sent to Sancian with a rescue party. Meanwhile, the two priests escaped from their captors and made their way to the opposite end of the island. A Chinese gunboat heard the news flash, went to Sancian, and spotted the priests on the beach and rescued them before the American ship arrived.

On another occasion, a reactionary flare-up brought on a strike during which Chinese refused to work for foreigners. The situation was especially bad at Yeungkong, where the people grew belligerent and the missionaries were not safe on the streets. Again Lane asked for U. S. help to remove the missionaries by ship and again there was a delay. The British governor of Hong Kong offered his own launch, which set out for Yeungkong. Expecting it, the missionaries were on a junk in the harbor, but the launch skipper didn't know this and when he couldn't find them he headed back. Some days later an American ship arrived and took out the Maryknoll Sisters; the priests and Brothers decided to stay on until the tension faded, which it did several weeks later.

Lane loved to play baseball, and every Saturday afternoon he would go out to the park, change into a uniform, and get into a game. This scandalized French missionaries in the city who sent a complaint to Rome. Rome wrote to Maryknoll suggesting Lane seek some less public form of recreation and he was forced to give up the game.

In 1925, he received orders from Maryknoll to go to Manchuria, learn the language, and prepare to initiate Maryknoll's new mission there. The bishop in Manchuria was a Frenchman, and at the moment Lane entered his office for the first time the bishop had just finished reading in a French publication for missionaries in China a report about Lane's baseball activities. He greeted Lane with "And we will have none of this."

For a month, Lane was the only Maryknoller in Manchuria. He lived at the seminary, studying the language—Mandarin—and the people. Frequently he took trips with Bishop Bloise to gain practical experience. From time to time he was able to go over to Korea to visit other Maryknollers. The area assigned to Maryknoll adjoined Korea; it was a rugged, mountainous country, about the size of New York State, and it included the cities of Darien, Fushun, and Antung. In February, 1927, Father Joseph P. McCormack, of New York City, arrived, and he and Lane took over the territory. By fall, other Maryknollers were there and the work began.

For a long time all of China had been ruled from Manchuria, the origin of the Manchu dynasty. Gradually the Chinese absorbed the Manchurians, and the government moved south to Peking. Manchuria was rich in coal and iron ore. As China weakened, Russia and Japan fought for the important northern territory. In 1904, Japan took control; in 1932, Japan permitted a puppet government at Mukden and the region became known as Manchukuo. When the Maryknollers started there, several seething dangers existed. Adjacent to Russia, the area was a caldron of Communism. The presence of thousands of Japanese served further to remind the Manchurians that they were a dominated people. Outside of the cities the land was rough and lawless; the hills were full of Mongol bandits. Travel was difficult, in places impossible. There were four million people in the Maryknoll district, of whom some four thousand were Catholics: many of them lived in such remote corners of the country that they had not seen a priest in years.

Lane adopted Walsh's motto—go slowly but go forward. Aware of the conflicting tensions in the country, he realized that the whole thing might blow up under him any minute. Thus he felt his most important work would be to organize a native clergy as quickly as possible. Establishing his headquarters at Fushun, he immediately opened a seminary. Because of a school shortage, he had no trouble attracting students: he had twenty in a few days. The problem was housing them. The only space available for them was one room at the mission, twenty by twenty feet, and into it they all went, to sleep, to eat, and to study. When the first Maryknoll Sisters arrived, Lane asked them to take on the training of Chinese girls for the Sisterhood so that there would be someone ready to carry on their work in case the Americans were forced to leave. In two years, he had a dozen Maryknoll priests strategically assigned to cover the vast area; he said he could have used a hundred. Five Chinese priests, trained by the French, were working with him. One Auxiliary Brother had been sent to him, plus five Maryknoll Sisters; the Sisters had ten Chinese women in training for the religious life.

Lane felt that, given a bit more time, he could sink roots to a permanent depth. If for any reason his staff had to leave, they could take the seminarians and postulants along to a safer place, continuing their training toward the day when they could return. Then, in 1929, came the unexpected orders to report to Maryknoll for the general chapter. Like Pat Byrne in Korea, Lane did not expect to be away long and, again like Byrne, he was alarmed to find himself elected to the council of four assistants, obliged to remain in the United States. Three years later, however, Rome announced that the Fushun district was about to be made into a prefecture and asked Walsh to appoint a superior qualified to become its prefect-monsignor. It was a happy day for Lane when he was relieved of his position as second assistant of the society and reassigned to Manchuria.

"I feel I'm getting out of prison," he said. Actually he was going into one.

The man saddest to see Lane leave Maryknoll was Pat Byrne. Although Lane's departure indicated that it was possible for an assistant to be reassigned to the Orient, Byrne dared not hope that such an occasion would occur twice. Lane had also acted as superior of the seminary. Now Byrne took on the assignment. The students kept him busy; this plus his other duties occupied him enough so that he did not feel entirely useless. If affairs continued undisturbed he expected to remain at Maryknoll for the ten years of the present administration, until 1939. Then, with luck, he would not be elected to anything and he could go back to Korea.

His major concern was Walsh. The man was not looking well, he tired easily, there were times when he did not seem fully aware of what was going on around him. As subtly as he could, Byrne, as vicar-general, assumed more and more of Walsh's responsibilities and he urged Walsh to take a long vacation.

More amused than annoyed, Walsh said, "I am puzzled by the growing effort around here to get me away. Am I so feeble that none of you trust me in my job any more?"

"On the contrary," said Byrne, "we want you to go away so that when you come back you can be on the job longer."

Walsh grew serious. "I'll be going away soon enough; I'm long overdue." Somehow he managed to keep going. In June, 1934, he ordained Maryknoll priests for the first time, a special joy to him because now he had not only provided their training but by his spiritual heritage as a bishop he granted them their priesthood. There were eighteen of them; the ceremony was long and exhausting; Walsh could hardly stand at the finish.

Construction on the seminary was still going on and the noise was often too much for Walsh. He moved out of his quarters into an apartment in the Maryknoll Sisters mother house. It was only a hundred yards from his office, but frequently he was too tired to walk it and had to be driven. There were days when he remained in the apartment and conducted his business from there. He had long since stopped taking his meals with the seminary faculty and they were therefore surprised one July noon when he entered the refectory and took his accustomed place. He chatted amiably, as he always had, then he raised his voice to the familiar tone that indicated he had something to say.

"Monsignor Byrne," he said.

Byrne looked at him quizzically. On giving up the Korean prefecture he had also given up the title that went with it and was now addressed as Father. "Yes, Excellency?"

"I have something to say to you." Walsh paused and looked out the window. "The last time I had a similar message for you we were in the midst of a blizzard, for which you claimed innocence. I don't know whether or not you are innocent of this July heat, but I won't embarrass you by asking. There is, however, no reason why you should remain here to suffer with the rest of us. You are going back to the missions."

Jolted, Byrne got up from his chair and made his way quickly to Walsh. "I'm going back to Korea?"

"No. To Japan."

"Japan?"

"Yes, unless you think you're too old a dog to learn new tricks."

Catholicism was first brought to Japan by Saint Francis Xavier in 1549, at a time when Japan, like the rest of the Orient, refused to permit foreigners into the country. Nevertheless, Xavier managed to stay in Japan almost three years and in that time he baptized over five thousand people. Other missionaries followed him; within fifty years there were three hundred thousand Japanese Catholics. Once again, Christianity was considered a foreign influence by those who ruled, and persecutions broke out, some of the worst persecutions in history. In one year in Nagasaki, thirty-seven thousand Christians were put to death. Mass crucifixions were common throughout the country. The rulers proclaimed that Christianity no longer existed in Japan; it seemed true. Then, in 1854, American battleships steamed into Yedo Bay, and with that Japan opened her doors to the world.

It was in 1865 that Father Petitjean, a famous French missionary, arrived as chaplain to the French embassy. He built a small church on a hill where twenty-six men had been crucified over two hundred years before. One day he noticed a group of people standing outside, looking up at the cross atop the church, and he went to them.

A man asked warily, "Have you a shrine here to the Lady Virgin?"

Petitjean said yes and led them inside and showed them the statue of Mary.

The man asked, "Was it the Teacher-King who sent you here?"

"I have been sent here by the Holy Father in Rome," Petitjean explained.

Someone asked, "Have you any children?"

"I am a spiritual father," said Petitjean. "A priest of my religion is forbidden to have children."

Smiles passed among the group. A woman said, "The hearts of all here are the same as yours. At Urakami nearly all have hearts like yours."

It was incredible. Two hundred years had gone by without a single priest in all of Japan and yet the faith was alive, kept alive by parents who had baptized their own children and passed on to them the precepts of the Church. After two hundred years, there were still some fifty thousand Catholics in the country.

But the troubles were not over. With a priest in the country, interest in the religion was revived, but the government announced that Christianity was illegal and that anyone practicing it would be punished. In the next six years, two thousand more Japanese died because they were Catholics. At last, in 1873, freedom of religion was officially granted. But this did not bring on any rush into the Church. Fifty years later, when Maryknollers in China were winning sixty conversions a year per priest, the missionaries in Japan were lucky to get four.

The area consigned to Maryknoll centered around the inland city of Kyoto, some hundred and fifty miles south of Tokyo. Kyoto had been the capital of Japan for a long time; it was still the nucleus of Japanese culture. Painters, sculptors, writers lived there; the city had seven universities; the finest artisans of the country resided in the suburbs. Such an atmosphere should have been conducive to the intellectualism which made men ask questions and accept truths. There should have been many converts. However, the reverse was the case. There were over two thousand Buddhist and Shinto temples in the city. At the lone Catholic church there were two priests, both Japanese, one so old he could no longer work. The younger priest, Paul Furuya, was busy enough with fifteen hundred Catholics he had and had no time to proselytize. Also, there was a broad spirit of materialism in the city. It was almost impossible to convince anybody to change his life merely for spiritual benefits.

Byrne was determined to try. He studied the language, he made himself known at the universities and cultural organizations, he visited hospitals and the rural areas where the poor lived, he requested Walsh to send on more men. Just when he was ready to initiate various programs that would attract further attention he ran into an unexpected problem. Ecclesiastically, Kyoto was under the archbishop of Tokyo, and despite orders from Rome the archbishop was not prepared to turn the district to Maryknoll. Until this was done, Byrne could not really get going. At one point, the archbishop indicated a willingness to let Maryknoll have the rural areas surrounding the city. Not only was this contrary to Rome instructions, but experience had taught the Maryknollers that Catholic action was most quickly effective among the heavy population of a city and would spread on its own from there to country cousins. The confinement to the country would exceedingly hamper the Maryknoll effort. The situation was unpleasant and uncomfortable, and it required two years to resolve, finally in favor of Maryknoll.

On the day in 1937 when Kyoto was erected as a Maryknoll prefecture and Byrne once again became a monsignor, an old woman came to the church. She said she had tuberculosis, that she was poor and could not afford a doctor or hospital. "Will you keep me alive?" she asked.

"We'll do the best we can," said Byrne. "That's why we're here."

The news got out. Other tuberculosis patients arrived. It was in this way that the mission got started.

From the start Byrne felt an apprehension that also existed in Manchuria, Korea, China, the Philippines—wherever the Maryknollers were abroad. At home, comfortable between oceans, there was less of the fear because there was less knowldge of the threats. But the missionaries overseas were sure of it: there was going to be a war. It was only a matter of time.

XVIII

IN THE cemetery behind the Maryknoll seminary was a vault which, in the process of settling, had cracked, and whenever it rained the walls were purple with moisture and there were puddles on the floor. On the occasions Walsh visited it—to bury another man, to pray for the dead or on All Souls' Day—he would regard the damage wryly and observe, "I'm going to get wet when they put me in here."

And now the time had come.

In the autumn of 1934 doctors detected spots on his lungs. He had announced that he was going to China that winter, but the doctors said that if he was going anywhere it was to the Bavaria mountains for rest and treatment.

"That is idiotic," he said. "If I can't go to China I am going to stay here."

"If you stay here you will try to work," the doctors said. "You are going to Bavaria."

He went to Bavaria, but he did not rest. Sitting there staring at mountain tops struck him as a great waste of time. If he had to be in Europe, he might as well see something. He went to Oberammergau and saw the actors of the famous Passion play. He went to Konnersreuth and met Therese Neumann; he said Mass in her parish church and gave her Holy Communion and came away convinced of her sanctity. He went to Lisieux and visited the tomb of St. Therese of the Child Jesus, the holy Carmelite, and met her sister Pauline, also a Carmelite. He went to Nevers and prayed at the tomb of Bernadette; Price's heart reposed nearby. He considered going to Rome, but it was November, Christmas was coming: he wanted to go home.

From Maryknoll he wrote his sister: "I am continuing the 'loaf' treatment, leading something of a dog's life and being coddled as never before. If I don't come out of this a lazy man, I shall be surprised. Progress there is, though slow enough for one of my temperament. However, I am thankful for much."

He pontificated at the Christmas Mass at Maryknoll, then left immediately for Florida on orders for further rest. But Florida could not calm him any more than Bavaria. He would remain in bed a few days, expecting rest to work like some wonder drug, but when nothing seemed to happen he would get up and insisted on going somewhere. Toward the end of February, he started back to New York, but at Jacksonville he suffered a severe attack of coughing and weakness and had to be taken off the train for hospitalization.

A month later he reached Raleigh, where he spent a fortnight visiting the places Price had spoken about so often. He felt much better, which he attributed to North Carolina and to Price, and when he got back to Maryknoll he said he was fit for work. The refusal of others to let him work annoyed him. "You can't expect me to wither my way to the grave," he argued, but he was doomed to that.

Sixteen new Maryknollers were to be ordained at Maryknoll in June; Walsh would not let anybody talk him out of ordaining them himself. On his return he received a letter that brought tears to his eyes. It was from Ford. The Kaying prefecture had been elected to a vicariate and he had been named its bishop. "With your permission," Ford wrote, "I would like to come home to Maryknoll and be consecrated by you." He knew, he said, that it would be expensive and take time, but, he pointed out, he had been Walsh's first student at Maryknoll, he had been trained for the priesthood by Walsh, and now that he was about to become a bishop he wanted to receive the episcopal heritage from Walsh's hands.

Walsh cabled him: "COME HOME."

The Maryknoll chapel used by the students was more of an auditorium—inadequate for a consecration, so the church of the Sisters across the road was used. The ceremony took place on September 21. The coconsecrators were Bishop (later Archbishop) Thomas E. Molloy of Brooklyn and Bishop Stephen J. Donahue, Auxiliary Bishop of New York, who had been a classmate of Ford's. Molloy had been a curate at Ford's parish in his youth and had encouraged him toward the priesthood. Standing at the sacristy door was Walsh's physician, ready to step to his aid if the three-hour ceremony proved too much for him. He went through it without a pause.

It was his last public ceremony. After it, he did not leave his apartment in the convent until rooms were ready for him at the seminary on December 3. On December 5 he celebrated Mass in the chapel; it was his last Mass. By Christmas he did not have enough strength to read his breviary, but his rosary was always in his hand. On March 1, two Auxiliary Brothers were ready to make their *Propositum;* Walsh insisted they do so in his presence in his room.

At the end of the month, Archbishop McNicholas came to visit him and when he left the sickroom he said to those in the corridor, "Do you know what's on his mind? He thinks you're all working too hard."

In the first days of April, Walsh knew the end was near. On Thursday of Holy Week he was anointed. Now both his lungs were badly infected and he could scarcely breathe. On Friday a Sister asked him how he felt, and he replied with a smile, "Oh, as well as anyone has a right to feel on Good Friday."

On Sunday it seemed certain that he could last no longer. Someone said to him, "Easter Sunday is a good time to die."

Walsh said, "The Feast of the Ascension is better." Ascension Thursday commemorated the ascension of Jesus into heaven; the feast was a month off.

He managed to live through Monday, but on Tuesday the fight was out of him. He received Communion early in the morning, hardly aware of what he was doing. At nine o'clock he lifted his arms into the air and exclaimed, "God!" Then he whispered, "Jesus, Mary, Joseph!" In the next hour he repeated this several times. At ten, the faculty priests were brought in to give him their blessings, then they went into the adjoining chapel to pray. At twenty-seven minutes past ten Walsh died.

In the drawer of his night table letters were found—one addressed to the Auxiliary Brothers, one to the Sisters, one to the students, one to the priests. The letter to the priests was typical.

Dear Priestly Sons in Christ [he wrote]. I make no distinction since we are all missioners. Whether our daily tasks are in the homeland or on the field, we are of one heart and one mind, pledged to the evangelization of the world, with special interest in the people entrusted to our care by Rome.

I write in the expectation of my own departure, this time, with God's grace, for the life that changes not. You have been my comfort, my pride, my joy. I am fully aware that while much credit has been given to me because of my position in the society, my work would have been a failure without the help you have so generously given me.

I have known my limitations, and you have borne with them. God certainly uses the weak for His divine purposes. But, after all, our work is His work, and you will make no mistake if you look to Him for guidance. All that He seeks from you is generosity and ready willingness to use the opportunities—or to meet the difficulties—which will inevitably present themselves.

I have often urged you to appreciate what is good in other societies than ours. Keep up this spirit, but watch closely that loyalty shall be a shining virtue in your life—loyalty to the society, to your superiors, to one another. That we may be one in Christ is my prayer.

Keep me in filial remembrance and know that, if God finds me worthy, I will be your helper until we meet merrily in heaven.

Affectionately in Christ,

✠ JAMES ANTHONY WALSH

Now it was necessary to elect a new superior general. There was a great deal of paper work to be done, the personal files of Walsh to examine, evaluate, and file, and the Maryknoll staff was busy at it for several weeks. Since most Maryknollers were in the Orient, it was decided that the society's second general chapter could best be held there rather than expect the missionaries to make the long journey to join the few in New York. The meeting was held in Hong Kong in July and the new superior was elected: young Jim Walsh.

When he heard the news, Walsh said, "You've got the right name but the wrong man."

He went back to Kongmoon to clear up his affairs and to prepare his office for the man who would succeed him. He wrote a detailed report of all that had happened and indicated his plans for the future; the new man would be free to change them any way he wished. Then he packed everything he had because he was not sure that he would ever see China again.

Because he was a bishop and now the head of his society it would have been proper for him to travel with attendants, but he said that wasn't necessary; he would be all right. Early in September he arrived at San Francisco and went to the Maryknoll house there to say hello. A telegram was sent to Maryknoll announcing that he was in the country. He left for New York. Nothing more was heard from him for a week.

Then, one day at noon when the students and the priests were in the chapel at their prayers, word spread quickly that Jim Walsh was in the house. There was a flurry of excitement. Several priests got up and went to look for him.

They found him in the apartment reserved for the superior general, the place where James Anthony Walsh had died. A private altar was there and he was at it, vested in black, saying a Requiem Mass for his predecessor at the altar where the man himself had celebrated Mass so often for twenty-five years.

One priest went forward and knelt on the altar step to be Walsh's acolyte. The others knelt nearby. They did not see Walsh's face until he turned around to give them the greeting of the Mass: *"Dominus vobiscum."*

They saw the tears on his cheeks. They responded together: *"Et cum spiritu tuo."*

In the autumn of that year the remains of Fred Price were brought back to Maryknoll from Hong Kong and placed on the hilltop next to those of James Anthony Walsh. After twenty-five years, the two men who had given America its place in the mission affairs of the Catholic Church were united again—in both worlds.

XIX

HARRY M. BUSH decided to become a Maryknoller one afternoon while reading *The Field Afar* during his days at Boston College High School. He entered the Vénard in 1925; in 1933 he was ordained and received his mission crucifix. He was sent to Ford at Kaying. If a man could handle himself in the Hakka dialect within a year he was considered outstanding; Bush managed to do so. Tall, lean, with smooth black hair and glasses, Bush was soft-spoken and a little shy: a gentle man.

Comfortable in the language, he was sent on brief assignments to stations near Kaying to get used to the people. In April of 1935 he was ready to go it alone. Up at the Shakchin station, Patrick Malone was about to go on leave; Ford assigned Bush to fill in for him. Bush took off for Shakchin determined to do a good job; on Malone's return maybe Ford would give him a place of his own.

He did very well at Shakchin. The people liked him, they trusted him on sight, they did what they could for his comfort in the rugged mountain town. Affiliated with Shakchin were several out-stations, some in villages thirty miles away. The only way to reach them was to walk. On the morning of April 30, Bush decided to visit the village of Vou Shak, about twenty miles away. With him went his houseboy, whom he called Friday, a fourteen-year-old student named Tsac Gou, and two of the Shakchin dogs. The first day, they made Lam Tsai Piang, a village fourteen miles out, where there were two Catholic families. They spent the night there. In the morning Bush said Mass. After lunch they were on their way.

They were in the mountains on narrow paths when suddenly three men sprang out of the brushwood and pressed rifles against Bush's chest. Immediately they bombarded him with questions: who are you? where are you from? where are you going? what is your country? who are these others? One of them reached for Bush's arm. He shook off the man, turned and ran back down the path, waiting to hear bullets follow him. He had gone about a hundred yards when four men leaped at him and aimed their rifles at his head.

He was trapped. He was sure the men were bandits, but Friday called out to him, "Father, don't be afraid. They are regular soldiers in search of bandits and have orders to stop everybody and question them."

But Friday was wrong. The bandits tied Bush's hands behind his back with a rough hemp rope, then looped it around his neck so that if he moved too much he would strangle himself. They tied Friday and Tsac Gou the same way. Then they were led through the mountains to a hide-out.

One of the dogs went along with them, but the second ran off and found his way back to Lam Tsai Piang. When the people saw the dog they expected Bush to come along shortly, but when he did not appear that night or the next morning they knew something had happened to him. They waited another day to be certain, then they sent a messenger to Vou Shak to see if Bush was there. He was not. By the time the messenger made the fifty-mile trip to Kaying to tell Ford that Bush was missing, a week had passed. Ford rushed to the Nationalist general in command of the district and asked for help to find Bush, he wired the United States vice-consul in Swatow that an American was missing in the mountains, and he cabled Maryknoll that Bush had disappeared and was presumably kidnaped. The general sent out a search party, the vice-consul notified the government that every co-operation would be expected, and at Maryknoll there was nothing to do but pray.

The bandits were unusually amiable. Apparently pleased with

having captured a rich American, they chatted with Bush about his travels and their travels as if they were all merely on another trip together.

"What is going to happen to us?" Bush asked the man holding the end of his rope.

"That is up to the chief," the man said.

The chief would say nothing. They hiked through the mountains for two hours until they reached the hide-out, then the chief went away. That night when he returned, Bush heard him speaking with one of the guards.

The guard asked, "How much will we get for him?"

"They ought to give us two or three hundred dollars," the chief said.

They? Who are they? Bush considered the price low if the bandits expected to demand the ransom themselves from Ford. He remembered talk he had heard of how people were being kidnaped and sold to the Communists who were cleverer at getting ransom. Were the Communists the "they"?

The chief looked in at Bush. Bush said, "I heard you talking. Are you selling us to the Reds?"

The chief said, "Yes."

At midnight the Communist agent arrived and after a short talk with the chief he led the gang and the captives across the mountains to a cave where the captives were put under guard for the night. Next morning, another man arrived, a well-dressed man evidently a Communist officer. He spoke to Bush.

"What is your name?"

"Harry Bush."

"You are American?"

"Yes."

'What are you doing in China?"

"I am a Catholic missionary."

"From where?"

"Shakchin."

"Your chief is at Kaying?"

"Yes."

"You know who we are, don't you?"

"You are Communists."

"You are right. Now think of some plan for your release."

"I have no plan," said Bush. "There is nothing I can do."

"You can write to your country," the man said, "to President Roosevelt. He will ransom you."

Bush said, "Suppose you went to America and were taken captive—would you write to Chiang Kai-shek?"

"Of course not. He doesn't know me."

"Well, neither does President Roosevelt know me," said Bush. The man went away.

In the afternoon they were given a meal of cold rice and cold green vegetables and toward evening they were taken out of the cave. The well-dressed man was still there.

"We are taking the man back where we found him," he said. "He is of no use to us."

"All right," said Bush. "Take the boy, too."

"No, we will keep him. He may be of some use somehow."

"A little boy that size? You don't need him."

"We will keep him. But get rid of your dog."

"I don't know if he will obey me. He isn't mine."

"Get rid of him."

The dog did not understand. When Bush told him to go away he thought Bush wanted to play. When Bush scolded, the dog looked puzzled. It was only when Bush kicked toward him that the dog ran off into the forests.

That night, with a guard holding each arm, Bush was led off into the mountains. Close behind came Tsac Gou with his own guards. They had walked about an hour when Bush heard a familiar whimper at his heels. It was the dog.

At daybreak they slid down a steep embankment into a camp of a hundred Communist soldiers. Most of them were still asleep. The well-dressed man ordered two of them to get up and give their bunks to Bush and the boy. In the late morning Bush was awakened by the smell of roasting meat. On the floor near the bunk he saw the hide of his dog; outside the door was the dog's skinned body on a spit. Later he was brought a bowl of hot rice and a plate of the meat but he refused the meat.

"What's the matter?" the soldier asked. "You're not hungry?"

"Today is Friday; I can't eat meat," Bush explained. "Besides, I liked that dog."

The days emptied into each other, a jumble of night hikes, of cold food, of caves, of lean-tos, of rain, of morning frosts, of hunger, of aching bones, of stiff muscles. One night four more prisoners were brought in—two old men, another who was the principal of a primary school, the other a young man who did not speak much and was very afraid. On another night a man who was an opium addict was added to the group; deprived of his drugs he went into withdrawal torments and there was nothing anybody could do for him. Later the wife of a rich merchant and her teen-age daughter raised the number of captives to nine.

How much time had passed? A week? Surely more than that. A month.

They had taken away all his things; he was not permitted his breviary or his rosary. They had taken away Tsac Gou's rosary too. Bush found a piece of soft wood and made eleven notches in it with his thumbnail—one for the Our Father, ten for Hail Marys —and he gave it to the boy as a prayer stick. "We must keep praying," Bush said. "We must keep praying." Every morning he recited as much of the Mass as he could from memory.

Somehow they would have to escape. He told Tsac Gou, "I don't know how we can do it or when, but when you see me take off you run too. Run until you find a river, then follow it downstream. That is important. Downstream. That will take you out of the mountains and you just keep running until you reach a village."

He had some note paper in his pith helmet and dropped bits of it along the path so that any possible rescuers could follow them, but the bandits caught him and beat him with a rifle.

He observed that after the bandits ate they always grew tired, so he decided the best time to try and escape was at such a moment. His chance came in the sixth week. After an afternoon meal one man was left to guard him and the boy. Bush watched the bandit become heavy-eyed and begin to nod. When he thought the bandit was asleep he got up quietly and moved toward the trees.

"Where are you going?"

Bush turned. The rifle was pointed at him. He made a gesture of washing his hands; the bandit understood. Bush stepped behind a tree. The bandit relaxed and soon seemed to be asleep.

Tsac Gou was watching carefully. Then Bush gave him the signal: now.

They ran. The ground was wet and the brushwood was thick. Running, slipping, tripping, Bush struggled downhill. A branch caught at his face and pulled off his glasses; he could not see a foot ahead. He heard the rifle shots at the hilltop. It was useless to run any further. He let himself roll downhill and hid prone in a gully. An hour passed and he thought he was safe. Then he felt a heavy foot upon his back.

"Here he is. I found him."

But they did not find Tsac Gou. At nightfall he was still missing. He had escaped.

After that, they did not leave Bush alone for a moment. The guard responsible for his escape was particularly rough on him. He was kicked, shoved, cursed. From the first night, shackles had been put on his ankles during sleep; now they were never removed. The sneakers he was wearing were in shreds; his feet bled as they walked.

A few days after the escape attempt, lookouts reported that government soldiers were in the area. The chief was worried. He would not let any of his men go down from the mountains to get food from farmers and they had nothing to eat for four days but soup made from sweet potato leaves. Each day the soldiers came nearer. At times Bush could look down and see them probing the valleys but he would not call out to them because he knew that then all the prisoners would be killed.

The bandits were edgy and afraid. By accident one morning the group was broken into two parts: Bush was with three other prisoners, the chief, and two bandits.

The chief said, "I'm going up the hill for a look around."

After he was gone awhile, one bandit—Sen Tsat by name—said to the other, "We must find the others. You go look for them; I will guard these." He waited until the other bandit was out of sight, then he said to Bush, "Father, what do you think, shall I shoot the chief and lead you out to the soldiers who are waiting not far away? The chief refuses to surrender, and another day here in hiding will probably mean starvation for all of us. It is seven lives or one. Shall I shoot him?"

"Well, Sen Tsat," said Bush, "as a Catholic priest I will not commission you to take another man's life, even though it may mean freedom for us."

Sen Tsat turned to the others. "What do you think? Shall I do it?"

"Yes," they said. "Do it."

He went up the hill in the direction the chief had gone and after a few moments a shot rang out. When he came back, he said, "All right. Follow me."

They all went down the mountain and across a valley to a place where the soldiers had set up camp. The surprised commanding officer asked many questions, then he ordered Sen Tsat to lead a contingent of soldiers back to the mountains to free the other prisoners and capture the bandits. A meal was prepared for Bush and the others. After it, the officer gave Bush some clean clothes, bandaged the infections on his feet, and gave him a horse to ride. It was evening when they reached the town of Vongpi. Father Charles Hilbert was there with a truckload of Catholics, and they all gathered around Bush and shook his hand, patted his back, and told him how glad they were to see him.

"Are you all right?" Hilbert asked.

"Yes," said Bush, relieved and with the repressed fear of seven weeks now sending tremors through him, "but I've got the darnedest feeling that I'm going to have a good cry."

"Go ahead," Hilbert said. "You've been through hell."

And yet there were glimpses of heaven:

Sister watched the litle girl come slowly across the convent garden. She was very tiny. Her dress was torn, dried mud was caked upon her bare feet and legs, malnutrition had caused most of her hair to fall out. She came forward slowly, as if she were prepared to be ordered out. Sister watched and waited.

At last there was just a little distance between them. The girl looked up a Sister with big black solemn eyes set in a thin pale face. "I am hungry," she said. "I am very hungry."

"Where are you from?" Sister asked.

"Off there." She nodded back to the mountains.

"Where do you live?"

"No place."

This was the worst of it: the children, the little girls, unwanted, thrown out by their families, little vagabonds who roamed the hills and the roads begging for something to eat. Scarcely a day passed without at least one of them wandering in, but this one was the littlest, the saddest. There was a certain wisdom in her face that came from suffering among people she knew would do nothing for her.

"Come," Sister said.

They went around to the kitchen where Sister Ellen Mary was, and Sister said, "There is a little girl outside who is hungry. Do you have anything for her?"

"I have no cooked rice," Sister Ellen Mary said, "and there is nothing hot. But I'll fix her a sandwich." She cut two slices from a loaf of bread that had been baked that morning and she put cold meat on it and lettuce and salt and pepper and she took it outside. When she saw the tiny creature she was so stricken that she stopped. Dear God! Then she went to the girl and said, "Here you are."

The girl had never seen a sandwich before and didn't know what it was. She accepted it cautiously, examined it a moment, then took a bite and gulped it down. She took another bite.

When Sister could resist the child no longer she knelt beside her and took her into her arms. The girl seemed unaware of the affection; she had had no experience by which to recognize it.

Sister asked, "Is it all right?"

The girl nodded without looking up.

If only she would smile. If only she could be brought out of her sadness. In a tone any ordinary child would have caught as a tease, Sister said, "But I am hungry too."

The girl remained bent over the sandwich.

"I am so hungry," Sister said. "I haven't eaten for so long."

The child stopped. She regarded the sandwich for a moment, then lifted it to Sister's mouth. Touched, Sister took a little bite, then drew away.

The girl moved the sandwich to her. "Eat it all," she said. "It hurts to be hungry."

XX

FEBRUARY 5, 1936, was a cold day at the Tunghua mission in Manchuria. Cold or hot, the work had to go on. Early that morning, Father John W. Comber, superior of the mission, looked in on Clarence Burns, his newly arrived assistant who was slowly recovering from a serious case of dystentery.

"How are you this morning?" Comber asked.

"Still a little weak"

"You'll be all right. We all have to go through it."

"It sure went through me."

Comber said, "I have to go to Fushun today to see Monsignor Lane; I should be back tomorrow. Think you can manage on your own?"

"Sure. I'm O.K."

Alone in the house, Burns decided to try his legs. He managed to reach the window and he looked out onto the compound. He saw Wu, the chief catechist, arriving and heading for the room in the school he used as his office. A few minutes later Chiu, one of the teachers, came through the mission gate, waved at Burns, then entered the school. Everything seemed to be in order. The children would be arriving soon and the day would begin.

The compound was white with snow, white roof tops stretched beyond the compound walls, on the mountains in the distance snow filled the long narrow gullies like streams of white lava. It all looked like a Christmas card, slightly soiled. The past Christmas had been Burns's first in China, his first away from his Toledo home. Considering this, he scratched his cheek appraisingly, and realized he needed a shave. It was to be his last shave for nine months.

At nine, he glanced out the window again and saw Chiu talking to a stranger. Wu came from the schoolhouse and joined them, then they all advanced toward the rectory. Burns went into the hall to meet them.

Wu said in English, "There is a sick call, Father. This man"—he indicated the stranger—"says a farmer is dying out in the country."

"I'll get my things," Burns said.

"Are you well enough, Father?"

"Well enough. I'll take the horsecart; I can ride comfortably in that."

"It is cold, Father."

"I'll dress for it."

"Father, you will not go alone?"

Burns looked at Chiu. "Can you come?"

"Yes, Father."

Wu said, "I will go, too."

"We'll manage, Wu."

"You must be careful, Father. You never know what will happen on the roads. You and Chiu can ride in the wagon. I will go ahead on my bicycle to be sure the way is safe."

Burns smiled at Wu's concern. "It really isn't necessary, Wu. I'm sure Chiu and I can take care of ourselves."

"I think I should do it, Father." And he left the house.

The day was colder than Burns expected. He huddled inside his heavy coat and pulled it tighter. They were an hour from Tunghua on the quiet empty road with the mountains rising sharply on both sides. Chiu, aware that a silent priest was usually a praying priest, said nothing as he guided the horse between the drifts. They went on for another hour.

They passed a small farm. Four men were standing there. One of them called out and Chiu stopped the horse. They came nearer and one of them asked, "Are you the Father from Tunghua?"

Chiu answered, "He is."

The four men drew revolvers from under their coats.

Chiu said, "What is this?"

"You are our prisoners," the man said. All four climbed aboard the wagon. One shoved Chiu aside and took the reins. They rode on.

Chiu said in English, "They are bandits, Father. We're in trouble. Don't do anything to excite them because they may shoot us."

They went on for another mile. At a turn in the road Burns saw Wu in front of a farmhouse, standing beside his bicycle. He raised his hand to signal Wu out of the way, but Wu already saw the strangers in the wagon and realized what had happened. Instead of darting into the woods, he stepped into the road to stop the horse. At that instant, eight more bandits came from the farmhouse, brandishing revolvers and rifles. The wagon stopped and the men surrounded it.

Wu said, "Don't harm the Father. He is a sick man. Today he got up from his bed for the first time to come here because he thought he was needed."

"Shut up," the leader said.

"Take us," said Wu. "Take the old man and me, but leave the Father go."

The man ignored him. "Get off the wagon," he ordered Burns and Chiu.

Wu said, "Don't make the Father walk in the mountains. He will die."

The leader examined Burns with a glance, then told two men to bring a sled from the house. Burns was tied on it, and then they all took off into the hills. Up and up they went until nightfall, and it was then that they came upon a cabin. They all went inside. One of the men made a meal of rice, but none was given to the prisoners. The leader appointed three men to guard the prisoners and two to go outside as sentries; the remaining seven curled up on the dirt floor and fell asleep.

At nine, a sentry came in and woke the leader. "There are soldiers on the mountain," he said.

The leader said, "Put out the fire. We will go."

They went up to the top of the mountain and spent the night

in the heart of a raging blizzard. In the morning they went on to the farm of a cohort. On the way, Burns's sled broke through the ice on a river and he was drenched. By the time he reached the farm he had a high fever and pains in his chest. Worried, the bandits decided to remain at the farm until Burns was better; this required ten days. Wu nursed him; the elderly Chiu devoted himself to the only help he could provide: prayers.

During this period, Burns perceived from conversation he overheard that the bandits with him were part of a larger gang and that eventually he would be turned over to a higher echelon. Two teen-age boys who had been kidnaped and were now being trained to become bandits brought his meals; Burns questioned them about the organization but they said only that they were not permitted to talk to him.

Burns was just beginning to feel well when the leader came to him. "We will have to move on," he said. "The Japanese soldiers are close by again. We will send the old man back where we found him."

"Very well," Burns said. "Let Wu go, too."

"No, we will keep him in case you are sick again."

This time they traveled two days, resting only a few hours at night, until at last they reached another hide-out. A few hours later a gang of fifteen more bandits appeared, and the leader said to Burns, "I am Captain Chang. You are now in my charge. Our main camp is surrounded by soldiers and we cannot go there, but we will move on to another place."

They went deeper into the mountains to a cluster of dilapidated huts, and from the air of finality about the bandits Burns concluded they would remain there a while. March passed; April moved quickly. There was still snow on the ground and the nights were desperately cold.

Burns told Wu, "We must try to escape."

"It is dangerous, Father," said Wu.

"We must take the chance."

"The mountains are full of bandits. If we escape from these others will catch us."

"We must try, Wu," said Father. "Now, here is my plan. The men are relaxed; they will get careless. We must watch them

cautiously to learn their habits. When the time comes, we must
go separate ways, but work your way east to Korea."

"To Korea?"

"There are many missioners in Korea and they will help us."

"All right, if you say so, Father, but it will be dangerous."

"I know, Wu. Let's ask God to help us."

The chance came a week later. It was afternoon; an unexpected
sun gave the mountains a lazy tone. Most of the bandits were
napping; a few played cards. As was their custom, Burns and
Wu began to walk back and forth in front of their hut, stretching
their legs. The card players recognized the habit and gave it
small attention. On each round, Burns and Wu extended their
distance, moving nearer and nearer the trees.

Then, tensely, "Now, Wu, now!"

In a moment they were in the forest, Burns running north, Wu
running south. Burns prayed they would both escape, for whichever was caught would certainly be killed. He ran on, zigzagging
between the trees. Then he heard the cries and the shots. He knew
he was too weak to run far, but he had hoped for more time.
Now they were after him. Ahead he saw a hollow tree. He ducked
into it and crouched in a dark corner; if they did not see him he
could go on after they gave up the search. He closed his eyes and
listened.

Then, "Come out of there!"

Captain Chang was furious. "You idiot! You fool!" he shouted.
"I should kill you right now."

"Go ahead," said Burns. "Then my troubles will be over. But
as long as I'm alive I will try to get away."

"You will get away alive only when your ransom is paid."

"It will never be paid."

"That is your loss, not mine."

"I have nothing to lose."

Chang slapped Burns brutally across the face. "And you have
that to gain."

They broke camp immediately and moved out. They hiked all
night and all the next day, until even the bandits were complaining. But Chang would not pause. Night came again. Burns saw
lights ahead and hoped it was their destination because he knew
he would not last much longer.

It was a farm, bigger and better equipped than the last, and there was a barn where Burns and Wu were locked in a small room. Burns had no idea how long they were locked up before they were permitted out for the first time—under strict guard, nor had he any idea whether or not the priests at Tunghua or Monsignor Lane at Fushun had given him up for dead. They had not, but they privately doubted that they would ever see him. When Chiu had returned to Tunghua and told of the kidnaping, the priests informed the Japanese occupation commanders who immediately started a search, but the country was big and the winter storms were bad and the search was frequently interrupted.

May passed, then June, July, August. On some days the room in the barn was so hot that Burns and Wu had to strip down to bear it. The barn was crawling with lice, and what peace came with night was quickly destroyed by battle against the insects. Being allowed outside was a luxury, being allowed to wash was a salvation from madness.

Bandit gangs came and went all summer, and all of them wanted to see Burns. He was a prize captive; he was different from them. They examined his thick beard and his nose—for them enormous. They questioned him about himself and were astonished by what he told them about his country, his God, his Church, his priesthood, and its vows. The moments with them were like little sermons for Burns to give and he consoled himself that even his imprisonment allowed him to remain a missionary.

September passed.

One day Chang said, "We can go to the main camp now." He said no more. He had never forgiven Burns for the escape attempt. Even as Burns talked to the men and Chang stood a short way off chatting with other officers he gave no sign that he was aware of the priest.

They traveled through the mountains for a week, arriving at last at the camp. In the center was a huge barracks that housed over two hundred men. In nearby huts lived officers with their wives, and set aside was a big house for the commander. Burns never saw him. Burns stayed in the camp only a few days when, for security's sake, he and Wu were removed to a hut half a mile away and put under heavy guard.

Burns explained to Wu, "They're hiding us here in case the Japanese search the camp."

"How will the Japanese ever find the camp?" Wu asked in wonder.

But they did. About November 1 their campfires were spotted in the next valley. Search platoons fanned out, and one night they passed so close to the hut that Burns could have called out to them, had there not been revolvers at his forehead and Wu's.

It was necessary to move on. Chang chose twenty men to aid him in an attempt to go deeper into the mountains to elude the Japanese. For over two weeks they were on the run, fleeing with little rest, little sleep, little food. No place was safe. The soldiers seemed to be everywhere.

A bandit said, "Captain Chang, this is too dangerous. Why don't we get rid of those two?"

"I will give the orders," Chang said.

"I know, Captain, but the men are getting afraid and angry. But we have had these prisoners for almost a year. There is nothing to show for it, and now the soldiers are on our tails. We may all be killed for two prisoners who have been nothing but trouble."

Chang said, "I will decide what is to be done."

"Yes, Captain. I just wanted to tell you that the men will not stand much more. It would be simpler if we shot these two."

"I will decide."

"Yes, Captain."

The man was right. The past year had been difficult and fruitless. With the Japanese popping up all over the place it had been impossible to make ransom arrangements; rumors from Tunghua indicated that the ransom would not be paid anyway. Indeed the bandits were troubled. Unlike soldiers, they were not held together for any national purpose but purely for their share from robbings and kidnapings. For nine months there had been little to give them—all because of the risk involved in trying to collect ransom for a man who should now be either free or dead. Had it all been a mistake? Would it be wiser now to end the woes by killing Burns? It seemed so. But . . .

Chang went to the gully where Burns and Wu were being guarded. "We are in trouble," he said simply.

"I suspected as much," Burns said.

"This is a tight one; I'm not sure I can get my men out of it."

"I understand," said Burns, "and I realize I am the cause, but I don't know which of us is to blame."

"The men want me to kill you. Without you we can move faster and we would have a chance to escape."

Burns studied Chang, waiting.

"But," said Chang, "I cannot bring myself to do it. I know it will probably cost me my own head, but I cannot bring myself to kill you."

Burns said nothing.

"And I'm not sure why," Chang went on. "You have been brave; I respect bravery. Never once have you shown fear; I like that in a man. You know that even this minute I could kill you if I wanted to, but you don't seem to care. I can't understand where you acquired such courage—maybe from your religion. I've heard you discuss it with the men: I suspect you may even have infected some of them with it. I don't understand these things, but I know I can't change them by killing you. What puzzles me most is that you do not hate me. You should, you know, and if you did it would be easier for me to decide to kill you. And yet I somehow feel you don't."

"I don't," said Burns. "That, too, is part of my religion."

"Very well. You shall live. In a few minutes I will lead my men away. You remain. When we are gone, you can find your way to the soldiers."

"Thank you, Captain. The only way I can repay you is to pray for you."

Chang almost smiled. "That might be a waste. Pray for my country."

He called a command to his men and in a moment they moved out.

Wu was silent, then, "They are gone, Father. Let's go home."

They walked in the direction they thought the soldiers were but they could not find them. "That's odd," said Burns. "Five minutes ago the place was full of them."

"Maybe they have swept around to cut the bandits off," Wu suggested.

There was nothing to do but go onward, hoping they would not encounter another gang of bandits that might take them prisoner again. They walked on and on, through the first day, the second, the third. They had no idea where they were. They walked a fourth day and a fifth; still they saw no one. They had nothing to eat but grass and green leaves. It was on the seventh day that they made their way out of the mountains and began to cross a wide plateau. In the afternoon of the eighth day they came upon a hamlet of a dozen huts. The people took them in and gave them some food.

"How far is the nearest village?" Wu asked.

"Luitaokomien. It is five miles."

"Do they have a telegraph there or a radio?"

"No, but they have a truck. They can take you on from there."

"How far is Tunghua?"

"Two hundred miles, at least."

Burns said, "Do you feel strong enough to go on now, Wu?"

"Yes, Father. I want to go home."

They started out at a quick pace but after an hour their week of stress slowed them and by the time they reached Luitaokomien night had fallen and the village gates were closed. They banged on the gate and called to the guard, and in a little while they saw a man's face in the glow of a lantern atop the wall.

"Who's there?" the guard cried.

"It is the Father from Tunghua," Wu said.

"I can't open the gate," the guard said. "Come back in the morning."

"But bandits may come," Wu argued.

"I cannot open the gate."

"Get the commanding officer," Wu said. "The Father of Tunghua is here, the one who was kidnaped."

The face disappeared and about ten minutes later several men, all armed, were on the wall looking down. There was a sound of chains, then the gate was opened and more armed men came out. Some were carrying lanterns. They neared Burns and Wu.

One asked, "Which is the Father?"

"I am," said Burns.

A lantern was lifted and the man examined Burns's beard and his nose. Another man searched him and Wu. "They have no weapons," he said.

The first man seemed unsure of him, but he said, "All right. Take them inside. Put a guard on them for the night. And double the guard on the wall in case this is a trick."

They were taken inside and the gate was closed and locked. They were safe.

Four days later—on November 17—they were back at Tunghua, nine months and twelve days after their kidnaping. They both needed medical care: they had lost weight, suffered from malnutrition, they had infected sores on their legs and backs, and their teeth had gone bad. But they were safe. Safe.

In the Masses he said thereafter Burns kept his promise: he prayed for Manchuria. He also prayed for Captain Chang, confident that his prayers were not a waste.

XXI

AFRAID that kidnapings mibht be on the increase, Monsignor Lane sent a telegram to all missions: "STRONGLY URGE AVOID ALL UNNEC-ESSARY TRAVEL UNTIL CONDITIONS SAFER."

It was an essential caution and the Maryknollers accepted it glumly. Not being able to travel was a great sacrifice. A mission station itself was like a sun: no matter how cold-hearted against Christianity were the people who lived near its rays of charity and prayer, it sooner or later penetrated and then came the con-versions. Travel, on the other hand, provided the important occa-sion of reaching the isolated Catholic and offering him the sacra-ments which, because of distance and difficulty, he went too long without. Travel also meant contact with the remote pagan or Buddhist or Confucian, a chance to talk to him about the Church, to show him the Church at work and to win him, slowly, slowly, to Christ. A thriving mission surrounded by a forest of uncharted paganism was like a ship in a bottle: it was nice to have but it wasn't going anywhere. Travel in the hidden corners of the mis-sion field provided the Church with somewhere to go. It gave far roots to the oak the mission itself was. It also gave the missionaries a chance at adventure, at roughing it, at being on the road—a contagious aberration which all of them happily suffered because they felt it made them missionaries indeed.

From Lin Kiang, in the southeast corner of the Fushun prefecture near Korea, Father Jerry Donovan, of Pittsburgh, wrote Lane: "You should have seen how happy my mule was when I showed him your telegram."

This was a typical Donovan remark. From his first days at the Vénard he was known for his humor, his smile, his light disposition. He came from a truly Maryknoll family. While he was at the Vénard his brother Joseph was studying at Maryknoll; when Jerry went to Maryknoll his brother Tom entered the Vénard; all three became priests. His oldest sister was a nun.

Ordained in 1928, he was assigned to the Wuchow mission, but before his departure he developed a bad case of peritonitis and surgery so weakened him that he was not able to leave for the mission until 1931. He went to Manchuria. After learning the language and assisting at various stations, he was assigned to Lin Kiang to fill in for another priest who was going home for medical care.

Before Lane's telegram arrived, Donovan already had had his experiences with bandits—bandits of the more popular type who were well mannered and well meaning. When such bandits took a victim's shoes, they gave him a tattered pair of their own; if they took his coat they gave him a worn jacket of their own; if they took his money they gave him some trinket they had. Once when bandits stopped Donovan and led him into a gully to their chief, the man said, "Stupid! We don't stop this man: he is a Father."

Donovan therefore felt that Lane's orders were unnecessary for the Lin Kiang district but out of obedience he adhered to them. He spent the next months building up the mission itself, never going more than a few miles from the town and then only in the company of enough people to discourage bandit attacks.

In July, 1937, the priest Donovan had replaced returned. Lane called Donovan to Fushun to assist in the central administration of the prefecture and to be pastor of St. Patrick's parish at Hopei, directly across the river. Compared to Lin Kiang, he might now just as well have been in New York, but he adjusted quickly to what struck him as big-city life and was happy at it.

On October 5, he had plans to go over to Fushun with another priest but each time he was at the door, ready to leave, some other task arose that required his attention. He sent the other priest on alone, promising to follow when he could. Evening came. The church bell summoned the people for Benediction. Donovan decided to remain for the ceremony. He went into the sacristy, put a white surplice over his cassock, and entered the sanctuary.

At that moment a stranger arrived at the mission. He stood for a while in the compound, looking around, until he saw Lao Kao, the handyman. He stopped him and said, "I want some medicine."

"Come back in the morning and see Sister Maria," Lao Kao said, and went on his way.

But the stranger did not leave. He went to the chapel and entered the sacristy. Francis Liu, a seventeen-year-old seminarian, was there, preparing the incense for Benediction.

"Where is the Father?" the stranger asked.

"Out there," said Francis Liu, nodding toward the sanctuary.

"I want to see him. I have a note."

"He will be free in a few minutes."

"I cannot wait." The man wandered out into the sanctuary. The people saw him and murmured, disturbed. Donovan saw him, got up from his *prie-dieu*, genuflected, took the man by the elbow, and led him back to the sacristy.

"What do you want?" Donovan asked.

"You," the man said, and he took out a revolver.

Francis Liu cried, "No, no!"

"And you," said the man. "Come along."

"We'd better obey, Francis," Donovan said.

They preceded the man out of the church and across the compound. Outside they saw Lao Kao. The stranger handed him the note and said, "Give this to the foreign devils."

They went on. At the gate, the man ordered Francis to remove his surplice. The boy did, dropping it on the ground. He also dropped the censer and its live coals that he was still carrying. Beyond the gate were three more men. They tied the priest and the boy with ropes and started off to the mountains.

Lao Kao ran into the church and cried, "Father has been taken by bandits."

Sister Veronica Marie moved quickly. "Go after them," she said. "Get some men and go after them. I will notify the police."

The people rushed from the church. In the distance they could see the bandits, Donovan, and the boy entering the foothills. Donovan's white surplice was like a marker against the dark trees. A few of the mission men started to follow from a distance merely to keep an eye on the group in order to aid the police. Half an hour later a squad of twenty police entered the hills. Lane was notified; he in turn notified the American consul at Mukden, the Apostolic Delegate at Hsinking, the American Legation at Peking, and all mission stations. The Japanese commander at Fushun immediately organized a search.

The kidnaping had been so daring that nobody believed it would work. Surely the bandits would not get far. Optimism was so high that, the next morning, Lane wired Maryknoll: "BANDITS ENTERED FUSHUN HOPEI PARISH CHAPEL YESTERDAY AT SIX P.M. TOOK DONOVAN. GOOD PROSPECTS EARLY RELEASE."

The note given Lao Kao indicated that the authorities would hear from the bandits soon. The search went on, hopefully but cautiously so as not to panic the kidnapers.

Even Donovan was hopeful. He told Francis Liu: "Don't worry, son. Everything will be all right. We'll be out of this in a day or two. Just pray."

The bandits were overjoyed with their good catch. In the hills they joined with the rest of their gang, about twenty in all, led by Swang Shan, a well-known bandit chief. They were sure of the ransom, confident of happy days ahead for them all. Swang Shan told Donovan, "It is going to be fifty thousand dollars for you or we choke you and pitch your bones in a cave."

"Have it your way," Donovan said, "but you're wasting your time. My Church hasn't got money to throw away like that. So don't set your heart on it."

Swang Shan laughed. "Words are cheap the first night out. We will wait and see."

The bandits were young; Swang Shan himself was only in his twenties. They joked and teased among themselves constantly; they seemed too good-natured for violence; Donovan remained optimistic. When his shoes became battered by the rocks and mud, they gave him a pair of sneakers. His trousers were better made than theirs: they took his and gave him a cotton pair of their own, feeling that his cassock would keep him warm enough. However, they also gave him a jacket to wear on their night hikes. He did not like the stewed sorghum they ate, so they brought wheat flour for him to be made into dumplings. In such an atmosphere it was difficult to believe their fatal threats.

On the eleventh day they reached a lean-to high in the mountains. Swang Shan said, "It is time now for the boy to go back with instructions for the ransom." He gave Francis a note demanding fifty thousand dollars in small American currency, advising that instructions would be sent later for the payment. Two men guided the boy out of the mountains by a devious route so that he could not find his way back. A week later Francis was back at Fushun.

Strangely enough, the authorities at Fushun were never completely out of touch with the bandits. Soldiers and policemen stood by at strategic spots in the mountains, ready to attack once Donovan was freed. Actual contact was made by ex-bandits who volunteered for the assignment. Regular reports came back that Donovan was alive and in good health. There was no apparent reason to worry as long as negotiations could continue.

At one point Lane sent a note to Swang Shan, one copy in English, another in Manchurian. He said:

It is difficult for us to understand why you have taken him since he and our other priests have left their parents, their homes and their country to come to your country in order to do good and particularly to help the poor. You are asking fifty thousand dollars for the release of a man who has sacrificed his life for you and your people. You ask this money of a religious society which gives all it has to charity to help the poor, the old men and women, the orphans and the sick, to educate boys and girls. I cannot feel that you understand all this and yet demand money for the release of Father Donovan.

Four ex-bandits took the notes into the mountains, along with clothes and food for Donovan. Only one returned, and it was impossible to determine whether the others had been killed or persuaded to join the gang. On October 27, soldiers encountered seven members of the gang on a patrol and engaged in gunfire with them. One bandit was killed, and on him was found the English version of the note. Nobody could tell whether he had been killed on the way to having it translated by someone or whether the notes never reached Swang Shan.

There was world interest in Donovan. Each week the Vatican cabled for news; each week inquiries came from the U. S. State Department. All Manchurian Catholics were alerted for every clue. Many roamed the mountains looking for Donovan, and there were daily prayer sessions for his safety. Similar sessions were held at Protestant missions at Fushun, Darien, and Antung. The American press carried daily reports. Newsmen from Pittsburgh papers were at the Donovan house every day.

At the darkest moments there was still hope. In November a boy reported that while hunting he had stumbled into a bandit camp and that he had spoken to Donovan, who said he was well and sent a message that he should be released soon. In December villagers said the bandits had passed through with Donovan, that he looked all right and called to them to pray for him. In January soldiers said they saw the campfires of the bandits but did not attack for Donovan's sake. Lane put his faith in the experiences Burns had had during the nine months of captivity; the same could happen to Donovan.

Then, on the morning of February 11, 1938, came the dreaded news. John Davies, the American consul at Mukden, phoned Lane: "The Tunghua military report that the body of a foreigner was found on a mountain path near Huai-Jen and from the description we must conclude that it can be no other than Father Donovan. I will give you a further confirmation as soon as I have it."

The world's heart sank.

Two days later, Father Thomas N. Quirk, a Maryknoller, and Raymond Ludden, assistant consul at Mukden, flew to Huai-Jen to identify the body. A truck met them at the tiny airstrip and they were driven into town to a private home that had been turned into a mortuary. The town had put a guard of honor around the large Chinese coffin; the room was full of flowers. In the Chinese custom, a silk cloth covered the face and upper part of the body.

Quirk was trembling as he asked, "Please remove the cloth."

It was Donovan.

When he was found in the mountains there was a thick rope around his neck, with the stick used to twist it still in place. The rope had bitten an inch into his flesh and the mark still showed.

On his temple was a bad bruise: evidently a bandit had mercifully struck him unconscious to escape the pain of strangulation. He had been barefoot. From the condition of his legs and hands and face it was apparent that wolves and wild dogs and rats had been at him. He was cold and stiff; a doctor estimated he had been dead a week or ten days before he was found.

"It is Father Donovan," Quirk said, and then he dropped to his knees.

Coupled with the horror of the outcome was the astonishment that the bandits could have been so cruel. No one had expected it. There must have been an influence deeper than mere kidnaping, and a hint of it was discovered in the official report from the Japanese military on how the body was found:

> At six o'clock on the morning of February 10 the Nagashima unit of the Manchuria Pacification Force arrested a Communist bandit named Fu-sheng, who belonged to what was called the First Anti-Japanese Communist Army of the Northeast. Fu-sheng revealed to them that the dead body of Father Donovan had been abandoned in the neighborhood of Niu-Wei-Tou-Shan. In close cooperation with the Kurosaki unit of the Japanese garrison here at Huai-Jen, the Nagashima unit began an immediate search. By ten o'clock, at a point some two hundred yards from the base of the mountain, they discovered the remains of the murdered missioner.

So that was it. The bandits were joining up with the Communists. No one dared guess what this would portend.

Monsignor Lane made arrangements to bury Donovan in the Catholic cemetery at Fushun, but from Maryknoll came cabled instructions to send the body home. Donovan's younger brother Tom was then stationed in South China and had been unable to reach Fushun in time for the Requiem ceremonies that had been held there. However, he went to Japan and accepted his brother's body from the captain of the ship that brought the coffin from Manchuria and arranged for another ship to take it on to San Francisco. He was able to say his own Requiem Mass in the presence of his brother's remains, then went aboard the ocean liner to see that the coffin was put in a proper place.

It had all been a horrible thing, a vicious thing, and yet there was a certain glory in it. Undoubtedly, Jerry Donovan had been kidnaped not only because he was thought to be a rich American but also because he was known to be a Catholic priest. Now that the Communist influence in the affair was known, it was evident that Donovan would not have been released even had the ransom been paid. It was becoming increasingly clear that the Communists did not want Catholic priests free to work in the country. There was no other reason for the murder. Every caution had been taken to avoid harassment of the bandits. Friends in Manchuria and in America had offered to put up the ransom if the Church could not, and there was assurance that word of this had reached the bandits. Why the bandits had chosen to kill him when they did would forever remain a mystery, but those who knew Donovan during his lifetime and now knew the circumstances of his death were convinced of one thing: he had not been merely the victim of hunted kidnapers: he had been the victim of his priesthood. This made him a martyr. And that was the glory of his death.

Tom Donovan saw his brother's coffin safely aboard the ocean liner, then turned to leave. At the door of the cabin he looked back and said the words that were in every Maryknoller's heart:

"My, I envy you, Jerry!"

The
Fourth
Decade

XXII

JIM WALSH was certain there was nobody who envied him very much. As Maryknoll's second superior general, he was weighted with the responsibility of not only keeping the society going but nurturing its expansion as well. Having spent most of his priesthood in China, he had lost contact with all but his family and closest friends. Now he had to seek out new friends—friends with money, ones who were willing to part with it for the sake of the missions. He headed a Maryknoll family that, counting priests, Brothers, and students, numbered over five hundred, and they all looked to him for leadership, guidance, and support. Providing board and room for each one cost approximately a dollar a day, and in addition the Maryknoll constitution provided that each priest and Brother should receive a personal allowance of one dollar a day. The per diem expense of the physical maintenance of schools, seminaries, and various Maryknoll enterprises was even greater, but some of them, like farms and publications, not only earned their own way but brought in money as well. Financially, the missions were a debit. Priests and Brothers there had to be supported, so did catechists and teachers and doctors; educations and educational materials had to be provided, plus medical care, plus the care of orphans, the sick, and the aged. There was also the continual hunt for new vocations to be maintained. And with so many men involved, there were bound to be personality differences to be resolved. To be sure, Walsh had his council of four assistants: capable men though they were, by the nature of religious community life their authority was limited and they were at his desk every day with fresh problems. So it was no fun. But a man did not become a priest for fun, but to serve. And service meant doing anything that came along in the line of duty.

In November, 1940, Walsh's line of duty took an unexpected turn. Word had come from Rome that the Vatican had decided that all prefectures, vicariates, and dioceses in Japan held by foreigners were to be turned over to the Japanese clergy. There was no explanation. Maryknoll was affected because of Pat Byrne's work at Kyoto. A great deal of money had been put into it, a score of Maryknollers were there with Byrne as their monsignor, and now Rome had ordered that all jurisdiction be given to the Japanese. Aware of the growing world tension, Walsh wondered if the Vatican orders were given under Japanese government pressure. It occurred to him, on the other hand, that the Vatican might know more of what was about to happen in the world than most people and had taken the step as some kind of precaution. He knew he would never get the answer from Rome, so he decided to investigate in Japan. He went there with Father Drought.

They were in Tokyo only a few days when they perceived for themselves the consuming tension in the air. Already there was a war going on in Europe; a few weeks earlier, on September 27, Japan had signed a tripartite pact with Italy and Germany. The Japanese war against China, begun in 1937, had put most of the China coast in Japanese hands. The National Chinese government was being kept alive by supplies moved in from French and English holdings to the south, but now, under pressure from Tokyo, England had closed the Burma Road and France agreed to let Japan occupy northern Indo-China. The rope was being tightened around Free China's neck. Encouraged by this, the Fascists and militarists in Japan began to feel they had the power to defeat the only country that had not as yet bowed to them in the Far East: the United States. The Tokyo talk was that, comfortable with its growing strength, the Japanese were about to pressure America out of the Orient by diplomacy or by force.

At first, Walsh could not see the logic in the Vatican action.

The U. S. aid to the European Allies was mounting steadily and the experts predicted it was merely a matter of time before America entered the European war. As a world power, it was unrealistic to hope she could stay out of it. The Axis, however, was banking on the probability that America would delay getting into the fight long enough for them to level Allied power to the point where even the U. S. industrial might would not offer much help against defeat. Then, when America was in the European battle, Japan could engage her in the Pacific, thereby dividing her strength even further. It looked like a safe plan.

Rome foresaw that if the United States went to war against Japan it was inevitable that England, France, Belgium, and Holland would be forced into it also. These countries provided practically all of the missionaries in the Orient, and the missionaries were the prefects, vicar apostolics, and bishops in the Far East. Because of the war, such men would be taken prisoners, and that would mean that the Catholics in the affected Orient countries would be without a hierarchy. And the Church was hierarchal. To guard against the dangers of having an Asian church without a hierarchy, the Vatican wanted the foreign prelates to be replaced by Orientals as quickly as possible. Then, war or no war, the work of the Church could go on.

Walsh could see that now and he approved of it. He approved of it, further, because of his own convictions on the importance of not only a native clergy but a native hierarchy. The Church belonged to everybody; all races and nationalities deserved representation in its upper realms of authority, even at the top. Missionaries would continue to be needed, of course, but there was no reason they could not work as well under native ecclesiastical authority as under their own. With this in mind, Walsh considered it urgent to tour as many of the Maryknoll missions as possible to prepare for the eventuality and to plan accordingly.

He and Drought were in their Tokyo hotel room one day preparing to leave for Kyoto when there came a knock on the door that changed their lives.

Three Japanese men were there. One of them said, "Is it possible for us to see Bishop Walsh? It is very urgent."

"Of course," said Drought. "Come on in."

Walsh was across the room, reading his breviary. When he saw the three Japanese, he put aside his book, got up, and went to greet them.

The man who had spoken to Drought said, "I am General Muto Akira, director of the Central Bureau of Military Affairs."

"How do you do?" Walsh said. "You have met Father Drought."

Akira bowed, then introduced the men with him. He said, "I am here at the request of Yosuke Matsuoka, the Japanese Foreign Minister. He asks me to request a special favor from you."

"I'll do anything I can," Walsh said. They all took chairs.

Akira asked, "Bishop, do the people in your country realize the great risk of war that exists between your country and mine?"

"I'm sure millions of people are praying every day that it won't come to that," Walsh said.

"We must do more than pray," Akira said. "First let me assure you that the desire for war with America is not shared by all Japanese."

"I am happy to learn that," Walsh said. "I always felt it was true."

Akira nodded. "I can tell you that Mr. Matsuoka does not want war, nor does Prince Konoye, the Prime Minister. Nor do I, of course. But there are many who do—the Fascists and the militarists. And every day it is getting more difficult to restrain them."

Walsh knew he must be careful with his words. "I understand," he commented.

"Certainly," Akira said, "you can understand that relations between our two countries are not particularly happy at this time. Two years ago, as you know, our navy sunk that American gunboat *Panay* at Nanking. It was a serious incident, we all know. Frankly, I thought it would be the start of war between us. Instead, your Mr. Cordell Hull advised your industrialists to impose a 'moral embargo' upon us. That was almost as bad as war; we have suffered a great deal from it."

Walsh said nothing.

Akira went on. "Bishop, the Japanese people believe that a place of leadership in Asia is destined for us. Some feel we shall fill it through war; others hope it can be achieved peaceably by economic means. Prince Konoye hopes for the peaceful way. That is why he and Mr. Matsuoka have sent me to you."

Walsh raised his brows, waiting.

"Mr. Matsuoka," said Akira, "wants you to go to President Roosevelt and inform him that the Japanese government wishes to find some way to negotiate a peace treaty between our two governments."

"Me?" said Walsh.

Akira said, "You are well known in the Orient, Bishop. You have much influence and you are widely admired. You are also the head of an important American missionary society which surely is as much a factor in your country as it is in the Orient. You are also a religious man, a man of God; Mr. Matsuoka felt that you would want to do whatever you could for peace."

Walsh digested the suggestion, then said, "Of course I want to do whatever I can for peace, General, but I don't think you understand my position. It is true that I am the head of an important American mission society, but at the same time, politically speaking, I am just another ordinary American and the only time I have anything to say about what my government does is on Election Day. I don't know Mr. Roosevelt or Mr. Hull; I am not sure that I could even reach them; I am not sure they would consider me a reliable source of information. Furthermore, sir, I am a Catholic bishop, and in the past my Church has been accused far too often of meddling in politics. Whether this is true or not in other countries, in America we have stood steadfastly against any such conduct. General, I don't see what I can do."

"Then you won't help?"

"I can't help."

"Bishop, this is a matter of war or peace."

"I realize that, General, but as such it is a matter for the diplomats. I am a missionary; I want to help your people in every way I can, but I can do so only within the sphere of my position. If your government wants to negotiate with the United States, why don't you do so through the usual diplomatic channels?"

"That is not practicable at the present time," Akira said evasively.

"Then I don't know what else to suggest."

Akira stood up. "Thank you for your time, Bishop. Will you be in Japan long?"

"A few weeks."

"Perhaps I shall see you again." The General bowed and led his aides out of the room.

Walsh resumed his trip. At Kyoto he discussed the Vatican orders with Pat Byrne. Byrne knew about them and informed Walsh that Paul Furuya, the young priest who had been doing all the work at Kyoto alone before the Maryknollers arrived, had been appointed the city's first native bishop and that he had asked the Maryknollers to stay on and help him. The circumstances required Byrne once again to resign his role as monsignor, which made no difference to him at all: he was content to remain in Japan at his work. Walsh and Byrne discussed Akira's visit. They agreed that if war came the Americans would presumably be taken prisoners, but if the usual custom prevailed they would undoubtedly be repatriated on an exchange-of-prisoners basis. Meantime, everyone would continue at his assignment as normally as possible.

Three weeks later Walsh was back in Tokyo, preparing to go to Korea and Manchuria. To his surprise, General Akira returned.

"Mr. Matsuoka wants to see you," he said. "Are you free to come?"

"Why, yes," said Walsh warily.

"Good. I have a car waiting downstairs. Please come along as quickly and quietly as possible. We must not attract any attention."

"Can Father Drought accompany me?"

"I suppose that would be all right, since he already knows all about our previous meeting. But do hurry."

Twenty minutes later, Walsh and Drought, along with Akira and his aides and staff members of Prince Konoye and of Matsuoka, were seated with the Foreign Minister in his office.

"I appreciate that you came," Matsuoka began. "I would not have sent for you unless I considered this a matter of the most vital urgency."

Walsh said, "Sir, before you say anything more let me assure you that I have no authority whatsoever to speak or act for the government of the United States."

"I realize that, Bishop," said Matsuoka, "but you do have the authority to speak and act for peace."

"As I suggested to General Akira," said Walsh, "I feel this

matter should be handled through the American embassy here."

Matsuoka raised his hands in impatience. "It cannot be, Bishop, for a very simple reason. Your ambassador here thinks the secret code he uses for his messages to Washington is inviolable, but I can assure you that the code has been broken in every embassy in Tokyo, that every word that passes between your embassy and the State Department in Washington is decoded, recoded, and then sent on to every foreign capital in the world."

"Good heavens!" Walsh whispered.

"The Americans do not have a secret in Japan," Matsuoka said. He sank back in his chair. "Do you know General Hideki Tojo?"

"I know who he is—the cabinet member who heads the army."

"Yes. He also wants to be head of the government. He is the strongest advocate for war against America." Matsuoka leaned forward. "If he discovers one word of what is said in this room he will have all of us killed. I promise you that."

Walsh emitted a soft whistle.

Matsuoka asked, "Will you help us now?"

"Yes."

"Good."

"What do you want me to do?"

I want you to leave for Washington immediately," Matsuoka said briskly. "I want you to arrange a meeting with Mr. Roosevelt and Mr. Hull. I want you to tell them that Prime Minister Konoye offers this proposal: if the United States will lift its embargo against Japan, if it will allow us to buy raw materials on the American market like any other country, and if it will grant us the right to pursue our own economic expansion in Asia, Japan will break its treaty with Italy and Germany and will in no way help them in the European war. Also, we will withdraw our troops from Manchuria and China, and we will recognize the integrity of the Nationalist government. We will also promise that if at any time in the future it becomes necessary we will fight with the Chinese against Russia. Is that clear?"

"Perfectly."

"One more thing: the invitation to negotiate these points must come from the United States. We cannot do it in the face of General Tojo's rising influence. But if the United States suggests negotiations then we cannot refuse. Is that clear?"

"Yes."

"Good. When can you leave for America?"

"Right away."

"There is a ship tonight."

"I will be on it."

"Good. And just this: you are to discuss all this with no one but Mr. Roosevelt and Mr. Hull and any trusted aide they wish to include in the meeting. But no one else. There are spies everywhere; we can't take any chances. If there is going to be peace I want to be around to enjoy it."

Walsh and Drought were in Washington a month later. Through Catholic friends in Washington and through the influence of his brother William, a successful lawyer and Democratic leader in Maryland, Walsh was able to get word through to Hull that a meeting with the President was urgent. The meeting was held at the White House on Thursday, January 23, 1941, with Roosevelt, Hull, and Robert Walker, the Postmaster General; none of them knew exactly what they were about to hear.

Two and a half hours later Walsh had told them everything. Considering the proposals, Roosevelt said, "We can't ask for much more than that."

"Perhaps," said Hull, "but how do we know the Japanese will stick to any agreement they make? They're ready now to break their treaty with the Axis. At what point will they break their treaty with us?"

"That's true," Roosevelt said, "but that's also the risk. If there's a change in government, if Tojo gets power, anything can happen. What do you think, Excellency?"

"Mr. President," Walsh said, "I am only the messenger. I refused to express any opinions with the Japanese and I don't think I should do so here."

"Are you willing to continue as messenger if it's necessary?" Roosevelt asked.

"Yes, of course."

"Would you be going back to Japan this year anyway?"

"There would be nothing unusual in it if I did. I have many men there."

"All right. If we find it's necessary to contact Matsuoka through the channels now set up through you, we will appreciate it."

The negotiations that soon began between Japan and the United States came as a surprise to most people, even in high places. The Japanese ambassador was astonished to be called in by Hull and told that if his country had any proposals to achieve peaceful relations America would be interested in learning them. Foreign leaders wondered what was going on. The trouble was that there was too much going on. The proposals sent officially by Matsuoka to his ambassador in Washington differed somewhat from those he mentioned to Walsh, but this was essential for the sake of appearances. The Foreign Minister expected adjustments to be made through secret negotiations. Father Drought was kept on in Washington to advise Hull on any subtle insinuations in the negotiations that were intended to be flexible. In Tokyo, meanwhile, Matsuoka was having his troubles with Tojo. While, at cabinet meetings, pretending to be tough and immobile, he was also trying to prepare other government leaders for a treaty along the lines he had offered originally. The Japanese ambassador could bargain only on the terms given him officially by Tokyo and had no idea what was going on under the table. Thus, from the start the negotiations were doomed by the complications in Japan.

New problems arose when, completely unexpectedly, Germany signed a nonaggression pact with Russia. This was in utter contradiction to a mutual-aid agreement Germany and Japan had signed two years before against Russia and it bewildered the Japanese. In an effort to stabilize the situation, Matsuoka was sent to Berlin where he had long talks with Adolf Hitler on the future relations between the two countries. Hitler convinced him that the pact with Russia was the best way to keep the Russians out of the European war and he also assured Matsuoka that Germany was ready to give Japan a free hand in the Far East. Content with this, Matsuoka went on to Moscow and worked out a similar nonaggression pact between Russia and Japan. This brought about a peculiar situation: in its negotiations with America, Japan had offered to withdraw its troops from the Asian mainland and to fight the Russians if necessary, and now Japan had a nonaggression pact with the country everybody knew had been trying to take over China, if only in the Communist political sense, for twenty years. It was no wonder, then, that the American negotiators grew more and more suspicious. Then the whole thing exploded when, two weeks after Matsuoka returned triumphantly home, Germany attacked Russia and pushed her into the European war on the Allied side.

Walsh went back to Japan in June and was soon approached by Matsuoka for further discussions. Walsh said, "I have no messages for you except that the United States is wondering how you could expect to reach an agreement acceptable to your government and then keep it in view of what's happened in the past few months."

"I can do it," Matsuoka said. "If we can only come to terms I am sure I can get the cabinet to accept it, then the Emperor can make it law by rescript. But something dramatic must happen. The United States must take some step that will take the wind out of Tojo. Why don't they lift the embargo?"

Before leaving Maryknoll, Walsh had arranged with Drought to cable him any further developments disguised in mission-business jargon which he could then pass on to Cordell Hull. Now Walsh sent this latest message, which eventually reached Hull. Two things happened before Hull could act: on July 2, Japan conscripted a million men into the army—certainly no clue of peaceful intentions, and on July 25 the Japanese soldiers in northern Indo-China were ordered to sweep south and take over the entire country.

The next day President Roosevelt issued an executive order to freeze all Japanese assets in the United States. Before the week was out, Great Britain and the Netherlands issued similar orders. The United States then banned all Japanese vessels from American ports and put a rigid embargo on the sale of American petroleum to Japan. The Pacific war was shaping up.

Despite everything, Prince Konoye and Matsuoka still tried to work out a treaty with the United States. Practically every day for two months, Walsh sent coded messages to Drought at Maryknoll, defining in the mild language in which they had been put to him the offers Konoye and Matsuoka felt they could make. At the same time, stern demands for terms were coming through the Japanese embassy. On August 17, Prince Konoye suggested a meeting with President Roosevelt to discuss terms, but the State Department rejected the offer unless preliminary agreements were

THE FOURTH DECADE 231

reached first. The meeting was not held. Both Konoye and Matsuoka's positions in the Japanese government grew extremely shaky.

It was on the morning of October 14 that Konoye put to Tojo the idea that Japan should withdraw from Indo-China as a sign of good faith; surely then the United States would respond with a similar gesture, perhaps lifting the oil embargo, and then peace would be assured. Tojo rejected the idea fiercely, refusing to lose face by being the first to step back from the battle line. That afternoon Konoye sent for Walsh.

"There isn't much time," he said. "I can't hold General Tojo down any longer. Will you go to Washington immediately and tell them that?"

"Is there time even for the warning?" Walsh asked.

"I don't know," said Konoye. "I do suspect, however, that Tojo has found out about your role in the negotiations, and to prevent anything from happening too fast I suggest you do not leave for America directly from Japan. I imagine you are being watched. If you wish, take a plane today for Shanghai, giving the impression that you are going to visit your missions on the mainland. I can arrange for another plane to meet you there and fly you to Hong Kong where you can catch a ship to San Francisco. I hope you will do it, Excellency. I have a feeling this is the last thing I will ask of you."

Walsh reached Washington on November 15, too late. Both Konoye and Matsuoka had been thrown out of the Japanese government and Tojo was in charge.

"It is hopeless," Cordell Hull despaired. "It is hopeless."

There would be war. The question was when and where. For the sake of appearances, Tojo sent one more note to Hull: unfreeze Japanese assets, supply Japan with oil, pressure Nationalist China into a treaty economically favorable to Japan, then Japan would withdraw its troops from southern Indo-China and eventually from China itself. The American military leaders recognized this as the end and they urged Hull to stall, at least to the extent of supplying Japan with oil for civilian purposes, until either a treaty could be worked out or America could better prepare itself for war. Instead, Hull convinced Roosevelt to reply with a complete reversal of terms: you move first, then we will.

Jim Walsh was home at Maryknoll working in his apartment office, the radio softly playing, on the December Sunday afternoon when the first news flashes arrived from Pearl Harbor.

XXIII

WHEN the Japanese occupied major ports along the north and central China coasts, they took a look at Sancian Island to see if it was worth bothering about. The Nationalist Chinese had no military installations on the island. With the exception of a few scattered villages, the island was all farms, and the only trouble had been caused by a handful of bandits who lived in the hills. To make an impression, the Japanese burned several houses in the port town and set fire to some junks and sampans, then they left. The deeds were enough to frighten hundreds of islanders, who quickly packed their meager possessions and sailed across to the mainland to find safety in the Nationalist-held areas in the south. It almost seemed as if the Japanese made allowances for the refugees, for as soon as they had made safe crossings Japanese gunboats took up a patrol that thereafter cut the island off.

The only Maryknoll priest on the island was Sandy Cairns, stationed there since Sancian had been made part of the Kong-moon vicariate in 1933. From time to time he had assistants, but because the demands on the island were few the assistants were always assigned elsewhere to replace men on leave or who were ill. Cairns did not mind being alone; he often said, "You are never lonely when you serve God." Actually he was not entirely alone. A hundred yards from his rectory two Maryknoll Sisters conducted a school and dispensary. Whenever Cairns wanted to speak English or enjoy an American meal, he would go and visit the Sisters.

The rocky fields of Sancian had never produced enough food for the islanders. Now faced with the Japanese blockade, there was a serious threat of starvation. Something had to be done.

The Japanese who had come to the island did not seem a bad lot to Cairns. The commanding officer had inspected Cairns's living quarters and paged through his religious books, then said, "I have a Bible." When they went into the church, the officer had removed his hat and bowed to the altar. Cairns later suspected that the burning of the houses and the boats was done because the officer felt he had to make some show of authority. The failure of the Japanese to return convinced Cairns that the island would not be occupied.

But there was the blockade. Vessels trying to reach Sancian from the mainland were turned back; any ships attempting to break through were fired upon and sunk. Passengers on sampans from Sancian were taken prisoner and their crafts were set afire.

Each passing week saw greater food shortages on the island. Crowds began to form at the mission door every morning, begging for food. Cairns gave away all he had; the Sisters distributed all they had. One day there arrived at the mission a dozen emaciated boys from the far side of the island. While Cairns hunted around for something to feed them the cry went up that the Japanese were landing. Terrified, the boys vanished, apparently returning home as hungry as they had arrived. The warning cry had been a false alarm. Occasionally the Japanese did land, but their landings were only beachhead practices and they did not leave the shores. When the people got used to this they were not so much afraid.

Cairns realized that food had to be obtained somehow. Boldly running the blockade in daylight would be foolhardy; attempting a crossing at night was dangerous because of the rocks and swift currents off both shores. He devised this method: by leaving either Sancian or the mainland in the middle of the night with the aid of an experienced fisherman he could get his sampan safely away from shore. Then on his own he made the dash, arriving at the opposite shore just at dawn. He would get his bearings from landmarks and sail on to his destination. There were, inevitably, times when he was off course and thus remained longer at sea. On these occasions a Japanese pilot on dawn patrol often spotted him and fired on his boat, but the planes were fast and the sampan didn't look worth the trouble, and after a single unsuccessful run the planes usually went on their way.

Over the next months Cairns made trips as regularly as he dared, managing to supply enough rice to protect the islanders from absolute starvation. In one particularly good month he smuggled in twenty-six thousand pounds of rice but he urged his people to use it sparingly because if ever he was caught that would be the end of it.

On Sancian he had no outside contact of any kind with the world. His trips and his few hours on the mainland therefore enabled him to learn the news. He agreed with Maryknollers he met that war seemed a certainty. When they suggested to him that he might leave Sancian permanently he refused.

They told him, "You can get somebody else to smuggle the rice."

"It's more than the rice," he said, "and you know it."

They did.

On December 9, 1941, a contingent of Japanese soldiers, along with Chinese troops from the puppet government Japanese-held cities, came ashore. Cairns saw them head for the convent. He intercepted them and urged that they leave the Sisters alone. By the time they brushed him aside the Sisters were able to escape by a back door and hide in the hills. The convent was thoroughly looted. That night the Japanese departed, leaving the Chinese behind. At midnight Cairns led the two nuns to his sampan, put them into it, and pushed the boat out to sea, and in the morning they were safely on the mainland.

The Japanese returned on December 13. The commanding officer found Cairns in his office and said, "Your country and my country are at war."

This was the first Cairns had heard of it. "I was afraid that would happen," he said.

The officer said, "I can save you, if you leave with me now. Tomorrow Japanese from other places may come. And they will come to kill."

"That's very kind of you," Cairns said, "but I cannot leave."

"I won't take you prisoner," the man said. "I can see to it that you are put ashore on the mainland."

"I appreciate it and I admire you for taking such a risk with an enemy, but I must stay," Cairns said.

"You will be killed," warned the officer.

"I expect so."

The Japanese left.

Three days later the Japanese occupation force arrived. There was great panic on the island and nobody was ever sure exactly what happened that day. Against the unarmed island the assault was unnecessarily brutal. Again houses were burned, shops were looted, and people were shot simply for trying to run to safety.

What happened to Cairns was never learned. Natives later reported that the Japanese had gone first to the mission and dragged Cairns into the road. His houseboy, Ching, tried to fight off the Japanese; they took him along. The party moved down to the beach where Cairns and Ching were forced into a landing launch, the motor was started, and the boat left the bay.

It was said by some that Cairns was shot and thrown overboard when the launch was a few miles offshore. Others said he had been put into a sack and thrown overboard alive. And others said that he had been beheaded and then dumped into the sea. A few days later his hat was found on the beach. There was also some talk that he and Ching had been taken as prisoners to Japan, and in fact Cairns's name appeared on a list of prisoners published by the Japanese nine months later but there was no mention of the camp where he was held, no mention of Ching. Neither man was ever seen again.

On the far side of the international date line the day of the Pearl Harbor attack was December 8. That day Father William Thomas Cummings, of San Francisco, joined the army. Although he had been a Maryknoller for twelve years, a bad back kept him out of the missions until 1940, when he was sent to the Philippines. It was perhaps unusual that missionaries should be assigned to a country that was already completely Catholic. As early as 1898 the islands had more than enough priests to meet the needs. But that was the year when, as a result of the Spanish-American War, the Philippines became an American possession, and that was the year things changed.

Almost all of the priests in the Philippines had been Spaniards. After three centuries, they had produced only a handful of Philippine priests, none in executive positions. When the Spaniards were forced to leave the country they thus left behind great cathedrals and excellent universities without staffs. The Spanish themselves were to blame. They thought their paternalism in the Philippines would endure forever and out of this they failed to provide the country with its own strong native clergy, a failure which had already occurred in South and Central America and from which the Spanish had learned nothing.

As bad as this was, the American influence was worse. Most of the men appointed by the U. S. government to rule the Philippines were Masons, men with little sympathy for the dominant religion in the country. At the same time, they had little respect for the wishes of the people. Because the Church in the Philippines had staffed and directed the hospitals for the poor, the orphanages, and the homes for the aged, the Spanish government had demonstrated its own responsibility for social welfare by supporting these institutions. The American rulers put an end to such aid. Also, the Filipinos considered it perfectly normal for their children to study religion in government schools. The Americans put an end to that also. The Filipinos argued, they demanded, they threatened. But they wasted their time.

The American conduct in the Philippines shocked the world. The Spanish-American War itself had grown out of the flimsiest evidence of Spanish intervention in Western Hemisphere affairs and was erupted by the sinking of the USS *Maine* in Havana harbor, which many thought was a strange place for the ship to be, in view of the tense relations between the two countries. Added to this, the American behavior in the Philippines made much of the world question the nobility of intentions the United States had proclaimed in "freeing" Cuba, Puerto Rico, and the Philippines from what was called Spanish despotism.

The Vatican expected American Catholics to take on responsibility for the Church in the Philippines, but this was not easy to do. An American—Michael J. O'Doherty—was appointed archbishop of Manila, but as late as 1920 only two American secular priests had been given permission to enter the country on a permanent basis. Meanwhile, the islands were overrun by thousands of American businessmen and Protestant missionaries. Rome tried to meet the spiritual requirements of the enormous Catholic population by sending in some European priests, but again the number was as restricted to a minimum.

In 1926, Archbishop O'Doherty asked Maryknoll to come to his aid. In those few years he had already witnessed a spreading materialism that was endangering the moral standards of the country, and he could see in this, as he saw so clearly across the sea in China, the rising fields for Communist seedings. Maryknoll was short-handed and at first only Father Drought was able to come over from China to become director of St. Rita's Hall, a hostel for young men in Manila. The Maryknoll Sisters arrived and took on the operation of St. Paul's hospital, St. Mary's Hall, a residence for college women, a college itself, and some primary schools. Each year more priests and nuns entered the Philippines. Oddly enough, the only complaints about the increased Catholic activity in the preponderantly Catholic country came from American Protestant missionaries. Drought found himself embroiled in a public debate with one of them who was trying vociferously to convince the university students that the Catholic religion was bad for their brains. One Filipino who remained unmoved by the clamor was a young man named Carlos P. Romulo, who went on to become a famous editor, a Pulitzer Prize winner, an aide to General Douglas MacArthur, Philippine ambassador to the United States, and president of the United Nations.

But during the Roosevelt administrations a Catholic governor general was appointed to the Philippines and the anti-American feeling in the country began to diminish. Many of the Masonic abuses were corrected and the Filipinos once again could feel like human beings whose traditions, customs, and convictions were being respected. The Maryknoll work broadened; by autumn of 1941 there were some twenty Maryknoll priests in the country and fifty Maryknoll Sisters.

The Japanese chose the Philippines as the first major U. S. Pacific holding for occupation. At the very hour the Japanese navy moved against Pearl Harbor the army was poised for the attack on the northern Philippines. On the first day of fighting, Bill Cummings was at U. S. Army headquarters, offering himself as a chaplain. At first he was refused because the commanding officer at Manila knew of his bad back, but he immediately offered himself again, this time in such forceful language that the officer said, "That's the kind of fighting talk I like to hear. You're in."

In January he was out on the Bataan peninsula where the U. S. Philippine forces had retreated before tremendous Japanese assaults. By day he was on the battlefields, encouraging the well, comforting the wounded, consoling the dying; by night he was at Base Hospital One at every chore he could find. He was at the hospital when the Japanese bombed it twice in an hour, and it was only after he had calmed the panic-stricken amputees who tried to slither outdoors to safety that he turned to a nurse and said, "O.K., sis, put a tourniquet on my arm when you get a chance. I think I've been hit."

On Easter Sunday he erected a makeshift altar to say Mass for those who were free to come and it was on this occasion that, in his sermon, he spoke the words that became historic when he said, "By now we have all discovered that there are no atheists in foxholes."

That Mass was the last of his life. So frequent, so fierce became the Japanese attacks that there was not a moment's rest for anyone. It was soon obvious that Bataan could no longer be held and the retreat to Corregidor began. Cummings went along, leaving behind all his equipment. He was near the beach, awaiting transportation across to the island fortress, when the Japanese broke through the defense lines and captured almost twenty thousand battle-weary American fighters and sixty thousand Filipinos.

The next two weeks were a walking hell. This was the Bataan Death March, the eighty-five-mile trail of blood on which hundreds of men died or were killed every day. Weak and wounded himself, Cummings was back and forth along the line, giving his shoulder to a man who could no longer walk alone, easing to the ground another man who died in his embrace, feeding another his share of what little food was distributed, bending over another to provide shadow during the hours they were forced to sit in the burning sun.

In the prison camp he was the same, ignoring camp rules to go to a man who needed him, risking his life to obtain something to eat or drink for others. The Filipinos living near the camp knew him, and because of him they dared bribe the guards to get food and medicine through the prison fences. Never did his spirits drag; always he was busy among the sick and the dying, urging them to keep hope and to keep on. The first news of him came after a year's imprisonment, and of himself he said only, "Am quite well."

But he was not. He suffered the dysentery, the malaria, the infections that struck all the others, but even when he was too weak to move he kept on with his firm voice, encouraging those who were near. When fever scorched his body, and his lips were white from dehydration, he nevertheless dragged himself to dying men to bless them and absolve them in their last moments.

When the turning trend of the war destroyed optimism in Japan all efforts were made to bring in hordes of prisoners to give the impression that actually all was going well. Most of the prisoners came from the Philippines, Cummings among them. The clothes they had were shreds of the tropical uniforms worn in the warm country; aboard the winter transports sailing north men literally froze to death. Scores of them developed pneumonia, and this was what happened to Cummings.

To the end he continued his hopeful chatter in a strong clear voice—"It'll be different in Japan. They'll have to treat us better. We'll get food and there'll be doctors. You'll see. We've had the worst of it. Once we—"

Those who watched him die sat quietly for a few moments, then one of them said, "I wonder where he got all the strength."

There were some who knew.

XXIV

DECEMBER 8 was the Feast of the Immaculate Conception, the miracle of purity to which the Church in America was dedicated. Throughout the Orient, Maryknollers were busy with the holy day celebrations. In Manchuria, Lane had just returned from a special Mass when Japanese officers came to his house with news about the war. The Japanese in Manchuria had known the Maryknollers for almost fifteen years and had co-operated with them in many ways; they had seen the priests at work among the Catholic Japanese at Darien, and understood their motives and their aims.

An officer said, "I'm sorry, but you people are enemies now."

"It's strange, isn't it?" Lane said.

"I'm going to have to lock you up."

"I suppose you must."

"I've already ordered my men to bring in the missionaries at the other stations."

"Peacefully, I hope."

"Nobody will be hurt unless he resists arrest."

"What about the Sisters?"

"I'll give them a few more days. They will have to find someone to take care of the orphans and the old people."

241

"Yes, that's right. Will we be permitted to take personal things with us?"

"Like what?"

"Mass kits, for example. I'm sure the priests will want to be able to say Mass."

"Of course. Anything like that will be all right."

Within a week all the Maryknollers were in prison camps, along with Protestant missionaries, with citizens of other countries now at war with Japan, and with Chinese known to be Nationalists. At one point Lane discovered that Catholics in a prison camp to the north were without a priest and he asked that two Maryknollers be transferred there. The request was granted. In 1942 when the first exchange of prisoners was made Lane said he wished to stay behind to attend the Catholics who would not be freed. One of his assistants expressed the same preference. They were permitted to remain.

The Korean situation was somewhat similar. On the first war day, a Maryknoll Sister had gone into a chapel to prepare the altar for Rosary and Benediction, and she was surprised to find only one person there on the important feast day. "Where is everybody else?" she asked.

The Korean said, "They are afraid to be seen with Americans because of the war."

"What war?" Sister asked.

"Don't you know about it? You're at war with Japan."

Sister hurried across the compound to make inquiries of the priests, reaching the rectory just in time to see Japanese soldiers lead the priests away. Again the Sisters were given a few days to arrange for others to carry on their work. During these days the priests realized that they would not be allowed to return to their churches, so they instructed the Sisters to consume the Blessed Sacrament reposed in the tabernacles in order to prevent any desecration of the Sacred Species in the event of looting.

In both Manchuria and Korea, Italian and German missionaries were permitted to continue their work, as were French priests who avoided overt concern for the Free French Government. The native clergy worked on without interference—vivid proof of their importance in mission countries caught in world conflicts. When Pat Byrne had been recalled from Korea to join the Maryknoll council, Bill O'Shea, one of the six original Maryknoll students, was transferred from South China to replace him and eventually became a monsignor, then a bishop. With others, O'Shea was imprisoned at the war's outbreak, and as the prisoner exchange neared he realized his departure would deprive Korea of a bishop at a time when there was already a serious scarcity of them. He therefore arranged with Rome to resign his bishopric in favor of a Korean: the man was consecrated before O'Shea was out of the country. Again the importance of an available native clergy was displayed. Some months later, while hurrying through Grand Central Station to catch a train to Maryknoll, O'Shea dropped dead of a heart attack—the second death among the first five students to become Maryknollers.

The Maryknollers in South China were in a different position. Living in Nationalist China territory, they were subject to air attacks and constantly threatened with invasion. The Kweilin prefecture, separated from Wuchow in 1932, was in particular danger because of the nearby Flying Tigers air base. Evacuation of the coast swelled the Kweilin population from eighty thousand to four hundred thousand in eighteen months. Refugees stormed the mission night and day for food and medical care. Those who had fled the coast with only what they wore were given small amounts of money to tide them over until they could find a livelihood in the crowded city.

In charge at Kweilin was Monsignor John Romaniello, of New Rochelle, a short, chubby man who had become well known and well liked during his twelve years in China. In the midst of the panic he seemed to be the only calm man in Kweilin, busily devising emergency housing plans, finding qualified help for the government offices that moved in, organizing farmers to assure fast and fair food distribution. The mission was repeatedly hit by bombs; Romaniello was always the last to flee to safety. One day the mission buildings were pulverized in an air raid. After it the people saw Romaniello pick through the rubble for whatever was salvageable, then head for the river.

"He is going home," said one dismayed Chinese.

At the river he engaged in conversation with a boat owner, then hiked aboard a sizable houseboat. He turned to the worried crowd that had followed him and announced, "From now on, this is the mission." A great cheer went up.

U. S. pilots had been briefed to head toward the nearest Maryknoll mission in case they had to bail out or make a forced landing. An American bomber once skidded to a landing a few miles outside one of the missions and when the crew tumbled out they found themselves surrounded by what seemed belligerent Chinese. They all stared at each other expectantly, then one American held up his rosary. Immediately one of Romaniello's Catholic Chinese dug out his rosary, then turned to his countrymen with a speech that began, "We Catholics are winning the war."

In the Kweilin district alone, one Maryknoller guided eight downed pilots to safety. Another made two trips of two hundred miles to bring in pilots. All Maryknollers served as chaplains wherever they were needed.

Each day the invasion threat to Kweilin increased. Romaniello told his men: "We will stay here as long as we can to help the refugees. When the Japanese come in the north gate we will go out the south gate, but not before." That was what happened. Only when the advance Japanese patrols were already moving into the Kweilin streets did Romaniello and those with him ride their bicycles out to the air base to be evacuated.

Wuchow had no planes for evacuation, but there were plenty of planes overhead—all Japanese. This was the mission area that Bernard Meyer had built up against the most immobile opposition. Called home in 1936 for medical treatment, he was replaced by Frederick A. Donaghy, of New Bedford, Massachusetts, who became the Wuchow bishop in 1940; at that time Meyer was reassigned to Hong Kong. Because of its strategic location on the West River, Wuchow was the Japanese goal in a drive to slice Free China in half. By mid-1944, most of the city was in ruins and thousands had been killed. Thousands more piled into the city, however—refugees from the coast. Now the Japanese began their advance upon the city.

Bishop Donaghy advised his priests, "Your people come first, and when there is nothing more you can do for them take to the hills."

He was worried most about his seminarians, for upon them rested the future of the Church at Wuchow. Aware that the city

would soon fall into Japanese hands, he put the students aboard
a riverboat and sent them upstream with the faculty. Also aboard
the boat went such a variety of barnyard animals and fowl for
food that the boat resembled a floating zoo. After two days of
rowing they completed the first leg of their trip, then they hiked
thirty-five miles up into the mountains to a walled mission station
that Meyer had built fifteen years earlier which later proved too
inaccessible for use. Now they could only hope that the Japanese
would not find out about it. They were there just a day when ten
more Maryknollers came up the hill with the same idea in mind.

Nobody dared rest. They posted a guard so that there would be
time to move farther back should the Japanese move near. Farmers in the valley knew they were there and, whenever it was safe,
went up with news. As the Japanese fanned out from the river
there were days when the valley was full of them, but the mountain
tops looked cold and bleak and empty, and the Japanese did not
think there was anyone up there.

A month passed. Some of the priests were growing restless. Also,
the unexpected ten helped deplete first the food supply and then
the funds faster than had been anticipated. Four of them volunteered to try to reach American bases far to the south to get some
kind of help, and it was decided that if they made it, one of them
—Arthur F. Dempsey, of Peekskill, New York, a veteran of fifteen
years in China—would work his way back.

It was rugged travel, from mountain top to mountain top for
four days, skirting farms and villages, passing within a few yards
of Japanese patrols, then on to a river full of rapids for two more
days, deeper and deeper southward until they were safely behind
Free China lines. When at last they staggered into a U. S. air
base and explained how they had come, intelligence officers called
their success phenomenal: the woods even around the base were
thick with snipers. A telegram was sent to Maryknoll headquarters
at Chungking, from where funds were sent to the base chaplain
for the Maryknollers. Now Dempsey was ready to begin the return trip.

A pilot suggested, "If you can guide us back to the mission we'll
fly over in a bomber and we can drop the money right at the
door."

Three hours later a Mitchell bomber made a run on the mission. The bomb bays were opened, a bombardier took a count, and a weighted wicker basket containing the money was delivered as promised: right to the door. The missionaries now had enough to support themselves for the duration of the war.

At Kaying, Frank Ford faced the familiar plight of too many refugees and too little food. To meet the problem, local farmers had to increase their rice crop many times, and to buy seeds they had to take out loans at interest as high as 300 per cent. When the crops failed—as they did due to a drought and a lack of help —the profiteers did not hesitate to confiscate farms. This only worsened the problem; a way to solve it had to be found.

Father James A. McCormick, of Clarks Summit, Pennsylvania, suggested a rice bank, from which farmers could borrow seeds for 20 per cent of the crop. The plan worked from the start. Even in a bad year, when only half the normal crop was produced, the farmers paid their bills so that the mission would have rice for the poor. Along the same line, McCormick organized a soap factory, a cloth-making factory, a training school for carpenters, and a glass factory. Thus Kaying was able to take care of itself during the war, and so successful was the co-operative program that it was extended into the postwar years, providing Kaying with financial stability that most of the country lacked.

Succeeding Jim Walsh at Kongmoon was Adolph J. Paschang, of Martinsburg, Missouri, who became a bishop in 1938, shortly before the Japanese began their occupation of the China coast. The Japanese blockade cut Kongmoon off from its waterway to Hong Kong. Caught in Hong Kong by the sea action was Father Joseph A. Sweeney, of New Britain, Connecticut, who ran the Kongmoon leper colony. His major worry was getting medicine back to the lepers. One day he found a Chinese boatman who was willing to try to run the blockade. They were out on the high seas when they were spotted by a patrol boat that ran them down and crashed into them, then left them to drown. After six hours in the water, Sweeney stumbled ashore on an uninhabited island. In the morning when he saw that he was isolated from the world he wondered if he had really been so lucky to survive. There was nothing on the island to eat, but he found a clear stream where he could quench his thirst. He realized that the

chances for a rescue were so remote that he put it out of his mind
and prayed instead for China and his friends who were there.
On the third day, weak from hunger, he did not believe his eyes
when he saw a small boat pop above the horizon and make for
shore. He dared not hope against a mirage until he saw a man
and boy come ashore and make a fire. Then he went down to
them and startled them when he stepped from the bushes. The
man explained that he and his son were fishermen and did not
plan to return to the mainland for a week.

"That's all right with me," said Sweeney. "I don't care how
long you stay, just so you're here."

They did not want to risk going all the way to the mainland
with Sweeney, so they put him off at an island village a few miles
downstream from the mission, then went to tell the mission where
Sweeney was. One of the priests went out for him on a sampan.
When he got home he did not have the medicines he had promised to bring, but he was there, and for the lepers that was medicine enough.

On December 8, the Japanese entered the Kongmoon mission
while Bishop Paschang was distributing food to a thousand refugees. Word spread quickly. Priests at other stations immediately
retreated into the mountains. After questioning Paschang for
three days, the Japanese moved him and three priests to Macao
which, by their blockade, they had practically turned into a
prison.

Paschang was determined to get back. On the Macao water
front he made contact with Free China guerrillas who were willing to help him make it. One night, accompanied by Father Anthony J. Paulhus, of Fall River, Massachusetts, he went down to
the water front where the two of them hid between barrels and
mounds of ropes until the signal was given that the way was clear.
At the side of each oarsman in the guerrilla boat lay a machine
gun. The oars were wrapped in cloth to muffle their sound. They
started out into the black night. At one point they passed within
a few yards of a patrol boat. They were so near the China shore
that they could hear the water lapping, when the searchlight fell
upon them and the patrol boat opened fire.

"Jump for it!" the chief guerrilla cried.

Paschang and Paulhus went over the side and as they ran up

the shore they could hear the soft thuds of bullets striking the mud at their feet. The guerrillas fought off the patrol boat and prevented a landing. For the next two weeks, the two Americans passed from the hands of one guerrilla band to the next, moving steadily toward free territory, and at last they made their way to Loting, in Paschang's diocese, and there they remained secretly at work for the rest of the war.

The Americans in the Philippines who were not caught in the fall of Manila took refuge in the mountains and were able to continue their work. Some of them managed to elude the Japanese for almost a year before they were captured by the thorough occupation forces and imprisoned. In Japan, Maryknollers were arrested and imprisoned the day the war broke out. Oddly enough, it was there, in their own homeland, that the Japanese war leaders discovered they had one Maryknoller on their hands they could not push around.

XXV

•

PAT BYRNE had become a celebrity in Kyoto. He was a brilliant man, a charming man, a good man. Slow though conversions were, public admiration for Byrne himself came in abundance. He knew all the intellectuals in the city of universities, he was a friend of the Kyoto political leaders, and the poor he had helped in his tuberculosis hospital, his outpatient clinic and his food kitchen were devoted to him. When the military police swooped up all the Maryknollers around Kyoto in a single afternoon, they left Byrne at home. Public opinion would not tolerate anything else. To be sure he was an American and by the fact an enemy, but in his five years in the city he had consistently demonstrated only friendship and affection. Perhaps now he could not be permitted to move around freely in his work, but he need not be put into prison. He was made a prisoner in his house.

It was a small house with no garden or promenade so he had little outdoor space to move around in. The kitchen was, he found, eight steps apart from the house, but nine steps if he walked in a curve; in the tiny alley he got his only fresh-air exercise. Indoors he exercised by taking loads of kindling in his arms and running around the spacious second-floor living room. People who observed this from outside wondered if confinement had driven the poor man mad. But after two months of this he was transferred to another mission building where there was a garden to occupy him with flowers and vegetables.

He was denied visitors: anyone caught in the house was liable to three days' imprisonment. However, his houseboy developed a method of signaling by clopping his wooden sandals on the porch to indicate when a policeman was coming or going, and in this way it was possible for people to sneak in occasionally with news and gifts.

He was allowed to keep his small library and receive Japanese newspapers and magazines. It was easy for him to read between the lines of war reports and see how, after the first year, the government was deluding the people on the progress in battle. The steady Allied northward advance, hinted at in the Japanese press merely as thwarted landing attempts, could only mean that the Japanese were being pushed back. His news, then, although by circumstances mostly presumption, encouraged him.

In addition to his garden, he busied himself with a language text; having had difficulty with Oriental languages, he produced a simple book for others like himself and called it *A Japanese Grammar for Boneheads*. He noted, "I think I've got a fortune in it."

Living at a mission, he had a private chapel available to him and was permitted to obtain Mass wine and Hosts from Japanese priests, so, more fortunate than many others, he had always the consolation of his sacerdotal faculties. At times the days passed very slowly, but he was not uncomfortable. He could wait.

And then it was all over.

There was panic in the land, a danger of riots and looting, a fear of the Amreican victors, a threat of prolonged guerrilla warfare. The government was in turmoil. Men who felt dishonored committed suicide, so did others who feared punishment, so did women who believed the Japanese propaganda about American brutality. A newspaperman in Osaka sought some way to end the horror and went hopefully to Archibishop Doi of Tokyo.

"Is there no voice in the country that can calm us?" he asked. "Is there no one respected by both sides who can bring us together?"

"I can think of only one such person," the Archbishop said. "Father Byrne, the Maryknoller, at Kyoto."

The reporter went to Kyoto and called on Furuya and told him what he had in mind, and together they went to see Byrne. That night Byrne and the reporter were on a crowded train to Tokyo. The next afternoon Byrne stepped to a microphone in a Tokyo radio station and spoke these words to the entire nation:

"The war is over. What can I say first of all to the Japanese people whom I have loved and who loved me as a brother for more than ten years? I shared your grief when the Emperor spoke to them and told them that they had fought a good fight, but now he wanted them to give up the war and turn to peace. I, an American, speak to you Japanese in the name of those soldiers about to enter your land to assure you that you need have no fears. They are not coming to these shores as invaders, with tanks, bayonets, and bullets, but merely as representatives of their country, taking occupation of Japan to help you once more to reconstruct and build on the new foundation of democracy. The eyes of the world are on this occupying army. You may rest assured they come peaceably.

"What can I say to you, the soldiers of my native land, regarding these people? Their feelings will naturally be mixed with emotions as they look upon the victors entering their land, where their homes have been destroyed or burned, their sons and fathers of families killed or maimed and wounded. It is only natural that they look with anger, fear, mistrust, and frustration at your arrival. Should you add to their present feelings by any ruthless attack upon women and young people in this land, I am afraid of what the consequences might be. So I urge you to co-operate with me as I assure the Japanese people that you will commit no degradations, that you will have good will and charity in trying to realize what these people, the real victims of war, have suffered, and will not do anything to add to the pain they endure.

"You are on trial before the eyes of the world. Any violence or immorality, any unjust or criminal act on your part will not only be a stain on your own character but on that of the nation you represent.

"I believe I may assure you, people of Japan, that the army

chaplains will do everything they can to remind our soldiers of their moral responsibility. The Military Police, too, will carefully protect your interests and will arrest anyone found violating the law. If there seems to be any violation of this protection which is your due, I have been assured by the Archbishop of Tokyo that he will appeal to the Holy Father in Rome, who in turn will make known to the whole world by radio and the press any form of injustice. Freedom of the press in the United States will co-operate so that such news will not be suppressed.

"I am not afraid because I know these Americans and trust them, but I can understand the fears of the Japanese people. Soldiers coming into Japan, I strongly urge you to come with kind hearts and be good friends of these people. You have fought hard and won a victory. I know you want to enjoy it and want to be proud of it, but please try to understand the distress of the Japanese and make your behavior calm and warm as representatives of a great nation. Perhaps after two or three months they will begin to understand you better, and then I think there will come an intimate friendship between you and them."

They were words heard by the world and praised by the world. Conjecture was offered as to what kind of speech a German or Japanese would have made in the same situation, but Byrne brushed it aside as irrelevant. The Allies had won, and now they should act like representatives of the civilization they fought to protect. Byrne was heralded on all sides as Japan's Number-Two American, second only to General MacArthur. When the ordeal of the occupation calmed, MacArthur wrote to Pope Pius XII: "In the early days of the Japanese occupation when everything was in confusion, Father Byrne was of great help to us. He was resourceful and courageous. He was looked up to by everybody."

Byrne was unmoved by the accolades. His reaction was typical of him: "Now let's get everybody out of prison camps and back to work."

Everybody wanted to do precisely that but it was not fully possible. First off, the Maryknollers who had been imprisoned were all in need of medical care. Those who had hidden out in the mountains were not much better off. Although only two—Cummings and Cairns—had died from wartime ordeals, others developed conditions which either subsequently brought on death or left them permanently disabled. These had to be brought home for treatment, and by this the mission field was deprived of experienced men who could have provided important training for the newcomers who had been ordained during the war and had to wait out assignments. Because of all the work that had to be done, every Maryknoller in the Orient begged to stay on and it became the unhappy duty of superiors to decide which of these could.

The work required the fittest men. Over a million dollars in damages had been inflicted upon mission buildings, some were completely destroyed. In many areas, reconstruction had to start at the ground. An added problem was finding the money to pay for everything, and this put a greater onus on the fund-raisers at home.

And there was something else. In the last days of the Pacific war, Russia got around to sending troops into Manchuria against the Japanese. Thousands of Japanese were taken prisoner and sent to labor camps in Siberia, most of them never to return. But worse, the Russian invasion gave the Communists a unique chance to make specific contact with the Chinese Communists. Before withdrawing, the Russians turned over to the Chinese all the Japanese battle equipment they had captured, plus most of their own. The Chinese Communists were now ready to resume their war against the Nationalists, which they did even before the Allied troops in the south were able to get out of the way. Furthermore, the occupation of Korea was divided between Russia and the United States, and instead of striving to rehabilitate the country until it could form its own government the Russians used the opportunity to set up Communist Korean puppets to establish a northern regime apart from the rest of the nation. At the same time, Chinese Communists claimed Manchuria as their own. Where there were Communists there could be no free Catholic Church: Maryknoll found itself locked out of two areas where mission efforts had thrived for twenty years.

Also, it was 1946—time for another general chapter. This time there were more Maryknollers at home than in the Orient, so the chapter was held in the States, at the Vénard. The new superior general was Lane, the pioneer in Manchuria.

Jim Walsh moved out of the superior general's apartment at Maryknoll with relief. His administration had been a difficult one, full of worry and heartache. The war had hampered the society's growth in terms of actual missions, but the heroism of the men in the Orient had earned much publicity and Maryknoll achieved new heights in popularity. As after every war, men who had seen death and suffering now sought new values and became more sensitive to God: they turned to the Church. Applications were heavier at Maryknoll than ever before. Many of the applying veterans had no college training, but they soon filled the halls of Maryknoll's preparatory schools at the Vénard, at Los Altos, at Cincinnati, St. Louis, and Glen Ellyn. Importantly, there was a great interest in the Maryknoll Brothers—the muscles of the society and the most difficult vocations to attract. While other societies went begging for Brothers, Maryknoll acquired an outstanding group, both in numbers and quality, and about 70 per cent of them were veterans.

But where to send them all? From his own experience, Walsh knew of the expanding Communism on the China mainland, and returning missionaries brought additional proof that it would not be long before the Bamboo Curtain would drop over all China with a deadly rattle. In the last years of his administration Walsh informed Rome that this problem would arise and he asked if there was any other place new Maryknollers could be sent to. He remembered that Price had always been interested in South America; he suggested it to Rome. The reply was yes, South America.

Now Walsh had the problem of what to do with himself. For the first time, Maryknoll had a living ex-superior general, on top of which he was a bishop. In all the Church, there was nothing so awkward to have around as an unemployed bishop, and Walsh was keenly sensitive to his superfluity. He made a special point of staying out of Lane's way so that he would not interfere in the new administration or even appear to. He took a little vacation, he traveled to major cities to make speeches about Maryknoll and his experiences in China, then he settled down at Los Altos to write. He produced a penetrating study of the mission factor in the Church that was rich in insight and thought, and he wrote shorter works on the missionary vocation that could well serve as yardsticks for vocation directors.

But he had not become a priest, a missionary, and a bishop to spend his best years as a writer. He wanted to go to work. Lane wanted to put him to work but it was difficult to find a place for him. No vicariates or dioceses were open in the mission field to appoint him to one, and although it was possible to assign him to a mission station as an ordinary missionary, his episcopal position required a certain protocol that would have made this a last resort. He wanted it. He wrote to Lane: "I know there's nothing worse than carrying an extra bishop on the books, so if you want to ship me off to some hidden station in the China bush I'll be happy to go and promise not to be a bother to anybody."

A Eucharistic Congress was scheduled for Australia in 1948. Cardinal Spellman of New York announced his plan to attend, and he wrote Walsh, inviting him to go along as his guest. Walsh was eager to go. The mere idea of it gave him the feeling of having something to do: at least he would get away from the attitude that he was a piece of luggage somebody had absent-mindedly left in the foyer of the Los Altos school. The entourage gathered at San Francisco and sailed away and everybody had an inspiring time in Australia. When the Congress was over, the Cardinal suggested to Walsh, "Now that you're in this part of the world why don't you go up and take a look at China? I know you want to, and your ticket can be adjusted without any trouble."

"I'd like to do that more than anything," Walsh said, and he sailed north to Shanghai happier than he had been for years.

He visited all of his friends and collected much mission data to give to Bishop Lane when he got back. He hoped to make a trip into the interior to survey the mission situation firsthand and he had a deep desire to see Kongmoon again, but the Chinese civil war had moved deep into the south and travel was dangerous so he took the advice of the Papal Internuncio at Shanghai and did not go.

But the Internuncio had other plans. "Do you know what China needs?" he asked Walsh one day. "An organization like your N.C.W.C. in America. Church affairs here ought to be co-ordinated."

The National Catholic Welfare Conference had been organized by the American hierarchy in 1919 to serve as a clearinghouse of information and a center for service on a national scale of Catholic works in the fields of social significance. It had proved highly successful and was eventually the blueprint for similar organizations in other countries.

Walsh conisdered the Internuncio's suggestion. "It is a good idea," he agreed. "At one time with the bad communications there was an excuse for the Church to be so loosely knit in China, but not any more."

"Yes," said the Internuncio, "and with current developments there is all the more reason for unification of action here. That is why I have organized what I call the Catholic Central Bureau of China. How would you like to run it?"

"I'd love it," said Walsh quickly and firmly.

"Is there any reason you must go back to America right away?"

"None at all."

"Then why don't you stay here a while until I see how Rome feels? It shouldn't take long."

"You've got yourself a guest," Walsh said happily.

Rome's reaction came with unusual speed, and it was hearty approval, both of the idea and of Walsh as executive secretary of the new organization. The appointment came as a complete surprise to Maryknoll. Bishop Lane asked Cardinal Spellman if he knew this was going to happen when he invited Walsh to Australia. Spellman replied that it was all news to him, that he had taken Walsh to Australia because he felt Maryknoll should be represented among the Americans there and also because he knew how much Walsh wanted to go somewhere. The suggestion to stop off at China was completely spontaneous, the Cardinal explained, but now he was glad he thought of it because certainly Walsh must be happy to be back there.

He was indeed. He rented office space in a downtwon Shanghai building and acquired an international staff of priests and laymen. He was, in effect, the executive secretary of the Church in China, responsible for the correlation of Catholic social and charitable works. It was, because of the war and the high costs of mission efforts, an impoverished Church. Its funds were to be provided by the hierarchy of China, but the bishops were all poor, and Walsh knew personally what that was like. He did not hesitate to use his own money to keep the organization going. There was a great deal to be done: everything was at loose ends and had to be woven together into a single, effective strand.

In addition to bringing order to what already existed in China, Walsh faced the chore of preparing for what was to come. True, a large part of China had been cut off from the free world, but in the enormous country there still remained a veritable continent for the missionaries to carry on. Anticipating their needs and problems occupied a major part of Walsh's time, but he thrived on it. As far as he was concerned the important factor was that the men were coming back. Throughout all history, war's special hells had forced missionaries to retreat and retrench but they had never surrendered. Their high purpose, measured in terms of eternity, equipped them with a holy patience that survived all of man's cruelties to himself. Whatever happened, whatever they were forced to suffer, the missionaries always went back—and they were coming back now.

Pat Byrne came back. He had remained in Japan until he saw that the occupation was going smoother and better than even he had hoped, then he went back to the States. He did not rest. He detected the embers of the wartime hatred of the Japanese and he was determined to extinguish them. Peace, he felt, was not merely the end of battle but the end of hate. He rejected the suggestion that he should rest and instead toured the country lecturing on Japan, explaining its people, its potentials, its promise. He said he believed that the occupation troops, right there in the land of the recent enemy, would learn to understand and to love the Japanese, and he hoped the rest of the Americans would take the time and trouble to look to the Orient with new eyes and recognize the good that could be achieved there by people who took an intimate interest in it.

Byrne continued at this project for almost a year. At the turn of 1947 he told Bishop Lane that he was ready to go back to Japan whenever he received permission. Lane granted it immediately. In early spring, Byrne was again at Kyoto at his familiar chores. He had learned that Maryknollers who spent the war in prison camps had nevertheless succeeded in converting over two hundred

Japanese, including some of their guards. This was a good sign:
apparently the Japanese, like all other people, looked for more
meaning to life when war took so much meaning out of it.
Furthermore, the Japanese had been deeply impressed to see
thousands of American soldiers file into churches every Sunday;
they were asking questions about Christianity and there was growing evidence of their satisfaction with the answers. Maybe something good would come out of the war after all.

On August 12, Byrne received a cablegram that almost made his
heart stop. It was from the Cardinal Prefect of the Sacred Colloge
of Propaganda, and it read: "CARDINAL FUMASONI COMMUNICATES
FATHER BYRNE APPOINTED VISITATOR APOSTOLIC KOREA, WITH
POWERS APOSTOLIC DELEGATE."

He read it several times, unable to believe it, then he put
through a telephone call to Archbishop Doi in Tokyo and he said,
"Your Grace, I have just received a cable from Rome and—"

"I have a copy of it," said Doi.

"What does it mean?"

"I guess it means what it says," said the Archbishop. "You are
going back to Korea. How do you feel about it?"

"I'm not sure," Byrne said. "I'll go if I have to, but after all
these years in Japan I— The point is I just don't feel I'm the man
for the job."

"The Holy Father seems to think so," Doi said.

There was no argument with that.

Maryknoll had also received a copy of the cable and released it
to the press. Congratulatory mail flooded Byrne, and in answering
one he said:

Your letter, Mother Irene, is edifying and encouraging to a poor
sinner to change his ways, but it is all wrong in one important aspect.
It saith thusly: "Your appointment is a signal mark of our Holy Father's
confidence and trust." No, Most Noble Sister, it is a signal mark of
our Holy Father's overconfidence and mistrust. If he only knew the
real Padre Byrne he would grab for his radio-phone and jangle the
hook up and down and be in a perfect stew until he had called up out
here and cancelled everything. I am hoping for the call any moment
now, and I say a prayer that the Holy Father's guardian angel will
shout in his ear and fix things up before it is too late.

In another letter he observed that the appointment meant he would become a monsignor for the third time. "You know what three strikes mean in baseball," he said.

More soberly, he became aware of a certain uneasiness about the appointment that gradually convinced him it was far more than coincidental. As much as he had loved Korea, he now loved Japan more and would have preferred to stay, but he sensed increasingly that if he stayed he would be rejecting a destiny that—he could not explain how he knew it—would determine his future for all eternity. Friends who measured only his outward attitudes suggested that he write to Rome and ask to have the appointment changed, and it was then that he revealed his inner apprehensions.

"I have even thought of that, too," he said, "but the thing that prevents me from taking that final step is the feeling that this is my last chance for heaven. If I miss this, I am afraid I shall also miss heaven."

No one had ever seen him so serious before.

So he packed his things and went to Korea, there to confront an enemy who was to provide heaven for him and for others as well.

The
Fifth
Decade

XXVI

IN 1948, the Chinese Communists held Manchuria and the northern half of China itself. Equipped with superior weapons supplied by the Russians, they pushed the Nationalists further south than when they had been routed by the Japanese in World War II. The Nationalists also suffered internal strife at the top level in an ill-timed struggle for power. Disgruntled soldiers were deserting the Nationalist army in huge numbers. Chaos in the south brought on extreme inflation that demoralized the people and destroyed unity of purpose against the Communists. Aware of these factors, the Communists wasted no time in taking advantage of them. With irresistible power they pushed southward. In a year they conquered the whole of the mainland, forcing the Nationalists to move their headquarters to Formosa. Thus the Communists fulfilled a conquest plan they had instigated twenty-five years earlier and which they were confident would be realized when, in 1923, the Western powers failed to go to the aid of the budding republic of Sun Yat-sen.

Now the Communist Party went to work to strengthen its control. It could count on about five million members out of a population of over five hundred million, but that was enough. Every profession, trade, and industry was organized. Peasants, youths, and women were enrolled in civic associations of a political nature. The party took over all forms of communication—the press, movies, radio. The police, the military, and the courts became political extensions of the government. In a matter of a few months there was scarcely a thing a human being could do in the course of an average day that was not shaded with political overtones—except pray. The party took that into consideration.

It was quite clear, in the Communist scheme, that unless a man's mind was completely controlled he remained a threat. The way to achieve that control was to control the things that might enter a man's mind. It would be rather difficult to control a man's prayers, but if the party could control when he would pray, where he would pray, and what he would be told to pray about, then the party's promise of freedom of religion in its manifesto could be fulfilled without the danger that freedom of religion would give rise to demands for other freedoms. Controlling religion gave the party the control over moral standards, and with such control there could be no one in the country to argue what was right or wrong. The first step in this direction was to get control of the churches.

There were about ten million Christians in the country, almost evenly Protestant and Catholic. The party realized that to pronounce that Christianity was a two-thousand-year fraud and declare that no good Chinese could adhere to it would be impossible to effect, so a different tack was taken. On the heels of the Communist conquest a propaganda campaign began that defined Christianity in its present form to be a foreign influence in conflict with the national purpose. If the Christian churches were to continue in China, they would have to sever their ties with foreigners and foreign institutions. This was no insuperable problem for the Protestant churches because of their traditional decentralized nature, but the situation was different for Catholics. Being Catholic encompassed a spiritual affiliation with Rome, the seat of Catholic authority. A man could not break that affiliation and still think of himself as a Catholic any more than he could pour all his blood in a bucket and think he could go on living. But that was the point. It was not a cluster of buildings on a Roman hillside that disturbed the Chinese Communist Party; it was the moral link between Rome and the conscience of every Catholic that would prohibit him from tolerating the Communists' demands to put his mind and body to whatever use the party

considered best for the country. To overcome that, the Communists had to remove Rome from the Catholic Church and substitute Peking.

There were at the time some fifty-three hundred foreign priests,
Brothers, and nuns in China. They came from every Western
country; their mere presence in China was evidence of the uni-
versality of the Church: they would have to go. And to defend the
party's scheme of things they would have to go not simply on government orders but on the demands of the people. Of the people,
the Catholics surely did not want them to go; the Protestants saw
in their departure threats to their own missionaries who had done
so much good for them, but the country's five million Communists provided enough people to shunt around to strategic loca-
tions to cause enough havoc to bring about the desired results.

For Maryknollers, the first trouble started in the Kongmoon
diocese, where Maryknoll in China had been born thirty years
before. After the Japanese pulled out of the area, Bishop Paschang returned to Kongmoon from Loting and tried to revive his
work. It was difficult; there had been so much damage. Progress
was slow because of poverty and general chaos, but spirits were
high because of the countless opportunities to help. After two
years of struggle to achieve some semblance of order, the Communists arrived, both the military and the organizers. Both went
quickly to work.

The propaganda barrage was directed first at the Chinese priests
and nuns. In speeches and in the press they were denounced as
"running dogs" of foreigners, and when they appeared in the
streets they were ridiculed by Communist organizers. They were
watched carefully for the slightest infractions of the constantly
changing laws, and when they were caught they were put into
public stocks, and tomatoes and eggs, already too scarce to waste,
were thrown at them.

The Communists disclaimed responsibility for the agitation
and defined it as a growing public sentiment. In light of it, they
said, they could not guarantee the safety of Maryknollers and
therefore forbade their trips into the unpatrolled hinterlands. For
the same reason, missions in the backwoods were closed. The
Maryknoll horizon was steadily decreased.

It was impossible and unwise to fight back. The Maryknollers went about their tasks as best they could and they urged their people to do the same. Encouraged by the lack of resistance, the Communists stiffened their drive.

At Loting, Father Robert P. Kennelly, of Norwalk, Connecticut, had taken over direction of the orphanage started by McShane. The importance of this institution was more than the prevention of abandoned infant roadside deaths: its presence in the city brought about a greater concern for the welfare of all children and the care of all the young was recognized as a precious responsibility and privilege. This humane attitude conflicted with Communist ideas that all people were, above all, wards of the state, which determined their futures.

A newspaper report appeared in Loting charging Kennelly with putting thousands of babies to death. The false details were gruesome and instead of being illustrated with pictures the story was illustrated with exaggerated cartoons. Nobody who lived in Loting any length of time believed it, but the charge was enough for the Communists to expel Kennelly from the country. After his departure he was tried *in absentia* and sentenced to two years in prison.

But there were others to take his place in prison. His assistant, Father Raymond A. Gaspard, was locked up for months. Brother Albert Staubli, a Swiss carpenter who had joined Maryknoll twenty years before and who had erected scores of mission buildings throughout South China, was accused of misusing public property and imprisoned.

Every Communist effort was made to detract from the Maryknoll works of charity. When the sick lined up each morning at mission dispensaries, Communist soldiers stood nearby, as if to protect the people from any Maryknoll attempt to drug them. The leper colony rectory, occupied by Sweeney and Father Carroll I. Quinn, of Baltimore, was taken over by Communist soldiers and the two priests were forced to put up cots in their chapel sacristy. Again an attempt was made to give the lepers the impression that they were being protected by their new masters, but the lepers knew better and paid no attention to them. When confronted by similar indifference elsewhere, the Communists had little trouble digging up enough phony evidence against a priest or nun to ship them out of the country or at least make them retreat to the confines of Paschang's headquarters at Kongmoon City.

A year passed before the Communists felt they had gained enough ground to tackle the popular Bishop himself. Their first thrust was to impose extra taxes on him, which both they and he knew he could never pay. Then they said that if he refused to meet the obligations of an alien in China he ought to get out. He ignored the hints. Then they ordered him out, and he ignored this too.

Then they put him under house arrest. Three times at gunpoint they forced him to telephone the Papal Nuncio at Hong Kong for money under the threat of torture. Their first demand was for forty thousand dollars. The Nuncio said exactly what Paschang expected: no ransoms. The demand was dropped to twenty-two thousand dollars, but still the Nuncio said no.

There was only one way to get rid of him and the Communists took full advantage of it. They concocted an idiotic list of charges against him, ranging from murdering babies to corrupting youth by conscripting boys into the priesthood, and they demanded a confession from him. When he refused, they dragged him to a public trial. Outside the courthouse, twenty Communist soldiers beat and kicked him, then he was turned over to a mob of party members who pommeled him about the face and head for three hours. A large quiet crowd watched, helpless against the cruel power that had taken over their city.

Paschang's persistent refusal to sign a false confession forced the delay of his trial. On the second day of his arrest, he was again taken out in the streets. A rope was tied around his neck and he was pulled, stumbling and falling, through the town. His wrists and knees were open messes of blood and raw flesh. Blood poured from him like sweat. Each time he fell, men pounded the back of his neck with the sides of their hands and women blackened his eyes until he could not see. Garbage was stuffed down his collar and crammed into his mouth.

But still he would not say that he had done the things that were charged against him. Realizing that he might die before he did, the Communists first went to his house and took all the money they could find and toted away all the furnishings they could carry. Then they put Paschang on a boat and took him down the bay to Macao and threw him ashore in the shallow water. They were satisfied now: they were rid of him.

The time came when there were only two priests left in the Kongmoon diocese—Sweeney and Quinn at the leper colony. They had been allowed to remain because the Communists had no one who was willing to replace them. Evicting them would mean that eventually the lepers would take to the streets in search of food and care, and the Communists did not want that. But their continued presence was like an enduring beacon of Christian hope in the darkened land, and this rankled the Communists. They decided at last that, whatever the consequences, the two priests would have to go. One day a squad of Communist soldiers arrived by truck at the leprosarium, and their officer told the priests, "You are to come with me."

"What for?" Sweeney asked.

"There is a new law that all aliens in the country must be registered," the officer said. "I have orders to take you to the county seat for the purpose."

The lepers were worried. "Are you taking the Fathers away?" one asked.

"For a while."

"Will they come back?"

"As soon as they register."

Sweeney and Quinn boarded the truck and were immediately surrounded by the soldiers. The truck roared away from the leper colony and into town, passing the county building without stopping. On it sped into the country, rounding the deep bay and heading northeast, not stopping until, late that night, it reached the boundary of the British territory of Hong King colony. The two priests were taken from the truck and pushed across the border.

The officer said, "There. Now you are out of China. If you make any attempt to re-enter, I have the authority to shoot you as invaders."

With that, the beacon of hope at Kongmoon blacked out.

Half of Korea was in spiritual darkness. The end of World War II shut off the northern sector to all foreign missionaries. Maryknollers returning to Korea or newly assigned to the country took up positions in the south, where the Church was still free to work.

Pat Byrne's appointment to Korea made him the papal representative to the hierarchy, and it was through him that reports of Catholic conditions in the country reached Rome. In the south, all was well, but affairs in the north were far from it. Early in 1949, two seminarians from the Pengyang seminary escaped to the south and brought startling news with them. Bishop Hong, who succeeded O'Shea, had been arrested and imprisoned. The North Korean clergy was disappearing, until now there were only six priests free in the country; all native nuns had either been imprisoned or simply turned out into the streets, their institutions taken over by Communist organizations. In one town, the arrest of parish priests caused a riot between the soldiers and the Catholics in which many were injured and which ended only when the priests, to protect their people, gave themselves up. In all, the two seminarians estimated, some ten thousand North Korean Catholics had been killed because they refused to sign up with Communist agencies.

On the formation of the Republic of Korea at Seoul in 1948, President Syngman Rhee appointed an ambassador to the Vatican. In return, the Vatican named Byrne Apostolic Delegate to Korea and made him a bishop. This was more than he bargained for, but he took it all in a light vein. Protocol required that he now be addressed as "Your Excellency," a formality that so amused him that in turn he often referred to himself as "My Excellency." His work was now apart from Maryknoll, but he took a Maryknoller, Father William R. Booth, of Brooklyn, as his secretary, and he was in frequent contact with Father George M. Carroll, of New York City, who headed the Maryknoll work.

By summer, 1949, the young Korean republic was in a severe state of jitters. Rumors seeped across the 38th parallel that the Communists in the north were building up a huge army, and there could be only one reason for it. The south, complying with occupation agreements, had cut down its forces to a constabulary unit; practically all American units had been withdrawn to Japan and Hawaii. Out of its growing pains, the Rhee government made many bad starts and many errors. Inflation raged. The average man's monthly salary was scarcely enough to support his family for a week. So there was much petty crime in the country, and many who would not resort to it chose the alternative common among Orientals faced with an intolerable situation: they committed suicide.

On Sunday morning, June 25, 1950, Byrne said his Mass early, had breakfast, glanced at the newspapers, and prepared to go to his desk to get at some personal correspondence. His plan was changed when he heard a jeep skid into his driveway. Glancing out, he saw Father Carroll slide from behind the wheel and hurry into the house. Byrne stood up to greet him.

"Pat," Carroll said as he rushed in, "the North Koreans have attacked."

"Are you sure?"

"I said Mass this morning for the Americans at the Sabingo base. Everybody's been called out."

"How serious is it?"

"This is it, Pat," Carroll said.

Byrne started for the door. "The city must be a mess," he said. He opened the door and called, "Somebody find Father Booth for me." Then he turned back to Carroll. "What are you going to do?"

"I've already ordered all Maryknollers to stand by for evacuation to Japan."

"Good."

Booth came in.

Byrne said, "Bill, the Communists have attacked."

Booth sent Carroll a questioning glance.

"It's true," Carroll agreed. "They're already deep into the country."

Byrne said, "Bill, George has ordered all Maryknollers to get ready to evacuate. You'd better pack up and go with him."

"What are you going to do?" Booth asked.

Byrne had already made up his mind. "I'm staying."

"Then I'll stay too," Booth said, adding to Carroll, "if it's O.K. with you."

"You sure you want to?" Carroll asked.

"Yes."

"All right."

Booth asked Byrne, "Is it O.K. with you?"

Byrne measured Booth with gratitude. "I wish you would. But there may be trouble."

Booth shrugged. "We've been expecting it."

"O.K.," Byrne said; then to Carroll, "What shape was the town in when you drove here?"

"The crowds are beginning to head south already."

"I thought as much. Bill, is there much food in the storehouse?"

"We stocked up just last week."

"And clothing?"

"A couple of big boxes from Maryknoll we haven't opened yet."

"Get some of the houseboys to help you pack it all on the pickup, then let's head down to the south gate and pass it out. These people are going to need anything we can give them. Is there any cash in the house?" Booth told him how much. "O.K., bring that along too." Booth left.

Carroll said, "Pat, I'd better get moving. I've got a lot to do."

"All right, George," Byrne said. "Good luck."

Carroll knelt in front of Byrne and said, "Give me your blessing, Pat."

Byrne blessed him, and when Carroll stood they shook hands. "I'll see you, George," Byrne said.

"Yes, Pat. I'll see you. And God bless you."

"I hope He will."

Byrne went to his room and searched through closets for clothes to give to the refugees, then returned downstairs and went to the garage where Booth and the houseboys were finishing their work. Byrne said to the houseboys, "You'd better get to your families now and be on your way south. Thanks for everything; your jobs will be waiting for you when this is over. Bill, give them some of the money to hold them for a while."

There was brutal panic at the south gate. The broad avenues funneling to the exits were packed with terrified people who carried all they owned on their backs. Battered cars, groaning with age, inched through the crowds. Policemen struggled fruitlessly at traffic control, then gave up. Women screamed, children cried, the old who had seen many attacks upon the city waited quietly in glum resignation. Byrne and Booth parked as close to the gate as they could, then gave away the things they had brought along. On Monday they collected more food and clothes from the departing Maryknollers and returned to the gate. They were there on Tuesday when the Maryknollers paused at the truck to say good-by as they left the city.

Wednesday morning, Byrne was in his office, reading his breviary, when the South Korean troops retreated past his house. Street fighting broke out, but Byrne went on with his prayers. He did not look up when a jeep pulled to his front door, nor did he move when a North Korean officer barged into the room.

"I want your jeep that's in the garage," the officer said.

"It isn't mine; it's Father Booth's," Byrne said.

"I don't care whose it is. I want it."

Byrne reacted with a shrug of nonresistance. An hour later other soldiers arrived and entered the garage after Byrne's car. He went to them and said, "That's private property, you know."

"We need it," a soldier said.

"Maybe so, but suppose some general comes along and wants my car for himself. What will I say to him?"

The soldier had no answer, so he left, but he was back in half an hour with an official confiscation order and drove the car away. Aware that the looting would soon start, Byrne packed his vestments and sacred vessels and sent them to the Korean pastor of a nearby church. The articles were no sooner gone than the Communist soldiers returned and began ransacking the house.

Byrne's objection was mild. "You don't have to break everything," he said.

An officer turned on him. "You believe in heaven, don't you?"

"Certainly."

"That's good. You'll soon be going there."

The house was in ruins. That night, Booth found just enough coffee to make a cup for each of them. As they were sipping, Byrne said, "Do you know what day this is? The twenty-ninth. Maryknoll's Foundation Day. Happy birthday."

"Same to you," said Booth. "And many of them."

They could no longer live in the house, so they decided to move into the residence of Seoul's Bishop Paul Ro, who then happened to be in Rome. They knew that sooner or later the Communists would come after them; they felt safer in Ro's house because, with all other Americans having fled, it seemed the last place to look for them. They were careful not to step outdoors in the daytime. For safety's sake—and also because of the heat—they put aside their cassocks and dressed in khaki shirts and slacks. Daily reports came to them on affairs in the city. All foreign missionaries—Protestant or Catholic—who had not escaped were imprisoned in a downtown office building. The city suffered shortages of all kinds, and diseases were breaking out. Suicides were rampant. Korean priests were trying to achieve some kind of order, but few of the city's thirty thousand Catholics were able to get to Mass. Churches were being looted; the Sacred Hosts were being scattered on the ground and trampled upon by Communist organizers who had moved in with the troops.

And the Communists were looking for Byrne. From what they could discover he had not left the city, so a platoon of soldiers were assigned to hunt him down. Captured missionaries were questioned about him, but they said they did not know where he was—which was true. Possible hide-outs were checked off, and gradually the hunt narrowed to Ro's residence.

At five in the evening of July 11, Byrne looked out his window and surveyed the garden: no one was there. Unknown to him, soldiers were watching the building from beyond the wall. Confident that all was well, Byrne stepped out onto the upper porch. The soldiers saw him. In an instant they were in the garden and in the house. A jeep roared up and an officer led the search. The Korean priests tried to hide Byrne and Booth, but it was hopeless. They were found and hauled away with only the clothes on their backs and an hour later they were locked in a small office in the downtown building with fifty other people.

The next week was all hell. Every day Byrne and Booth were taken to the basement where a hundred Communist officers interrogated the prisoners about every moment of their lives. The slightest variance in details between interrogations was sufficient grounds for execution. Those who survived were put on trial. At his trial, Byrne was told, "You will broadcast a denunciation of the United States, of the United Nations, and the Vatican or you will die."

"Then I will die," Byrne said.

In his crowded cell, there was no water or toilet facilities and no one was permitted out except to be questioned. The windows were locked; anybody who opened one or broke one was shot. Food provided was a cup of thin rice soup a day. The cell above was occupied by women, and there was a great deal of traffic in it. Helpless men with Byrne were kept awake all night by the screams of the tormented women.

A shred of hope appeared when the prisoners were told they would be moved north. This could only mean that the American forces had regained the lost ground and were approaching the city. The prisoners, about a thousand of them, were put on a train and taken to Pengyang, where Byrne had started his missionary career twenty-five years before. It was a strange homecoming.

The Pengyang prison had once been a school: it lacked all facilities for so many prisoners. In the seven weeks there, hundreds developed dysentery and worms, and there was no doctor for them. But the interrogations continued, and the beatings and the executions. Unaware that the prisoners were there, American pilots bombed the city and the school was hit. It was only when American ground forces pushed toward the 38th parallel that the prisoners were moved on.

Again they were put on a train, this time for what was ordinarily a ten-hour trip to Manpo on the Yalu. It took a week. By now, hundreds of captured American soldiers had joined the group. Many of them were wounded and sick, but they got no medical care. The train traveled only by night; by day, those who had died during the night were buried in adjacent fields.

It was now the middle of September and it was growing cold along the Yalu. The Manpo prison had also been a school; at one time there had been stoves in every room but now they were all removed. At night the buildings was like an ice house. In command of the prisoners was an officer called the Tiger, and he had the sensitivity of one. At Manpo he called the prisoners out in the freezing dawn and made them strip to the waist for calisthenics. One after another, they fell to the ground from exhaustion, starvation, and disease. Pneumonia became as common as colds.

Manpo was a bedlam. From the south came defeated North Korean troops, retreating before the Americans, and from the north came Chinese "volunteers," crossing the Yalu to get into the fight. It was impossible to keep the prisoners there long. After a few days, the Tiger announced:

"We are going further north, into the mountains to Chung-gangjin. It is a hundred miles and we will have to walk it. I warn you now that anybody who drops out of line will be shot."

From his past travels in the area, Byrne knew what the trip would be like. There would be snow in the mountains, cold and high winds, and no shelters. The morning the march began, he paused to step upon a mound, from where he gave absolution to the long lines of prisoners, for he knew that this would be a march of death.

It lasted eight days. During it, ninety-eight American soldiers were shot for not keeping the pace set by the guards; it was impossible to count the civilian dead. A lieutenant was executed for helping a soldier whose frozen feet had made him immobile. A French nun lost her balance in the stiff wind and fell over; she was shot before she could get up. Byrne's shoelace became undone and his fingers were too numb to tie it himself. A civilian knelt to help him and Byrne bent over, watching. A guard came from behind and kicked Byrne so violently that he went sprawling.

Despite his own hardships, Byrne used his waning energy to help the others. A Methodist missionary had lost his blanket and Byrne insisted that the man take his. The missionary's feet were freezing; Byrne went among the soldiers to borrow an extra pair of socks, then put them on the man himself. Booth offered Byrne half of his blanket one night when they happened to be together during a rest period and Byrne accepted it, but Booth awoke later and found that Byrne had wrapped him in the blanket and had moved aside.

At Chunggangjin, Byrne developed pneumonia, and yet when the order for calisthenics was given he went outside with the other men to suffer through it. That night he had a high fever and severe chest pains, but he hoped that with rest he would recover. At midnight, however, the Tiger burst into the barracks, pulling the prisoners off their mats. "Come on," he said, "we're moving on. Get up! Everybody up!"

Byrne could not get up himself; two men had to help him. "Where are we going now?" he asked the Tiger.

"To Ha Chang Ri, four miles from here."

Covering the four miles took all night and Byrne had to be carried the last few yards. The surviving prisoners stumbled into dirty, cold mud huts and let themselves drop to the bare-ground floor. Someone called out for food, but a guard said there would be nothing that day.

Booth held Byrne in his arms. "This man is sick," he told the guards. "He should have a doctor."

"No doctor," the guard said.

"Give me some hot water—anything to take the chill out of him," Booth said.

"Take him to the hospital," said the guard.

"The hospital?" Booth was surprised.

"The last hut on the path."

It was a small hut, filthier than the others, and in it was a Protestant woman missionary doing her best to give some comfort to the dying who were brought to her. On a stove in the hut was a pot of thick bean soup. "It is all I have," the woman said, "but it may help him."

It helped enough to keep him alive for four days, but even Byrne knew that he would not recover. On the third morning, he asked that one of the priests come to him, and with soft gasps he said the prayers of the dying.

Then he said, "I consider it the greatest privilege of my life to have suffered together with all of you for Christ."

He closed his eyes, surrendering himself to death, and it came to him at dawn of the next morning.

XXVII

Two years passed before the world learned Byrne had died, for it was not until then that the United Nations prison-camp inspectors located the survivors of the death march in the mountain village. And yet there were a few people who sensed he was gone, people who had loved him well and long and who, when only miles separated them, still felt him near but who somehow knew that now eternity had stepped between them. Frank Ford was one of these persons. Byrne had been one of his teachers during his early seminary days and they had been close friends over the years. When news came from Maryknoll that Byrne was missing, Ford, like all the others, thereafter spoke his name at the Commemoration of the Living at Mass. But when the months passed and there was still no word of Byrne, Ford began to say his name at the Commemoration of the Dead.

Ford himself did not have far to look for samples of Communists at work. On its southward trek in the civil war, the Communist army had moved right past his door, leaving organizers in its wake. They arrived with many promises, but Ford had beat them to it. The co-operatives he had started during the war continued with growing success. If there was one place in China where the Communist bait of material welfare was wasted, it was at Kaying. The people, to be sure, were not rich, but they had enough to meet their needs, and they had hope for the future. Also, the religious atmosphere was healthy. When Ford arrived at Kaying there had been only six Catholics, and they attended Mass in a small room of the house he bought. Now he was ready to build a cathedral—and there were more than enough Catholics to fill it.

The Communists, then, had to use different tactics at Kaying. They began by harping on foreign intrusion into Chinese affairs, progressing to the condemnation of Chinese who collaborated with the foreigners, then the public denunciation of the foreigners themselves. At Kaying as elsewhere the Communists at first promised freedom of religion, but their propaganda against foreigners soon made evident their opposition to religion that had come from outside the country. It was up to the priests to explain to the people that it was not simply the foreign religion the Communists opposed but foreign morals: morals, at least, foreign to Communists.

Ford viewed the Communist expansion with scientific care. He kept extensive records on known Communists at Kaying, on Communist activities and Communist anticipations. Through this he hoped to understand them better and thus be better able to defend himself and his work. He also felt that blueprinting the Communist technique would be helpful to the clergy in other countries in the event of Communist infiltration. Knowing the enemy, it would be easier to deal with him.

In line with his studies, he wrote this:

Perhaps the most glorious page in Chinese history is now being written by the devotion of both Chinese priests and Chinese Catholics. There has been little panic and there is a surprising demonstration of fidelity to their Faith. Almost overnight the Catholic Body has been recognized even by puzzled pagans as the one anti-Communist force in evidence throughout China, not necessarily an endorsement of the Nationalists' regime but clearly taking a stand on moral and doctrinal grounds. The Church, hitherto perhaps too aloof and esoteric, could soon become a practical way of life that pagans understand.

But the Communists had a strategy that wiped out attempts to cope with them: when they could not win by argument they fought with brute force. In December, 1950, the Communists froze all American property in China; the following January they confiscated all American institutions. In carrying out this policy, they arrested several Kaying priests and nuns on December 3, 1950, and then they got ready for Ford.

They barged into his house on December 23. At the time, only Ford's secretary, Maryknoll Sister Joan Marie, was there with him, and both were made house prisoners. For the next three months, the Communists made a systematic study of Ford's files, noting all that he had recorded about them. On the basis of what they found, they prepared a bill of charges against him, accusing that he was harboring agents of the Kuomintang, that he was organizing a "black army" to rise up against the government, that he was preparing an underground campaign to thwart Communist reforms at Kaying. His principal target was said to be the newly organized Chinese National Catholic Church.

By early April, the Communists felt they had enough evidence against Ford in his own handwriting to take care of him and enough converts in the town to provide a suitable demonstration. On April 14, Ford and Sister Joan Marie were taken from the house and led through the streets to the courthouse. Demonstrators lined the route and threw rocks and garbage at them as they walked by. At the public trial the court's case was so well organized, Ford's records so cleverly distorted, that even his old friends began to wonder if possibly he had been deluding them all these years.

The court's decision: Ford and Sister Joan Marie were to be sent to Canton to be tried by delegates of the national party.

They were taken by a slow and circuitous route, stopping off at towns along the way to be paraded in front of the people. Their hands were tied behind them, connected by rope to a noose around their necks, and heavy packages were put in their hands so that the weight pulled their heads painfully back. In each town, they were forced to pass between shrieking rows of people who beat them with clubs and sticks. One day their ropes were put on wet so that as they dried they bit into their flesh. Another day, a boy thrust a stick between Ford's legs, tripping him. When he fell, the mob pounced on him.

Not once did he make any effort to ward off their blows, not once did any expression of resentment enter his eyes. Throughout the ordeal he made only one comment. He said to Sister Joan Marie, "We are going to prison in honor of Christ, and it is no disgrace."

At last they reached the People's National Prison on Yellow Flower Road in Canton and they were assigned to separate sections. Then the Communists began the slow, relentless, brutal campaign to brainwash them. They were awakened every morning at six and taken to separate rooms where skilled interrogators worked on them ceaselessly for twelve hours, cajoling them, threatening them, beating them. They were questioned repeatedly on every moment of their lives, every thought they ever had. With fiendish skill, the interrogators remembered every word they said, throwing back the words if there was any deviation in their stories. Some days they were forced to stand under burning lights and listen to harangues against the United States, the United Nations, and the Catholic Church, then they were quizzed on what they had heard and if they did not answer correctly they were beaten. The moment came when they were not sure if the answers they mumbled came by rote or by conviction. They hoped that the right answers would persuade the interrogators to go easier on them, but then they were asked if they believed what they were saying and when they said no the torture started all over again.

In this way they passed the summer, then the winter. They did not see each other, they could not communicate with each other or anybody else, each was not certain the other was still alive.

It was not until January, 1952, nine months after their arrest, that Sister Joan Marie caught a glimpse of Ford. They had both been taken outdoors for exercise, and she saw him through a crack in the wood fence between them. His hair had turned white and he had a long white beard. He was using a stick as a cane. Another prisoner was with him, a trustee, and the man tried to walk Ford too fast. Ford spoke to him. The man squatted in front of Ford and Ford put his arms around the man's neck, then he picked Ford up and carried him back into the prison, past guards who stood laughing at him.

A few days later Sister saw Ford again in the same way. This time she noticed how emaciated he looked. She had only a moment to study his face: it seemed peaceful and calm and still intelligent. She judged from it that the interrogators had not as yet succeeded in breaking him.

She saw him once more, about two weeks later. She was scrubbing the floor of her cell; the bottom of the door was about four inches off the floor to provide ventilation. She heard footsteps and stretched on the floor to see who it was. Across the corridor was a staircase. She saw the forms of men approach it and begin to descend. Over the shoulder of one, slung like a lifeless sack, was Bishop Ford.

When week after week passed and she did not see him again Sister was not too perturbed. After all, she had already gone months without a look at him. Evidently he was ill: maybe he had been put into a hospital. She prayed for him, as she prayed for herself and other Maryknollers she knew were in prisons. She knew that whatever she had suffered Ford must have suffered more because of his importance in the country and the victory his submission would be for the Communists. At times she wondered how she managed to survive the mental and physical brutality, but she did. She was ill herself, but she had retained her self-control, and when she remembered what she had gone through she shuddered for Ford.

She began to notice that the interrogators sent for her less often as the second summer passed. Had they given up? Had they realized at last that she would never surrender to them?

On August 16, she was taken to a room where she had never been before, and she was told that the man at the desk was a prison official. For the first time of all the occasions she had been summoned she was invited to sit down.

The man said to her, "Bishop Ford is dead."

Her heart sank but she tried not to show it. "When did he die?"

"In February. On the twenty-first."

"Why have you waited until now to tell me?"

"There were many complications."

"How did he die?" she asked.

"He was not well. The doctors did everything for him they could. They say he died of old age."

Old age? He was only sixty.

The man handed Sister several photographs. "These were taken after his death."

The pictures showed him on a bed, dressed in the Chinese-style padded robe and wool skullcap he usually wore at Kaying in winter and which he had on the day he was taken from his house. The beard he had when Sister last saw him had been shaved off. His eyes and cheeks were sunken and his hands were bone thin. On one side of the bed stood a nurse, on the other a doctor.

"May I have these?" Sister asked.

"They are for our files," the man said.

"Can you make copies for me?"

"The negatives have been lost." The man passed a document to her. "This is an official report of his death. You will have to sign it."

"But I know nothing about his death except what you told me. Why is it necessary for me to sign this?"

"For our files." He gave her a pen. "You will have to sign it."

She read it quickly. It was full of medical terms and it meant little to her. She signed it.

The full impact of Ford's death did not strike her until she was returned to her cell. She felt very alone and helpless and suddenly the fight went out of her. When her evening meal was brought she was too weak to touch it. The prison officials showed a concern she never expected from them: when, in the morning, she was unable to rise from her cot several people came to see her and she was moved to the prison hospital where she received overwhelming attention. She deduced that they did not want her death on their hands as well as Ford's.

Two weeks later, when she was feeling better, her clothes were given to her and she was ordered to dress. She presumed she would be sent back to her cell, but instead she was led to the front door and to a car. She was taken to an old cemetery on the outskirts of the city, then to a particular plot. The headstone on it was the rough granite slab commonly used and upon it in red paint were written the Chinese characters for Ford's name and the word "grave." And the date: February 21, 1952. The paint was still wet.

There was no way she could be sure Ford was buried in the grave, but she said a prayer for him, wherever he might be. No one spoke to her during these moments. Then she was taken back to the car. From the route, she realized she was not going back to the prison. The car sped out into the country, roared through towns and villages, onward for the rest of the afternoon. It was not until the car made the broad turn at the base of a mountain and Sister saw the English guards at the Hong Kong border that she knew for certain that it was all over.

However horrible the ordeal, it was fitting that a Maryknoll Sister should share it with Ford. He more than anyone else guided the work of the Sisters in China and was responsible for innovations that gave almost revolutionary scope to the nature of the Sisterhood. When the Sisters first went to the missions, it was to work with Ford at Yeungkong; he built their first mission convent. And when he was assigned to Kaying his first request was for Sisters.

Ordinarily, even at home, the Sisters led sheltered lives, forced upon them by a public opinion that the circumstances of their vocation made them too fragile for the brutal facts of the cruel world. They were expected always to be soberly demure, to travel about at least in pairs, to concern themselves only with their prayers and their duties of teaching, nursing, or office work. Ford felt they could do much more.

China was a man's country, with the woman three paces behind her husband. If she kept her house well, did her share of work in the field, and produced enough sons, she was fulfilling her proper role as a human being and little more was expected—or tolerated —from her. In religion, she became a Christian only if her husband did, and most often he did not think this was necessary. In church she sat apart from him, frequently in a separate chapel with other women. Ford saw the shortcomings in this arrangement. It was more in the nature of the woman, the mother, to set the moral tone of a home, to see that the children were properly raised, and that religious obligations were met. The father might well be the disciplinarian, but it was the mother's influence that could make severe discipline unnecessary. To try to change the situation by discussing it with men would be, Ford knew, a waste of time. But there was a way the change could be brought about.

The Sisters. Ford was always grateful for their services in the schoolroom, the dispensary, and the office, and he was well aware of the spiritual value of their prayers. In addition, he felt the apostolic purpose of the missions could be better served if the Sisters took a more active part in it. If the Chinese woman could be reached only in her home, then the Sisters should go there.

Ford therefore instituted a new program for mission Sisters that greatly expanded their field activities. Just as priests took trips into the bush to make conversions, now the Sisters went. Arriving at a remote town, they took residence in a Chinese home where they could make contact with the women. Through the women, the Sisters learned who was sick in town and treated them. They got to know the children and gave them the rudiments of education. In the kitchen, they taught women sanitation, better cooking mehods, easier laundry methods, simpler house-cleaning methods. During all this they talked to the women about religion. At night, when the women gathered apart from the men, the Sisters were with them, becoming their friends by sharing their interests and problems. They often stayed on two or three months, gradually breaking through the Chinese woman's resistance to strangers and her refusal to think about anything without her husband's permission. Women began to discover they had brains and could make decisions, and when they decided to become Catholics they went ahead with it whether their husbands did or not. Experience had shown that with a Catholic mother in the house, raising Catholic children, it was only a matter of time until the father perceived the vitality of the new influence surrounding him and joined the Church himself.

At the mission station, convents became rallying places for women. The Sisters were put in charge of sodalities, which elsewhere was considered a priest's job. And where in the past the Sisters normally disappeared behind their closed doors at sunset now they were busy at evening classes for women in catechism and domestic sciences. Often men who could not attend daytime classes by a male catechist found themselves studying religion at night with the Sisters, and once they got used to the idea that their women teachers might know more about something than they did they relaxed and learned.

The program soon proved so successful that when requests came from distant villages for someone to come and teach religion, Ford did not hesitate to send Sisters instead of the usual catechists. Some people doubted the wisdom of this, wondering if the accepted delicacy of nuns could endure against the realities of Chinese life without personal shock or scandal. Ford pointed out that the Maryknoll Sisters were attracting women from all walks of life, women who had worked in factories, or newspapers, in shops, in emergency wards, in slum areas, and he was sure there was not much about realities they didn't already know. They revealed their practicality when they complained to Ford that their religious garb was often too cumbersome for the flat sampans and bicycles on which they had to travel in the bush; Ford told them to simplify it.

From the original six secretaries who went to work at Hawthorne in 1911, the Sisters grew, at the end of 1960, to some fifteen hundred. From the first six to go into the first mission in 1921, they have spread throughout the Free Orient, Pacific islands, Latin and South America, Africa, and the Japanese, Chinese, Mexican, and Negro concentrations in the United States. In 1932, a special house was built on their property at Maryknoll for those who sought the cloistered life, and from there since has emanated a steadily growing horizon of prayer to enrich the congregation's work throughout the world.

And the Maryknoll Brothers grew. From the first two who went to Hawthorne they increased in fifty years to almost two hundred, this during an era when vocations for the Brotherhood were scarce everywhere. One reason for the scarcity was the deepening materialism in the country that discouraged men from entering a work in which they would receive practically no pay, no promotions, no privileges. Also, it was said of Brothers that either they were aspirants for the priesthood who could not make the grade or square pegs who couldn't fit into the world's round holes. Their religious life was supposed to be incomplete because they did not have the spiritual consolations of saying Mass or absolving sin. Thus many men who thought of entering the Brotherhood were discouraged by their families, their friends, or themselves.

But this was not the case at Maryknoll. Each year, more and more men arrived who wanted to be Brothers and nothing else. They included college professors, scientists, executives, craftsmen of all trades, farmers, truck drivers, accountants, printers, policemen. When their number outgrew their facilities at Maryknoll they moved into new buildings at Brookline, Massachusetts. Then, in 1959, they themselves constructed a training center back at Maryknoll, and when they returned they occupied as a residence the expanded house where the first Maryknollers lived, now practically a shrine to the society.

In the missions the Brothers were, perhaps even more than the priests, all things to all men. Their first task was construction work. Just as Brother Albert gave China a new skyline, so did Brother William Neary, of North Adams, Massachusetts, in Korea and Japan, Brother Damien Walsh, of Wheeling, West Virginia, in Africa, and Brother Gonzaga Chilutti, of Philadelphia, in South America. Once the mission buildings were up, the Brothers put in the lights and heating systems, kept the mission cars and boats running, ran the dispensaries and kitchens and offices, grew the vegetables and tended the animals, printed the textbooks and the catechisms, then taught from them. And in the process of doing all these things they trained natives in the skills, thereby providing a means of livelihood to men who had had none before.

As important as what they did was how they did it, for as vital as a Brother's talents was his attitude. If in the past fifty years there was one vanishing trait among Americans it was selflessness, and yet no man could be a successful Brother without it. To be humble, to be free of intellectual pride, to be self-effacing and self-abnegating in good balance and good humor were prerequisites to the Brotherhood. Only a man of spiritual maturity could possess them: they were the stuff of which saints were made.

Brother Gonzaga had it. By trade he was a mechanic. Before going to Maryknoll he had been with the Trappists, but he put aside the cloistered life he loved in order to take an active part in the missions. When his Maryknoll training was completed, he was assigned to the Pando vicariate in Bolivia. For seven years his days were full of work, and he made the work a prayer. Invariably he was the first one up in the morning, anxious to have the chapel ready for Mass, and late at night, when others had fallen exhausted on their beds, he could be heard in his workshop repairing any of the contraptions that were forever breaking down. The mystery about him was how he did so much. He could be busy on the motor of the mission boat that plied the Beni River, but in the same day he would fix a child's broken toy, help an Indian paint his house, change the plugs on the pastor's jeep, repair a Sister's damaged typewriter, hurry to a distant outstation with fuel, and spend a few hours in the dispensary. And yet he never complained that he had too much to do; he complained merely that he didn't have enough time to do all he should. His failing—if it was one—was that everything was important to him, whether it was his work itself, an old woman who wanted to talk about her ailments, a young man who wanted to discuss his forthcoming marriage, a child who tried to smile him out of a piece of candy, or a barnyard animal about to give birth. Whatever he was doing, he never hesitated to turn his full attention to whoever or whatever popped up in the midst of it. To be able to do this with love, patience, and sincerity was a special virtue as well as a rare fault.

He was a very pious man, with a deep devotion to the Virgin Mary. He mentioned her in every conversation and called on her for help regardless of how small his plight. When hard work and irregular hours brought on stomach trouble and he was forced into the hospital he observed that he had fallen ill on the Feast of the Presentation and recovered on the Feast of the Immaculate Conception, and he said, "I guess Mary knew when I needed a rest and when I had enough of it." He also had a vital respect for the sacramental faculties of priests. Once he was driving in New York with a priest and they came upon a car accident. They both got out to see if they could help, and it was Gonzaga who first suggested, "Maybe somebody needs absolution." Later he observed as a gentle reprimand, "Too often when an emergency of death arrives a priest becomes preoccupied about many things and forgets what he should do as a priest." It was his way of saying that as long as priests had the faculties to get people into heaven they ought to work at it every minute.

He died as he lived. Early in 1952, Bishop Lane went to Bolivia on an inspection tour. Because most of the missions were along the Beni River it was decided to make the trip on the mission boat. Brother Gonzaga worked on the boat for days to have it in perfect shape—a major chore because weather and misuse at the hands of natives had taken their toll. Dissatisfied with the motor's slightest knock or groan, Brother Gonzaga asked to go along in case anything went wrong.

For four days Gonzaga did not leave the boat to eat or sleep. When others went ashore to be feasted at a mission, he remained aboard, satisfied with a sandwich and a cup of coffee, one eye always on the motor as though it were some demon out to ruin Lane's visit. At night he slept outdoors on planks stretched over the motor pit to be sure that no one else touched it. He had placed holy cards all over the boat and a picture of the Little Flower in the pilot's cabin, saying, "The trip is under her protection." But he did not spare himself in providing protection of his own. One night he was drenched by rain, but in the morning he was contented with "Well, the motor's dry."

On the fourth day a mission visitation was completed in the afternoon, and it was decided that to save time they would proceed to the next mission, eight hours away. Gonzaga took food aboard for dinner en route. As he prepared it, he kept darting up to the pilot's cabin with advice for the priests who were taking turns at the helm, continuing at this during his meal.

When dinner was over, Lane and the priests put chairs at the bow where they could relax and watch the scenery. Gonzaga gave the wheel to a native, then sat on a stool in the passageway at the mouth of the motor pit. He called out, "Hey, look at the beautiful sunset!"

They looked at it, then glanced up at him to acknowledge his pleasure in it. He was sitting there, smiling down at them, his rosary in his hands. Moments later there was a great noise, glass broke, the lights went out, and sparks flew from everywhere; the boat lowered in the river and began to take on water.

Lane and the others ran back to see what had happened. They discovered that a giant tree had toppled from the shore, falling directly into the narrow passageway, striking Gonzaga and pushing him down into the motor pit. They thought the tree was pinning him down, but actually he was free of it. One priest gave him absolution before they all hurried down into the pit to him.

They carried him to a bunk. His eyes were open and he was breathing, but he was unconscious and gave no sign of pain. They examined him and detected broken bones in the neck and back. As they tried to make him comfortable, each priest blessed him and gave him absolution, then they all knelt at his side to pray. A native craft came alongside; its passengers removed the tree from across the boat, then towed it on to the mission ahead. Gonzaga was dead before they arrived. It was only after they had carried him to the mission, put him on a cot, and prepared him for burial that someone realized what a proper day it was for another Maryknoller to go to heaven: it was the Feast of the Apparition of the Blessed Virgin at Lourdes.

XXVIII

LANE sent cables to Maryknoll stations across the world, asking prayers for Brother Gonzaga, but there was one mission where the prayers could not be said. That was at the Tungan mission, in the Kwangsi Province of South China, seven hundred miles west of Canton. The cable was not delivered to Tungan: for over a year the mission had been a prison.

In October, 1950, Father Robert W. Greene, of Jasper, Indiana, was the Tungan pastor, and with him were two new missionaries —Gregory Gilmartin, of Waterbury, Connecticut, and Irwin Nugent, of Dorchester, Massachusetts. These three had big plans for Tungan. Greene had fifteen years of experience in China, at Kweilin, as a chaplain with the Americans during the war, and now Tungan. Greene felt he understood the Chinese and how to best reach them; there was much he wanted to do for them.

The three were just settling down to work when the Communists arrived. First came a military unit of a thousand men, well-trained, well-ordered men, and by their presence they indicated that the Communist element in the country had stretched its control deeper and deeper across the land. Greene braced himself for trouble, but it did not come. On the contrary, one soldier painted on the mission walls the Chinese characters for freedom of religion. That was hopeful. Also, the mission had the only clinic in the area and the soldiers came for medicine. They told Greene how they had met Americans and fought at their side against the Japanese during the war. One soldier had been wounded and proudly showed Greene where American doctors had removed the bullet. More hope.

But then the army moved out and the organizers moved in and that was the beginning of the end.

First, the priests were told they could not leave the mission grounds. Then the people were told they could not go to the mission. The three Chinese nuns assigned to the mission were ordered away. For a while they lived with families in town, but when they realized that the people with whom they stayed were being arrested or fired from their jobs the Sisters split up and went back to their own homes.

On April 9, 1951, Gilmartin was given an hour to pack, and he was taken to Canton to be expelled from the country. Three days later, Nugent was likewise expelled. This left Greene alone at the mission, and he also expected to be sent on his way shortly. Instead, he was put under house arrest, confined to two rooms in the rectory. That day he watched the Communist organizers strip his chapel of his altar, pictures, statues, and pews, replacing them with chains, stocks, and instruments of torture: the chapel was turned into a jail.

Greene had an unusual stroke of luck. When he was confined to the rectory there was stored in the attic an assortment of Mass vestments, a Mass kit, some Communion Hosts, a few bottles of Mass wine, and a sack of wheat. Thus he was able to say Mass every day of his imprisonment. Even during the weeks when a guard stayed in the room with him constantly, he was able to go upstairs at dawn and say his Mass before the guard awoke. From the Masses Greene derived the strength to preserve his sanity.

He was appalled by the change that came over the people who had been his friends for years. His cook, Ah-Hui, was taken away from him and Greene did not see the man for over a year. Forced to cook his own meals, Greene was allowed to go into town under guard once a week to buy rice, vegetables, and eggs. Each week he noticed that fewer of the merchants were willing to sell to him, until at last there was only one. Children who had attended the mission schools began to taunt him in the streets, spitting at him and calling him the vilest names. Adults who at one time were willing to die for him now turned their backs on him. At first he excused it all as fear, but then gradually became aware of the results of clever propaganda.

The mission convent had been turned into a Communist headquarters and each day crowds were brought out from town for outdoor lectures. Greene could not help but hear them. They were masterpieces of delusion. The speakers began by appealing to fine instincts—patriotism and family loyalty, then they twisted them by false logic into instruments of Communism. The speakers were intent and loud and convincing. Like catechists, they quizzed their listeners on previous talks so that by repetition the people came to believe the things they were saying. If they needed further encouragement to the new faith of China, they had only to witness the daily executions of those who refused to believe.

The sadness was that they did believe so readily. They grasped at Communism as the panacea for all of China's woes. Although the Communists gave them no material aid, they accepted the promise of a better future. They quickly adopted Communist tactics: children informed on their parents, brother informed on brother, town informed on town. Any old grudge could now be revenged with a lie, and because the Communists accepted the lie the liars came to believe themselves. Fear became a weapon in the hands of those who were afraid; hate became the defense of those who a short time ago were the hated. How much of it was effective brainwashing and how much of it was mere effort to survive no one could tell. Either way, it all served the Communist purpose.

Greene's interrogation began soon after his confinement. Every day he was led to a tribunal in the convent where he was questioned about every moment of his life, over and over. Sometimes he was required to give his answers in writing. He was charged with posing as a priest but actually being an American spy, with giving comfort to the Nationalist guerrillas by granting them medical aid at the mission, and with perverting the people by affiliating them with a foreign ideology—Christianity. The questions were put to him so heavy with *non sequiturs* that they often confused him and often he was not even sure whether his answers

trapped him. After one twelve-hour session, he was jolted awake
in the middle of the night by the realization that he had admitted
to paying a guerrilla to shoot a Communist soldier on the compound, whereas he knew perfectly well the soldier had injured
his hand chopping wood.

His rooms were searched daily. One morning a peculiar assortment of items was taken: an ordination picture of himself, a
U. S. insignia he had worn as a chaplain, and a toy medal decorated with blue stars that a boy at home had given him when he
left for the missions and which he forgot he had. Months later
he discovered the reason for it.

The interrogation of Greene stopped suddenly and without
explanation, but it did not mean peace for him. Being restricted
to his room, being unable to speak to anybody prevented him from
sending or receiving mail, from keeping a diary, from reading
anything but his breviary; all combined to drive him close to
madness. Added to this, there were daily executions outside his
window, the screams of tortured men and women wafted to him
from the chapel day and night, and the shouted lectures of the
Communist organizers pounded at his head for hours every day.
Sheer inactivity ripped his nerves. The fear of renewed questioning put his body in a state of constant cramps. Week after week
passed this way; only his Masses gave him anything to hold on to.

Then in January, 1952, almost a year after his house arrest,
the interrogations resumed. They were worse than before, endless,
penetrating, overwhelming. The guard was taken out of his
rooms so that, between interrogations, he did not even have the
comfort of another person's presence, even a person to whom he
could not speak. The simple fact of being so utterly alone caused
him physical pain. Despite the danger in it, he decided there was
only one thing he could do. At Mass he consecrated two Hosts,
one to consume then and the other to place in a pyx in his room
for adoration whenever he got the chance. The danger was one
of desecration: if the Communists found the Host they would
certainly defame It, and Greene felt he would be involved in the
responsibility. He hid the pyx in a metal cash box and wrapped
it in a towel and put it in the small second room. Whenever he
returned from being questioned, whenever he was sure he would

be left alone for a while, he knelt before his unusual tabernacle in the True Presence and absorbed the strength that no human being could give him.

On the morning of April 3, he was again taken to the convent for questioning. The official behind the desk was a man he had never seen before and he wondered what the change meant.

The man said, "Now we are ready to deal with you. We have checked on you and we have conclusive evidence that you are not a priest but an American spy."

"How did you manage to do that?" Greene asked.

The man tossed him a photograph. It was quite obviously a composite, and not a good one, but it explained what had happened to the ordination picture, the U. S. insignia, and the toy medal that had been taken from him a year earlier. They had all been blended into one false picture that made him look as if he had been photographed in his black suit with the insignia on his lapel and the medal on his chest. It was a ridiculous picture and Greene said so.

"That's what I expected you to say," the official said, "so I have gathered a few people who can testify to the charge."

Then began an eight-day private trial, a parade of people Greene knew and many he didn't know—all with fantastic lies about his conduct in China. It was bad enough to hear his friends lie but the lies of strangers were so frustrating that he could just sit there and gape. Worst, his old cook, Ah-Hui, was brought in, and for three hours the man went through the Ten Commandments, listing the times he had seen Greene violate them. No priest, Ah-Hui said, would act like that; therefore Greene was not a priest.

Most terrifying for Greene was the refusal to let him go back to his rooms at the end of the day. Instead he was put into the cell that had been made out of the chapel sacristy. His great worry was the consecrated Host in the cash box. If It was found It would surely be desecrated. He begged to be allowed to live in his rooms but they would not let him. One desolate night he took a straight pin holding his shirt together and put it to his wrist to puncture his vein. He realized what he was doing in time and said aloud, "No. You are a priest. You can't do it."

The following Sunday—Palm Sunday—he was taken into town for a public trial in the town square. Again, for a whole week, the witnesses came, all swearing that he was not a priest, that he had confided this to them and proved it by his conduct. Greene tried to shut his ears to it all, repeating to himself over and over, "You are a priest. You are Bob Greene, a priest, a priest of God. You are a priest."

Again Ah-Hui proved the worst of all. He cited again Greene's violations of the commandments—in cursing people with God's name, in not saying Mass on Sundays, in denouncing his own dead mother, in stealing and killing and taking women—on and on he went. He added a new fable: he said Greene had kept him under drugs during his employment at the mission in order to enslave him.

The trial ended on Easter Sunday. When it was over, the official acting as judge called out to the crowd, "You have heard the evidence. How do you decide?"

The cry went up, "Kill him! Kill him!"

"The people have spoken," the man announced.

Taken back to his chapel cell, Greene was informed that he would be beheaded in the morning. He asked if he could spend his last night in his rooms, but he was refused. He worried all night about the Host, awake until dawn saying a rosary on his finger tips to ask forgiveness for his part in the desecration.

In the morning he was taken again to the convent. The man who acted as judge was there. So was another man—a Russian general.

The judge said, "I have received a telegram from the office of Comrade Mao Tse-tung. Your sentence has been changed. You are to be expelled from the country."

"Thank you," Greene said.

"Don't think you are getting away with anything," the man declared. "We've gotten what we wanted out of your trial. We've destroyed the Church in this district. We've proved that Mao is great and kind and merciful in letting a criminal like you live. You're not going to get away anyway, because we're going to take over America in ten years."

"I hope you don't," Greene remarked softly, "but that is up to God."

The Russian general said, "You say you're the chosen of God. Very well, then, we are the picked troops of Satan. We'll see who wins."

"Yes, we shall." Then Greene asked the Chinese, "Will I be permitted to go back to my rooms for a moment? There are some things there I want."

"We'll see."

He was returned to his cell briefly, then a squad of soldiers led him to the rectory. The sergeant said, "You are not to touch anything. Tell us what you want and we'll get it for you. And you can't take anything made of metal." Once inside, he asked, "What do you want now?"

Greene answered, "A pyx, a cassock, and a stole."

The soldiers had no idea what these things were, but instead of revealing it they drifted about the main room, picking up items and asking if they were what Greene had said.

"I think the pyx is in the other room," he said. "I'll get it."

"No." The sergeant stopped him. "We'll get it."

That could not be. Only the blessed hands of a priest could touch a pyx and its Holy Contents. Greene was quiet. The soldiers wandered about. They saw the crucifix on the wall and became interested in it. The sergeant, to show off his knowledge, began to explain it to them. A corporal stood near Greene.

Greene said, "If I can't go into the next room alone, come with me."

The corporal glanced at the busy sergeant: it seemed all right to go. He let Greene open the door to the smaller room and take the cash box from a shelf.

"You can't have that," the corporal said. "It's metal."

"I don't want it," Greene said. "But there's something in here that might interest you. I want to show you how we pray." He removed the pyx and opened it. Then he took the Host quickly and put It into his mouth.

"Don't do that," the corporal shouted. "Don't swallow that."

The sergeant came running. "What's happened?"

"He's put something into his mouth," the corporal said. "Maybe poison."

"Or a secret document," the sergeant suggested. "Open your mouth."

Greene opened his mouth; it was empty. "I was just showing the corporal how Catholics pray," he said.

They watched him for a moment, waiting to see if anything would happen. When it didn't, they let him pack a few things—including the pyx, even though it was metal—and they took him to a waiting bus.

The trip to Kweilin took all day because at each town Greene was ordered off the bus so that people could see him. They called him names, threw things at him, and said he should have been killed. At Kweilin he spent the night in a prison cell. All he received to eat was the water in which rice had been cooked. In the morning he was put on a train to Canton where he was given a hotel room and a meal. He saw himself in a mirror for the first time in almost three weeks. His beard was big, his face was covered with pus-filled sores. He asked for shaving equipment and a medical kit, but they were refused. Next morning he was put on the train for Hong Kong.

There were others on the train who were being expelled, and at the barbed-wire fence that separated the British territory from China there was a great deal of red tape. Each time Greene reached the head of the line, a few feet from the gate, he was ordered away. He wondered if the Communists could be so cruel as to bring him this far and then return him to Tungan for execution. At last he was the only person left. His papers were examined. Then, without a word, the Communists walked away in apparent disgust and left him standing there. He was afraid to look back at them; he was afraid to move to the gate lest they shoot at him for attempting to cross the border. A young Chinese soldier at the gate caught Greene's eye and nodded almost imperceptibly. Greene took the few steps. Nothing happened. He passed through the gate holding his breath.

Red Cross workers and British police were milling among the refugees. Greene tried to lose himself in the crowd for safety. A soldier stepped to him. "Are you the padre?"

"Yes." The one word revealed a year of fear.

The soldier put an arm around Greene. "It's O.K., Father. Everything will be all right. Come with us; you're free now."

Greene pressed his face against the young man's shoulder and stood there a long time, weeping.

XXIX

GREENE was the last of the Maryknollers to leave the Kweilin prefecture; the others were already expelled. The picture was the same all over China. Of the fifty-three hundred missionaries who were there in 1950 only fifteen hundred remained in 1952, and many of these were in prison. Others had been beheaded, bayoneted, burned alive, had their heads crushed between stones, had been dragged and beaten by mobs until they died.

If, however, the Communists thought that by producing long lists of martyrs in China they were exterminating the Church itself they were wrong. Since the birth of Christianity, one country after another tried to weaken the Church through mass murders but all they succeeded in doing was strengthening the Church elsewhere. It was happening again. For every priest who died in China, a dozen young men stepped forth in other countries to take his place. At Maryknoll, applications for studies were greater than ever before. Ordination classes were bigger than ever before. Where at one time a dozen new Maryknollers a year was considered good, now there were thirty, fifty, seventy-five.

With China closed, it was necessary to send the priests somewhere else. Although the Orient had been Maryknoll's first love, the society was not intended for the Orient alone. The young

298

priests were willing to go anywhere they could, anxious to go everywhere they could.

The switch of Maryknoll to South America began in 1942, steadily increasing over the next ten years until there were more Maryknollers in South America than there had ever been in China. Many of the China veterans were assigned there; most of the new men went there, to Bolivia, to Peru and Chile, to Guatemala and Mexico. Accompanying them were both Maryknoll Sisters and Brothers.

The Catholic Church in Latin America was in somewhat the predicament of the Church in the Philippines, only worse. Again the Spanish settlers had been content to convert, but there had been little effort to produce a native clergy. When revolutions forced Spain to withdraw from Latin America, there were millions of baptized Catholics but few priests. In the United States, for example, there was one priest for every six hundred Catholics, but in South America there was one priest for every fifteen thousand Catholics. Every South American city had big and beautiful and empty cathedrals, and in the back country were millions who called themselves Catholics but who, because of the lack of priests, had developed more pagan than Christian.

There were other factors. For many years, the Latin American dictatorships banned the emigration of foreigners, especially missionaries. With power in the hands of a few, so was wealth, so was education, and the Church fell into the same pit. In the field of education, governments saw no reason for schools in the bush country and the Church could not afford to provide them. Illiteracy, therefore, rated as high as 85 per cent in most countries. A similar shocking ratio of disease existed outside a few big cities. Vocations among the poor were extremely rare. The metropolitan middle class, what little of it there was, produced some priests, but the understaffed, inadequately equipped seminaries restricted their quality and thus life among the clergy was badly supervised. Sons of the rich who entered the Church usually did so, as in the Middle Ages, more as a career. Nevertheless, they became the Latin American hierarchy, and because of their affinity to the ruling classes, their backgrounds of comfort, and their inherited attitude toward the poor, some of them fell shamefully short of the men they should have been. It was no wonder, therefore, that for years the continent had few vocations, that paganism had crept into Christianity at the lower level, that the Church itself had a bad reputation. Repeated efforts by Rome to correct the situation—by papal letters, papal envoys, and reassignments—were to small avail. There just was not enough ready material for improvements, and governments would allow just so much improvement.

Maryknoll's offer to aid in the Latin American missions was good news to Rome and to the bishops who knew how badly they needed the aid. The offer meant men and it meant money. The mission generosity of American Catholics was well known. Now maybe something could be done.

The early Maryknollers in South America encountered many unusual problems. The native Indians, for example, had been left almost completely alone and lived in a primitive society unchanged for centuries. When the Maryknoll Brothers hired Indians to help with construction work the Indians insisted on toting sand by the handful. The Brothers tried to get them to use boxes, by which they could carry more. They were willing to, as long as they were watched, but the minute they were alone they reverted to carrying the sand in their hands—as they had always done. One Brother made a wheelbarrow for hauling the sand and taught the Indians how to use it. Next day, he saw they were still using their hands, meanwhile pushing the wheelbarrow around empty. Then when a building was finished the Indians were afraid to enter it because they were sure that anything obviously so heavy would not long endure and might one day crash down on their heads.

The native resistance to progress took many forms. The backwoods villages had a local variety of witch doctor, but the people had no experience with trained physicians and did not trust them. Deaths from malaria and tuberculosis were common. Simple contagious diseases that could be controlled by vaccination raged on because of the native fear of hypodermic needles. Rampant was a kind of blindness caused by contagion from infected flies, but the natives could not be convinced to kill flies whenever they saw them and to keep flies away from the eyes of babies. In the same way, the natives resisted all efforts to modernize their agricultural methods, with the result of widespread malnutrition.

And there were religious problems. In the first days of the early Spanish missionaries, South America had produced saints like Rose of Lima, Turibius, Francis Solano, and Martin de Porres, but when the Church's activities slowed down so did the continental spirituality. Maryknollers encountered a surprising number of baptized people in the back country, but they had been baptized by their mothers, who in turn had been baptized by their mothers who one day had met a priest. But people never went to church because there were none to go to, and they knew nothing about their religion because no one had taught them. The purpose of baptism, in fact, was not clear. One day a man brought a baby to a mission to be baptized—a hopeful sign until the priest learned it had been dead a week: the man could not understand why the sacrament could not now be given.

So the Maryknoll work in Latin America had to begin slowly but on a broad basis. Before different kinds of education could start, the missionaries had to explain why it should start at all. But once it started it rolled. In so primitive an area, the slightest progress was dramatic, and seeing it the people wanted more. Soon the schools were full and the hospitals were sending well people back to their farms. A doctor was found who could remove the growths from the eyes of those infected by the diseased flies: entire villages regained their sight. Better farming produced more food and people grew healthier. Adult education programs warranted the publication of newspapers in the remote territories where not long ago nobody could read.

And the newly built churches began to fill up. The time came when a native clergy was both possible and essential. In corners of the country that had gone decades without seeing a priest the Maryknollers uncovered vocations in every house. True, most of the boys fell out during their preliminary studies but that was common anywhere in the world. Enough students endured to encourage the missionaries to build a chain of seminaries across the continent in which Indian youths advanced closer each year to the time when the people themselves would be producing their own priests to direct the native Church within the framework of the Church Universal.

Reports of Maryknoll's success among the South American natives spread fast. In 1949, the Mexican hierarchy, having survived another wave of political anticlericism, invited Mary-knollers into the country to establish the Mexican Foreign Mission Seminary, thus to give Mexico its own mission society patterned on Maryknoll. By turning its attention to the foreign missions while still crawling out of the rubble of persecution, the Church in Mexico hoped for the same internal growth that the creation of Maryknoll provided in America within a few years after the United States itself was removed from Rome's list of mission territory.

The South American success also proved that Maryknollers could work effectively among other than Orientals. At approximately the same time Maryknoll entered Mexico, Rome asked the society to take on a large area in Tanganyika, Africa. It was a territory developed by the White Fathers for fifty years and was now about 5 per cent Catholic. Rome felt that with the additional priests Maryknoll could provide, future development would proceed at an accelerated tempo. The plan proved fruitful. In ten years the four Maryknollers who first went to Africa increased to seventy-eight priests, nine Brothers, and twelve Sisters, the two parishes increased to eighteen, the eight thousand Catholics increased to twenty-eight thousand. Thus on another continent Maryknoll fulfilled its purpose as the American factor in the world missions of the Church.

XXX

MARYKNOLL had come a long way. As the society approached its fiftieth anniversary, there were many landmarks to look back on. Of its first five students, three had become bishops—Frank Ford, Jim Walsh, Bill O'Shea. But of the five only Walsh was still alive. McShane had died of smallpox, O'Shea of a heart attack, Ford at the hands of the Communists. Alphonse Vogel had returned from the missions in such bad shape that he felt obliged to confine himself to parish work, which he did until his death in Kingston, New York, in 1944.

The survival of Maryknoll's first mission band was better. Price and Ford were dead, but Walsh was in Shanghai and Bernard Meyer was working out of Maryknoll headquarters, roaming the wide world producing new types of catechisms based on an effective teaching method he had devised. So only Jim Walsh was still in China—but nobody could tell how long he would last.

Walsh was, in fact, the only Maryknoller in China, the only foreign bishop there, quite possibly the only foreign missionary there. The eighteen hundred missionaries in China in 1952 were reduced to seven hundred in 1953, then to three hundred in 1954, of whom seventy were in prisons. Then the day came when, as far as anybody knew, there was only Walsh.

Walsh's work as executive secretary of the Catholic Central Bureau had got off to a good start. Correlating the Church's activities in so large a country was an enormous chore, but the bureau's staff was able and dedicated. Given time, they would have developed a thorough, efficient organization that would have met the needs of all China's hierarchy.

But there was no time. By the end of 1949, the Communists had occupied most of the major cities, including Shanghai. Restrictions on the Church quickly appeared, the expulsion of missionaries began, and others were already leaving. Walsh was opposed to the voluntary departures. He put the matter plainly when he asked:

"Nobody has any illusions about the Red determination to eliminate all religion. However, the question is: do we give them the field without the least struggle or do we keep at our work until we are put out?"

In a letter to the China Missionary Bulletin, published by Maryknoll at Hong Kong, he wrote:

At a time when the Catholic religion is being traduced and persecuted with the design of eliminating it from China, I think it is the plain duty of all Catholic missionaries—priests, Brothers, and Sisters, regardless of age, occupation or condition—to remain where they are until prevented from doing so by physical force. If internment should intervene in the case of some or even death, I think it should simply be regarded as a normal risk that is inherent in our state of life, as a necessary concomitant to our responsibilities and as a small price to pay for carrying out our duty, much as in the case of firemen and policemen who are sometimes required to give their lives in fires and robberies. In our particular case, moreover, I think that such an eventuality would be a privilege, too, because it would associate us a little more intimately in the Cross of Christ.

Our vocation is not simply our occupational work—the teaching, preaching and village visiting we usually do. It is something much deeper, permanent, indelible. It does not change if our work is impeded, if we are in prison or for any other reason. One of the necessary conditions to carry it out properly, I think, is to accept in advance every trouble and contingence in connection with it that Divine Providence puts in our way. If we start to pick and choose for ourselves, it is very hard to tell if we are carrying out our vocation or running away from it. I suppose that St. Paul had his mission vocation while in prison and that he carried it out there—also that such was God's plan in his regard. The only safe rule for a man with a mission vocation is, I think, to adhere to the clear indication of God's will—his appointed place where he finds himself—and to make no changes of his own volition. If he leaves China to escape imprisonment, how does he know it was not part of God's plan to let him be imprisoned for the good it might do?

"Enforced inactivity" is a term that needs some distinguishing. Activity does not depend on the place; it depends on the man. Suffering patiently borne is activity, so is prayer, so is any kind of mental work —things which can be done, one would think, in prison as well as anywhere. What is really meant is a change in activity. That is something of a hardship to many men, I confess it—especially to those who are lacking in the faculty of imagination. However, we can all learn something new, or at least we can try to do so. If an example of prison life will help the Church in China—as I believe any suffering undergone for God will do—then we are just being given another sort of activity for a time. There is no question of complete inactivity, I believe. That would be demoralizing and it is hard for many. Again, if ministerial inactivity is meant, that is, inability to care for Christians, visit the villages and so on, then we can only say that a priest or a father does as much for his flock by suffering for them—and maybe he does even more. Another thing which, to my mind, ought to be left in the hands of God.

He practiced what he preached. Within a few weeks after the Communist occupation of Shanghai, Walsh realized that his telephone was being tapped and his mail was being opened. Some mail did not even arrive. He then discovered that he was being followed. He took all of it calmly, but he warned his staff that they should now be extremely careful of what they said, did, wrote, and where they went.

Refugee priests, both Chinese and missionaries, began to arrive in Shanghai from the back country. Walsh put cots in his office and let eight of them sleep there. When it became apparent that they were not safe on the streets, he brought in eating utensils and food so they did not have to go out at all. He expected the Communists to barge into the office momentarily, but they still had not mustered the arrogance to do that. Meanwhile, Walsh continued to go about his business.

Unabashed, he made official contact with the government

whenever other priests came to him for help in getting away. Near his house was a parish church where he said Sunday Mass and preached. He did not hesitate to warn the people against affiliating themselves with the independent church the Communists were trying to establish. In this way he went through the entire Korean War period practically a free man. He had many friends in Shanghai, some of them important businessmen, and the Communists were reluctant to clash openly with him until they had cleaned up loose ends.

The first overt pressure on him came soon after the war, when the government mildly suggested it might be a good idea for him to leave the country. He replied that he could not leave: he had work to do. The government's reaction was to keep him at the work: a military guard was posted at the office door and Walsh thereby was put under an unusual form of house arrest. Foreign correspondents in Shanghai learned of it and immediately the story was all over the world. American newspapermen, banned from China, tried to reach Walsh by telephone from Hong Kong, Manila, and Tokyo. At first Walsh accepted the calls, but he knew his phone was tapped, he knew whatever he said would be exaggerated both by the reporters and the Communists, and out of this he knew might come reprisals against Maryknollers still in China and his friends in the city. Therefore, he asked the Maryknollers at Hong Kong to ask the reporters to stop the calls. This soon proved unnecessary; his phone was disconnected.

At Maryknoll there was great concern about him. Opinions were divided on whether or not he should leave China. In his position with the Catholic Central Bureau he was actually outside the sphere of Maryknoll jurisdiction, yet as a Maryknoller he was subject to it. A few returning missionaries of other societies stressed to Bishop Lane that Walsh was not actually achieving any good by remaining in China, that on the other hand he could do much harm to the native clergy by letting his presence serve as a symbol against the independent church. As long as Walsh was in China, they said, he was a thorn to the Communists and possibly blocked any compromise between the native clergy and the government.

A method of getting uncensored letters to Walsh through Chinese priests was set up, and in one such letter Lane put the question directly: What did Walsh plan to do? Walsh replied that he planned to stay, unless thrown out by the Communists or ordered out by Rome or Maryknoll. He suggested that a decision be cabled to him. If he was to be ordered out, the cable could say that his brother John had fallen seriously ill and that Walsh should hurry home. If he was to be permitted to stay, the cable could say that his brother John had safely come through an operation. Before deciding, Lane queried Rome for advice. The advice was that Pope Pius XII himself said the final decision should be left to Walsh. Lane cabled Walsh that his brother John had come safely through an operation.

Some months later a note arrived from Walsh, saying that the Communists had caught on to his private postal system and that no further mail should be sent to the Chinese priests in Shanghai. Then all went silent.

A year passed without news, then six more months. At last the Maryknollers in Hong Kong were able to report that a member of the British diplomatic corps, free to travel in China, had seen Walsh in Shanghai. He was well. He was living under house arrest in the rectory of Christ The King Church with two Chinese priests who had gone over to the independent church. The obvious intention was to give the public impression that Walsh, by living at the church, was in sympathy with the priests. However, Walsh refused to set foot in the church itself. He said his Masses in his room at the rectory and had as little contact as possible with the priests.

Then silence again.

In September, 1955, the Communists announced that they were ready to release twelve of the forty-one Americans still held in the Shanghai prison. Nine were to be released outright. Three would be released when they asked for exit visas. Walsh was listed as one of these three. He did not ask.

Again the silence.

Conflicting rumors came back: some had him in prison, others had him in a hospital, others kept him at the church.

There was nothing definite until March, 1960. On that day of March 17, the Communist government announced that Walsh, along with Bishop Ignatius Kung Pin-mei of Shanghai and twelve Chinese priests, had been tried for treason and found guilty.

The charges against him were that he was both an American and Vatican spy, that he had conspired against the government by opposing the independent church and urging others to do so, that he had perverted Chinese youths by making priests and nuns out of them, and that he had given active support to the Nationalists. The last charge was based on Walsh's activity during 1940 and 1941 when he was traveling between Japan and Washington as messenger of the peace negotiations. The Communists now knew of it. After the war, General Muto Akira, being tried as a war criminal, asked Walsh to prepare a document to show that he, Akira, had actually worked to prevent the war when he approached Walsh to serve as liaison. One of the Japanese terms had been a willingness to withdraw from China and give future support to the Nationalists against the Russians. Twenty years later the Communists used this in accusing Walsh of supporting the Nationalists against the Chinese people.

He was sentenced to twenty years.

There was no information as to when and where the trial had been held, what the evidence was, or who had given it. There was no indication of what Walsh had said in his defense, if anything. There was no way to tell whether he had been brainwashed. And there was nothing anybody could do.

The news was heartbreaking to Walsh's family in Maryland. His older brother, Judge William C. Walsh, took immediate steps to arrange a visit to Shanghai, but it was not until July that he was informed that the visit was permitted.

Judge Walsh and his wife arrived in Hong Kong on July 28, having agreed that Mrs. Walsh would remain there with Maryknollers while the Judge went to Shanghai alone. On the morning of August 1, he crossed the frontier at Shumchun and was greeted by a Mr. Wong, who identified himself as a member of the Chinese Red Cross. They traveled together that day to Canton by train. Next morning, Walsh was put on a plane for Shanghai, but bad weather forced the plane down at Nanchang and he spent the night at a hotel there. In the afternoon of August 3, he finally reached Shanghai where he was met by another Red Cross worker and a representative of the Chinese International Travel Service, a government agency. They took him to the Peace Hotel, formerly the Cathay, where he was given a room. It was not until the following afternoon, Thursday, August 4, that he was told he could see his brother for the first time at three-fifteen. A half-hour before, the Red Cross workers called for him and took him on the fifteen-minute ride to the prison.

Inside the prison wall was a small wooden shack, divided into two rooms by a partition. A guard in a white coat gave Walsh forms to fill out, then explained the prison rules. There was to be no discussion of Jim Walsh's trial or charges, only talk about family matters. No written messages were to be exchanged. No cameras or recording devices were permitted. Any gifts had to be checked by the prison and only essential items would be allowed. The visit would last thirty minutes. Judge Walsh was led into the second room. A photographer was sitting there.

A few moments later the door opened and Jim Walsh came in, accompanied by another guard and an interpreter. He looked thinner than he normally was, his hair was white, he was wearing a white short-sleeved sport shirt and dark trousers. He did not have his episcopal ring.

The two brothers stepped to each other and shook hands. The Judge put a hand on Jim Walsh's shoulder.

"Hello, Bill."

"Hello, James."

"It's good to see you."

"You look fine, James."

"How's the family?"

"Everybody's fine."

The interpreter said, "You will both sit down."

They sat opposite each other at the oblong table. The Judge said, "Everybody sends love and prayers. Bishop Comber—"

"*Bishop* Comber?"

"Yes, John Comber. You remember him. He was in Manchuria when you were at Kongmoon."

"Yes, and then he went to South America."

"That's right. He's superior general now."

"Well! And a bishop?"

"He was consecrated last year."

The interpreter asked, "Is this person a relative?"

"He is my religious superior," Jim Walsh said.

"You can discuss only family relatives."

"All right."

They talked about the family. Then the Judge asked, "James, do you want us to do anything about getting you out of here?"

The interpreter spoke quickly to the guard. Then, "You cannot—"

Jim Walsh said, "While no one likes to be confined I am not unhappy here, and I leave the future entirely in the hands of God."

"You cannot discuss that subject further," the interpreter said.

The Judge asked, "Can we smoke?"

"Yes."

The Judge took out a pack and offered his brother one. "Do you get the packages we send you with the cigarettes?"

"Yes. I have plenty. I'm not allowed to smoke much, so they last."

"I brought you a gift from your graduating class at Mount St. Mary's—a gold rosary. But the guard took it away from me."

"I suppose he would."

"Do you have a rosary, James?"

"No. Nothing. No breviary, no religious books. Nothing."

"You don't say Mass?"

"No."

"Maybe they'll let you have the gold rosary some day."

"I don't think so. It would be considered a nonessential item. But that's all right, Bill. I have these." He held up his ten fingers.

The half-hour went quickly. When it ended, the interpreter said, "The photographer will now take some pictures." Several shots were made.

"How about taking one outside?" the Judge suggested. "I'd like one of us standing up." The picture was taken.

The interpreter said, "The visit is over now. You will both be informed when you can see each other again."

The second visit, again limited to a half-hour, was permitted on the following Monday, the eighth. The Judge had a copy of the picture that had been taken outdoors and showed it. Jim Walsh laughed and said, "This makes me look older than you."

"Well, you're only a year younger, and when you hit seventy it doesn't make any difference any more." He dug into his pocket again. "Here are some pictures of my two grandchildren."

Jim Walsh took them. "They're cute. Real Walshes."

"Yes. Notice the square jaws."

"I did." He looked at the interpreter. "May I keep them?"

"Yes."

The Judge asked, "What about you, James? Are you all right? Do you need anything?"

"No. Everything is O.K. I have a comfortable bed in the hospital section. I get three meals a day, plain but sufficient."

"Why are you in the hospital section?"

"My age, I guess."

"Are you alone?"

"Another man is there. He speaks English, so I keep in practice."

"And your health is all right? What do you weigh now?"

"About one thirty-five."

"That's what you've always weighed, just about."

"Just about, James. Tell me about Cumberland. Has it changed much?"

"Oh, yes. Getting real fancy. All the stores have new fronts. And we've got a lot of one-way streets now; if you don't know the town you could go around in circles all day."

"The railroad tracks still across the end of Liberty Avenue?"

"Still there, still holding up traffic for hours when a freight goes by."

The half-hour ended but the guard made no move to interrupt them, so they talked on. Jim Walsh asked, "Are you seeing much of China?"

"I went to the opera the other night. I don't know what it was —all in Chinese. But it was interesting."

"I wish you had more time. You should go to Peking; it's a beautiful city. And I wish I could show you Kongmoon. The people are wonderful there."

"Maybe some day."

Jim Walsh smiled sadly. "Yes. Maybe some day."

Fifteen minutes went by before the interpreter said that the visit was over.

At the hotel, the Judge tried to remember everything his

brother had said, hoping to find somewhere a clue to how he really was, what he had really been through. But there was no clue. A priest in Hong Kong had said that once a prisoner had been tried and sentenced he was usually left alone; it was before the trial that the torture took place. But there were no scars on Jim Walsh's face to indicate he had been tortured, or at least they had healed. Nor was there any indication that he had been brainwashed. He seemed to be in full control of his faculties, he said nothing odd to indicate any mental imbalance. Evidently he had resisted the Communists and had been imprisoned just to get him out of the way.

They met for the last time on Thursday, the eleventh, and again they talked mostly of familiar things, of people they loved, of past events they treasured. When they saw that the time was growing short they faced the inescapable sadness.

"Well, James," the Judge said, "I don't know when I'll be able to get back here to see you again."

"Seeing you this time, Bill, has been the greatest human consolation of my life," Jim Walsh said.

The Judge said, "If they don't let me back in the country, I won't see you unless you get out."

"I guess so. Well, Bill, we will meet again in heaven."

The Judge could find no more words.

The interpreter said, "The visit is ended."

The two brothers looked deeply at each other and then they shook hands. Jim Walsh's guard opened the door and led him outside. The Judge stood there, staring at the door. He noticed a window and stepped to it and brushed the curtain aside, but the lower part of it was painted and he could not see out. His heart sank; desperately he wanted one more look. Then the guard with him came forward and swept open the window with a quick pull.

He saw him, walking ahead of his guard toward a narrow passageway across the compound. The Judge called, "James!"

Jim Walsh kept walking, but he looked over his shoulder and smiled and waved.

The Judge called, "So long, James!"

When the Judge returned to Hong Kong he was interviewed by reporters and the story of his visit with Jim Walsh was printed in papers around the world. Maryknollers everywhere—in South Korea, in Japan and the Philippines and Formosa and Hawaii, in Chile, Peru, Bolivia, Guatemala and Mexico, in Tanganyika, in Los Altos, Glen Ellyn, at the Vénard, at Maryknoll itself— they all read about this man who, fifty years ago, had been in the first Maryknoll class and was the second Maryknoller to be ordained, who with Fred Price had been the first to go to China and there had become Maryknoll's first bishop, and then had been the first Maryknoller to follow James Anthony Walsh as superior general of the society. Remembering these things about Jim Walsh, the one thousand Maryknollers went into a hundred chapels in a dozen countries and said a prayer for him. Praying, they remembered the last words he had spoken to his brother:

"We will meet again in heaven."

It was Maryknoll's invitation to the world.

Index

Divine Word, Society of, 45
Donovan, Rev. Gerald, 210-217
Douglas, Moses Hale, 40, 41
Downs, Rev. William, 156
Drought, Rev. James M., 173, 175
Dunn, Bishop John J., 42, 88, 112, 176
Dwyer, Mary, 83, 87

Falconio, Archbishop Diomede, 61, 62
Farley, John Cardinal, 42, 60, 82, 88, 89, 129
Field Afar, The, 43, 44, 45, 46, 55, 56, 83, 87, 170
Flagg, Dr. Paluel, 96, 112
Ford, Bishop Francis X., 93, 111, 114, 121, 142, 144 ff., 188, 246, 277-282
Freri, Rev. Joseph, 40, 41
Fumasoni-Biondi, Cardinal, 176
Furuya, Bishop Paul, 185

Gallagher, Dr. Frederick, 18
Gaspard, Rev. Robert A., 266
Gauthier, Rev. Auguste, 110, 116, 120
Gibbons, James Cardinal, 19, 40, 61, 63, 64, 76
Gilmartin, Rev. Gregory, 290, 291
Gotti, Cardinal, 72, 73, 74
Greene, Rev. Robert W., 290-297

Haid, Bishop Leo, 23, 25, 26, 29, 30, 31, 33, 53, 63
Harvard University, 36
Hawthorne, N. Y., 83 ff.
Herter, Christian A., 12
Hoban, Bishop Edward F., 97, 98
Hogan, Abbé, 38, 39
Hollger, Ernst, 83, 87
Hull, Cordell, 225 ff.

International Eucharistic Congress (Montreal), 17, 33, 47
Irwin, Rev. Michael, 28

Japan missions, 183 ff.
Jaricout, Pauline, 39, 40
Joan Marie, Sister, 279-283

Kaying, China, 144 ff.
Keller, Rev. James, 171
Kelly, Rev. James F., 174
Kennelly, Rev. Robert P., 266
Korea missions, 157 ff., 269-276

Lane, Rev. John I., 41, 43, 66, 83, 87, 129
Lane, Bishop Raymond A., 173, 175, 178 ff., 210, 214, 241, 290, 306
Latin America missions, 299, 300
Loting, China, 121, 155, 156, 266
Lourdes, France, 32, 77

Manchuria missions, 178 ff.
Maryknoll Brothers, 98, 182, 285-289
Maryknoll Sisters, 98, 133, 181, 283-285
McCann, Thomas, 83, 87
McCormick, Rev. James A., 246
McGlinchey, Rev. Joseph F., 65
McNicholas, Archbishop John T., 176, 189
McShane, Rev. Daniel, 95, 98, 131, 154 ff.
Mercy, Sisters of, 19, 27
Meyer, Rev. Bernard F., 111, 114, 121, 134, 135, 136, 137, 138, 151
Milan Foreign Mission Society, 39
Mill Hill Fathers, 39, 51, 64, 69, 80
Morris, Rev. John, 178

ABOUT THE AUTHOR

Glenn D. Kittler is the author of *The White Fathers, The Woman God Loved, Equatorial Africa: New World of Tomorrow,* and *The Papal Princes: A History of the Sacred College of Cardinals.* He has also written numerous articles for *The Saturday Evening Post, The Reader's Digest, Better Homes & Gardens, The American Weekly, Catholic Digest, Sign, Pageant,* and other national magazines. Formerly Associate Editor of *Coronet,* Mr. Kittler is now roving editor of *Guideposts* and writes a weekly column, *The New Apostles,* for the N.C.W.C. News Syndicate.

This book was set in
Baskerville and Bulmer type by
Harry Sweetman Typesetting Corporation.
It was printed and bound at
the press of The World Publishing Company.
Typography and design are by
Ernst Reichl